Australian Army Campaigns Series – 1

BATTLE OF CRETE

Revised and Expanded Second Edition

ALBERT PALAZZO

2007

Copyright
Army History Unit
Campbell Park Offices (CP4-2-31)
Canberra ACT 2600
AUSTRALIA
(02) 6266 4248
(02) 6266 4044 – fax

Copyright 2007 © Commonwealth of Australia

First published as ebook in 2005
Second edition published 2007

This book is copyright. Apart from any fair dealing for the purposes of private study, research, criticism or review as permitted under the Copyright Act, no part may be reproduced, stored in a retrieval system or transmitted in any form or by any means, electronic, mechanical, photocopying, recording or otherwise, without written permission.

National Library of Australia
Cataloguing-in-Publication listing

Palazzo, Albert, 1957- .
Battle of Crete.

2nd ed.
Bibliography.
Includes index.
ISBN 9780980320411.

1. World War, 1939-1945 – Campaigns – Greece – Crete. 2. Crete (Greece) – History, Military. I. Australia. Dept. of Defence. Army History Unit. II. Title. (Series: Australian army campaigns series; 1).

940.5421959

Title Page Image: Australian War Memorial: P02434.005.
Front Cover: Australian War Memorial P01495.002.
Back Cover Images: Australian War Memorial: ART27776; 106940 and P02053.007; Graphic Art by Mark Wahlert.
Typesetting: Margaret McNally, Canberra.
Printed by: Shannon Books Pty Ltd, Bayswater, Victoria.

CONTENTS

4	Preface to the Second Edition
4	Acknowledgements
5	The Eastern Mediterranean in 1941
13	The Situation on Crete
31	Air Attack on Maleme
52	The Descent at Prison Valley
73	The Landings at Heraklion
86	The Australians Defend Retimo
102	The New Zealanders Counter-attack
113	The Defence of the Galatas Line
121	End Game at Heraklion and Retimo
127	The Retreat to Sfakia
146	The Sea and Air War for Crete
160	Aftermath
166	Further Reading
169	British-German Rank Equivalents
170	Bibliography
174	Index

PREFACE TO THE SECOND EDITION

Battle of Crete first appeared in 2005 in an ebook format. The following year the Army History Unit asked me to prepare a print version of the book. The conversion to a traditional format was complex and led to the book's rewriting. During this process, I took the opportunity to add some material for which there had been no room in the ebook, and delete other sections that lacked relevance for a print book.

As I began this project the consensus of people to whom I spoke was that Crete's outcome had been a foregone conclusion, another inevitable German victory. My research, however, demonstrated that Crete was by no means a one-sided affair, and that the Germans won the island only by the narrowest of margins. *Battle of Crete* clearly shows that the difference between victory and defeat lay in a few decisions taken by a small number of commanders.

While accessible to the general reader, *Battle of Crete*'s primary audience is the Australian Army's junior leaders. I hope they enjoy this book. Command is their realm, decision-making their responsibility. Though now receding into the distant past, the story of Crete has lessons for both the present and future. Commanders at all levels will continue to have to face and make decisions. I hope that this book, in its small way, will provide some guidance for those who face that challenge.

ACKNOWLEDGEMENTS

Authors incur a great many debts in the writing of their books. I would like to express my gratitude to Roger Lee, Head of the Army History Unit, and his staff for the opportunity to undertake this project. In particular, I wish to acknowledge Glenn Wahlert for his efforts as the project's manager. The sector maps were the careful work of Keith Mitchell. The project's graphic designer was Mark Wahlert: the 2D, 3D drawings, the table and lesson layout, and the wire diagrams were the product of his talents. Jeff Isaacs provided the original artwork which is superb. Ian Kuring and Glenn Wahlert lent their invaluable assistance with the technical details for the weapon descriptions. The copyeditor was Cathy McCullagh and the typeset was ably completed by Margaret McNally. The index was the work of Michael Molkentin. The excellent cover design was the work of the Defence Publishing Service. The Australian War Memorial kindly provided many of the photographs, maps and other visual materials. I am indebted to the staff of the research centre and convey my grateful thanks to them for their assistance. Lastly, I must thank my wife Melissa Benyon for her patience with my prose and her service as my private editor.

BATTLE OF CRETE

THE EASTERN MEDITERRANEAN IN 1941

Prelude to Invasion

On 20 May 1941 the Second World War came to the eastern Mediterranean. Germany's invasion of the island of Crete marked the final phase of the conquest of the Balkans. The Germans had instigated their Balkan campaign on 6 April with simultaneous assaults on Yugoslavia and Greece. German forces, supported by elements of the Hungarian, Bulgarian, Romanian, and Italian armed forces, overran Yugoslavia in a matter of days. The Greek army, assisted by a small British expeditionary force built around 6 Australian Division and the New Zealand Division, could not stop the onslaught of the German Panzers. Athens fell on 27 April while the Royal Navy defied the *Luftwaffe*'s dominance of the sky to evacuate as many soldiers as possible in a Mediterranean version of Dunkirk.

Eastern Mediterranean Theatre
Drawn by Keith Mitchell

Adolf Hitler, *Führer* of Germany.
Australian War Memorial 044586

The German *Führer*, Adolf Hitler, had not planned a Mediterranean campaign for 1941; rather, his objective was the conquest of the Soviet Union. In fact, by early 1941 his plans for a June invasion of that country were well advanced. While Hitler certainly entertained strategic interests in the Mediterranean, these were of a more defensive nature. He wanted a secure southern perimeter in order to:

- protect the flank of the German army when it attacked the Soviet Union; and
- safeguard the Romanian oilfields at Ploesti from British bombers attacking from bases in the Mediterranean.

Ploesti was Germany's main source of petroleum. Such was German dependence on this oilfield that any British interruption to the flow of oil would almost certainly lead to the collapse of the Nazi war effort. As long as Greece remained neutral it provided Hitler with a buffer zone against British interference in his strategic plans.

ADOLF HITLER
FÜHRER OF GERMANY

Despite his humble Austrian origins, Adolf Hitler would rise to become one of the most dominant and destructive figures of the 20th century. Hitler initiated the Second World War in a bid to transform Germany into the strongest European power and to vanquish the disgrace of its defeat in the First World War. The result was six years of terrible global violence and racial extermination that almost witnessed the triumph of dictatorship over democracy. Ultimately, however, it was Germany that was destroyed.

Born in Austria in the city of Braunau-on-Inn in 1889, Hitler moved to Munich in 1913. After the outbreak of the First World War he enlisted in the German Army, serving in a Bavarian regiment. He rose to the rank of lance corporal and was awarded the Iron Cross.

After Germany's defeat Hitler returned to Munich where he deepened his exploration of ultra right wing politics and began to expound a political philosophy whose tenets included the enslavement or extermination of lesser races and the rise of Germany to world power status through the use of force. Postwar Germany, racked by hyperinflation, military humiliation, and economic collapse, provided fertile ground for his ideas. In the 1930s Hitler's National Socialist Party began to emerge as a political force on the national stage, enjoying increasing success in nationwide elections. In 1933 he was appointed Chancellor of Germany.

Exploiting the legal powers of the Chancellor's office Hitler moved to eliminate his rivals while securing power for himself. In 1934 Hitler took the title of *Führer* or leader. After his renouncement of the restrictions of the Treaty of Versailles, Hitler began the rearmament of Germany and the march to war. Initially, his conquests were secured through diplomatic means, as the leaders of Britain and France chose to appease Hitler rather than risk another Great War. Such effective diplomacy allowed Germany to absorb Austria, Czechoslovakia and Memel, occupy the Saar, and demilitarise the Rhineland.

Germany's invasion of Poland in September 1939 was the spark that initiated the Second World War. By the time of the Crete campaign most of Western and Central Europe was under German occupation and only Britain continued to defy the dictator. However, Hitler's unfettered ambition and ideological beliefs led to Germany's invasion of the Soviet Union and his declaration of war on the United States. Both proved disastrous decisions which would ultimately bring about his downfall.

Hitler also used his conquests to eliminate those European peoples that had no place in Nazi ideology or in the future society he planned to create. While the Jews were the primary target of extermination, other groups also slated for destruction were the Gypsies, and those suffering mental or physical defects. Hitler planned to allow the Slavic races to survive so they could serve as slaves for the superior Germany *Volk*.

Hitler did not survive the war to be tried for his crimes. On 30 April 1945 he committed suicide as Soviet forces approached his headquarters in Berlin.

SIR WINSTON S. CHURCHILL
PRIME MINISTER OF
GREAT BRITAIN

Statesman, politician and military commander, Winston Spencer Churchill was one of the most significant figures of the 20th Century. In the darkest days of the Second World War, Britain turned to Churchill for leadership through the greatest crisis the country had faced. He replaced Neville Chamberlain as Prime Minister of Great Britain after the Norway debacle, and steered his country through the disastrous 1940 campaign which saw the collapse of France. Refusing to concede defeat, Churchill provided Britain with the optimism and defiance the nation needed to see it through the Battle of Britain, and to lay the foundation for eventual victory.

Born in 1874 at Blenheim Palace, Churchill would combine the roles of political leader, wartime commander and literary writer during his extraordinary life. One of his greatest achievements was his receipt of the Nobel Prize for Literature in 1953. During the First World War he served as First Lord of the Admiralty and was a leading advocate of the Dardanelles campaign. Its failure almost cost him his political career, and for a time he served on the Western Front in command of a battalion. In mid-1917 he returned to cabinet as Minister of Munitions. During the interwar period he served in a variety of cabinet positions. At the start of the Second World War he again took charge of the Admiralty before becoming Prime Minister. Despite his crucial role in the British contribution to an allied victory, he was defeated in the July 1945 election. In 1951 he regained power and served as Prime Minister until his retirement in 1955. Churchill died in 1965.

Winston S. Churchill, Prime Minister of Great Britain.
Australian War Memorial 007835

British Prime Minister Winston Churchill and his military advisers were well aware of Germany's dependence on Romanian oil. Ploesti lay tantalisingly close—in a region with which Britain had gained great familiarity during the First World War. Since 1940 British diplomats had conducted secret negotiations with the leaders of Yugoslavia, Greece and Turkey in the hope of forging a Balkan League united in opposition to Germany. These talks failed to realise any firm commitments, however, because Britain had little to offer its suitors. The Balkan states knew that British power in the Mediterranean was already stretched thinly and it was not without good reason that they feared instigating a German reaction.

Oil security was also of importance to Britain. The Empire's lines of communication to the oilfields of the Middle East were vital to the prosecution of the war. In addition, the shortest route between Britain and the manpower and resources of India, Malaya, Australia and New Zealand was through the Suez Canal and the Mediterranean. German domination of Greece could imperil this line of communication. Thus Britain also had vital strategic reasons for keeping Germany out of Greece.

Benito Mussolini, Dictator of Italy
Australian War Memorial 062638

BENITO MUSSOLINI
IL DUCE OF ITALY

Benito Mussolini was born in 1883 in Predappio in the Forli region of Italy. Initially trained as a teacher he became involved in socialist politics at an early age. By the age of 25 he was on the staff of a socialist newspaper and had became an advocate of revolutionary change.

During the First World War Mussolini served as a private and was wounded in action. Following his discharge his political interest deepened and he started his own newspaper. In 1919 he founded the *Fasci di Combattimento*—the Italian Fascist Party. Mussolini's strong nationalistic message gained favour with Italy's war-weary population, and the Fascists gained strength through national elections. In 1922 the King, Vittorio Emanuele III, asked Mussolini to form government.

Once in office Mussolini gradually gathered power to himself, and the freedoms that the Italian people had enjoyed gave way to repression and totalitarianism. At the same time Mussolini's vision of a powerful Italy gathered momentum. It was no accident that the symbol of the Fascist Party was a bundle of reeds, the same icon used by the Romans. By 1926 Italy was a dictatorship and Mussolini *Il Duce*, or leader.

However the mismatch between Mussolini's talent and his grandiose vision for Italy's future doomed the nation to destruction in the Second World War. As a leader Mussolini centralised power in himself and was intolerant of criticism. He surrounded himself with sycophants and built a regime based on a web of propaganda that hid its many defects.

In 1939 Mussolini signed the 'Pact of Steel' binding Italy and Germany together. Mussolini initially hesitated to follow Germany into the Second World War, but when France's conquest appeared imminent he plunged Italy into the abyss. Italy was not prepared for war, and what followed was defeat in battle and increasing dependence on Germany.

After the allies invaded Sicily in July 1943, Mussolini was deposed and arrested. However German commandos liberated him and Hitler installed Mussolini as head of a Fascist puppet state, the Salò Republic. In 1945, as allied forces approached, Mussolini attempted to flee. On 27 April he was captured by partisans and executed.

Ultimately, the actions of Hitler's ally, Italian dictator Benito Mussolini, and the hapless Italian Army precipitated Germany's intervention in the Balkans. Hitler had already been compelled to come to Italy's assistance after its crushing defeat by the British Western Desert Force during Operation *Compass* in North Africa in December 1940. The rout saw the Italians lose tens of thousands of men captured, as well as the port of Tobruk and all of Cyrenaica abandoned to the British. In the Balkans Germany would have to undertake yet another intervention to rectify a different Italian mess.

On 28 October 1940, with little preparation or planning, Mussolini had launched his army into Greece from Albania, a country he had seized in 1939. Almost at once the Italians were in trouble—they barely outnumbered the Greek defenders, fielded outdated equipment, and lacked sufficient reserves of ammunition and food. The offensive ground to a halt not far from its start point.

On 14 November the Greek Army counter-attacked. The Italians' line collapsed and the Greeks pursued them into Albania. For a time it looked as if the Greeks would drive their enemy into the Adriatic, but the Italians managed to stabilise their line with the arrival of hastily dispatched reinforcements. The two sides settled into a winter stalemate.

Unprovoked Italian aggression did not move the Greek government to seek large-scale British intervention; rather, allied assistance was sought to protect Greece from the feared German response. Even then, the only assistance Greece was willing to accept amounted to a few Royal Air Force squadrons. However, even this meagre British foothold on the continent did not go unnoticed in Berlin.

On 13 December Hitler signed Directive 20, Operation *Marita*, the invasion of Greece. Soon after, ground and air units began to arrive in Romania, ostensibly as part of the German military mission to that country. In February German troops moved into Bulgaria. Britain followed these developments through intelligence provided by Ultra.

In February, in response to the growing threat to Greece's north, the British and Greek governments reached agreement on the deployment of an expeditionary force. Despite the obvious risks, Churchill favoured intervention and, on 7 March, British units began to arrive in Athens. The decision to commit ground forces led to two of the greatest British debacles of the war. First, the British contribution had barely arrived in northern Greece before it had to flee southwards, closely pursued by overwhelmingly superior German ground and air forces. Second, the troops the British had sent to Greece came from North Africa and their diversion brought to a halt the Western Desert Force's efforts in Libya. The timing of the redeployment of these battle-hardened veterans to the Balkans was unfortunate. On 31 March General Erwin Rommel unleashed the newly arrived *Afrika Korps* on the weakened British. The Germans trapped the 9th Australian Division in Tobruk and pushed the British back to the Egyptian frontier.

The final element of the Balkan campaign involved Yugoslavia. On 25 March Germany succeeded in pressuring the Yugoslav government into signing the Tripartite Pact, a mutual support treaty originally between Germany, Italy and Japan, but which now included Romania, Bulgaria, Slovakia and Hungary. Within days of its signing, however, an anti-Nazi *coup d'état* toppled the government in Belgrade. Hitler's furious response took the form of an order to his generals to 'smash Yugoslavia' and destroy 'the city of Belgrade'. Operation *Marita* was altered at the last minute to include the simultaneous invasion of Yugoslavia.

A Fallschirmjäger – gouache on board, 2005.
artist – Jeff Isaacs, OAM

The Decision to Invade Crete

The invasion of Crete was not part of the original plan for the conquest of mainland Greece. It was a separate operation which was authorised later as the Germans neared Athens. It also had its own Directive, No. 28, which Hitler did not issue until 25 April. Instead, the attack on Crete was a result of strategic opportunism by *Luftflotte 4*, the air fleet in charge of the Balkans, and the personal ambition of some of the *Luftwaffe*'s senior officers, particularly Generalleutnant Kurt Student.

Student was Germany's leading theorist on airborne warfare, and commanded *XI Fliegerkorps*, the *Luftwaffe*'s parachute and air landing organisation. Student and others argued that Crete was an important strategic objective for Germany. Possession of its airfields would prevent their use by British bombers—which would be in range of Ploesti—and extend the *Luftwaffe*'s reach to the North African coast. From bases on Crete the *Luftwaffe* could interdict British convoy movements throughout the eastern Mediterranean. Student also saw Crete as the first step in a series of aerial leaps leading to Egypt. His next target was Cyprus followed by Syria.

> ### GENERALOBERST KURT STUDENT
>
> Born on 12 May 1890 near Neumark in Brandenburg, Generaloberst Kurt Student came from a family of Prussian landowners who had traditionally entered military service for the state. His military career began at the age of eleven when he entered cadet school. Student was commissioned in the infantry in 1911 and, in 1913, he volunteered for flying training, the start of a career that straddled both air and ground warfare. In the First World War he served as a pilot, flying fighters. By 1916 he commanded a squadron.
>
> After Germany's defeat in the First World War the *Reichswehr*'s commander, Generaloberst Hans von Seeckt, selected Student for the force's hand-picked officer corps. Seeckt sent Student to the Central Flying Office where he applied himself to technological administration and the design of the future *Luftwaffe*. His career flourished. During this time, Student also returned to the infantry and commanded a battalion, continuing his affiliation with both forms of warfare.
>
> Once Hitler abandoned the restrictions of the Treaty of Versailles, Germany began to rearm and Student's career advanced rapidly. Among his appointments was Inspector General of *Luftwaffe* Training Schools, a position which included oversight of the parachute school. The development of parachuting as a new form of warfare soon dominated his thoughts. In 1938 he took command of *7 Flieger Division*, Germany's first parachute formation. By 1940 he led *XI Fliegerkorps*. Student retained command of all airborne infantry forces until the war's end.
>
> After Crete, Student continued to advance plans for the mass use of his *fallschirmjäger*, including the invasion of Malta, but Hitler refused to authorise any of these operations. Apart for a few small-scale drops, Germany's parachute soldiers spent the rest of the war fighting as foot infantry soldiers. In late 1944, Student, now generaloberst, commanded *1 Parachute Army* and helped stem the British advance in Operation *Market Garden*, subsequently moving to command *Army Group H* in the Netherlands.
>
> Student's role as a pioneer of parachute warfare reached its apex on Crete. Germany's severe losses and Hitler's reluctance to embrace parachute warfare saw the initiative in air mobility pass to the allies. Student was a highly decorated soldier, earning awards such as the Knight's Cross with Oak Leaves and the Golden Flying Award with Diamonds. He died in 1978.

General Kurt Student.
Imperial War Museum HU 32007

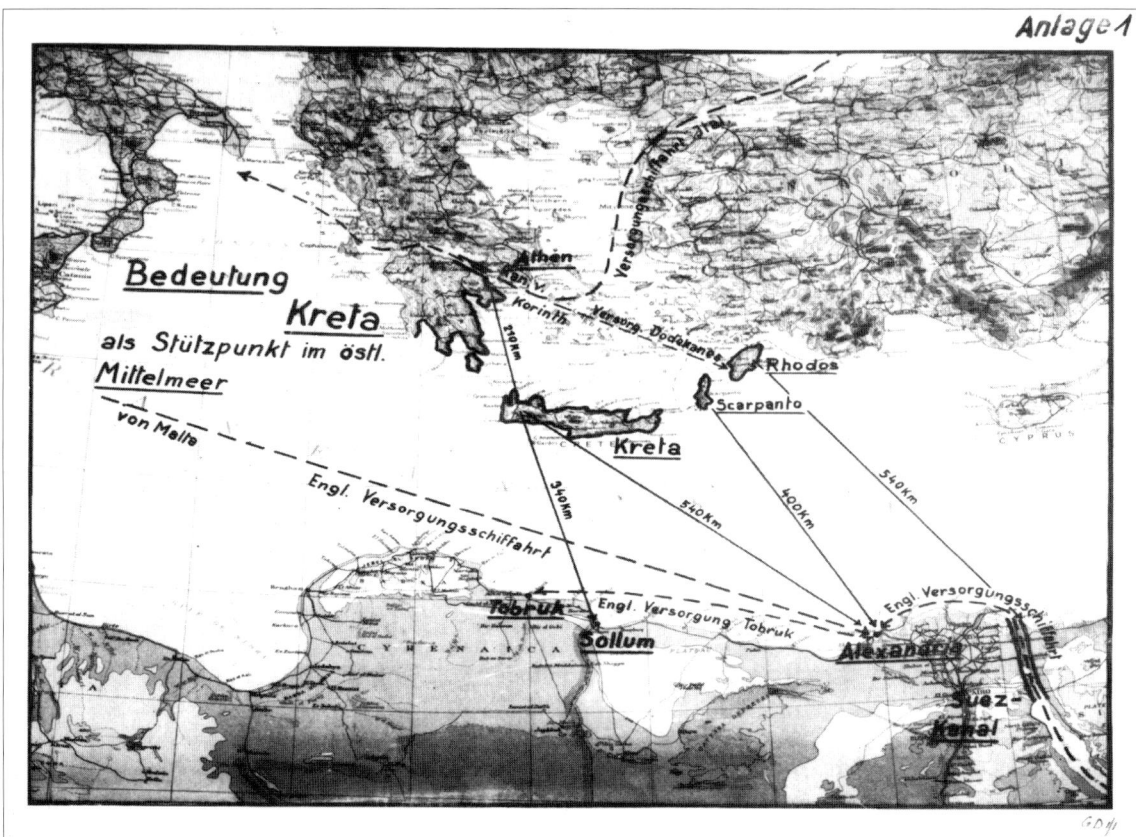

Map of Eastern Mediterranean showing British bases and convoy routes with distances from German and Italian airbases.
Australian War Memorial Map Collection

Student also had a personal agenda. As an advocate of parachute warfare he saw Crete as an opportunity to establish his specialty at the forefront of the German art of war, perhaps even rivalling the panzers. Success would increase the paratrooper arm's prestige and lead to its expansion. Student knew that a quick, low-cost conquest of Crete would give him the status with which to propose further opportunities to showcase his force. Reminiscent of its aerial origins, the Germans designated the invasion of Crete Operation *Merkur*.

THE SITUATION ON CRETE

The British Preparations

In November 1940 a British brigade group deployed to Crete. It assumed responsibility for the island's defence and allowed the Greek government to transfer the Cretan Infantry Division, a regular formation, to the mainland for service on the Albanian front. The brigade's role was to safeguard Crete from Italian forces based on the nearby island of Rhodes.

During the six-month interval between the brigade's arrival and the German invasion the following May, the British did little to improve the island's defensive capability. This critical failure is generally justified by a lack of materials, resources and manpower, and the absence of strategic direction and priority.

These explanations carry a degree of validity. Other areas of the Middle East Theatre, including the Western Desert and mainland Greece, had a higher priority for resources and were accorded more attention in Cairo and London. In addition, London was unable to enunciate a clear policy for Crete, although a number of potential roles were discussed.

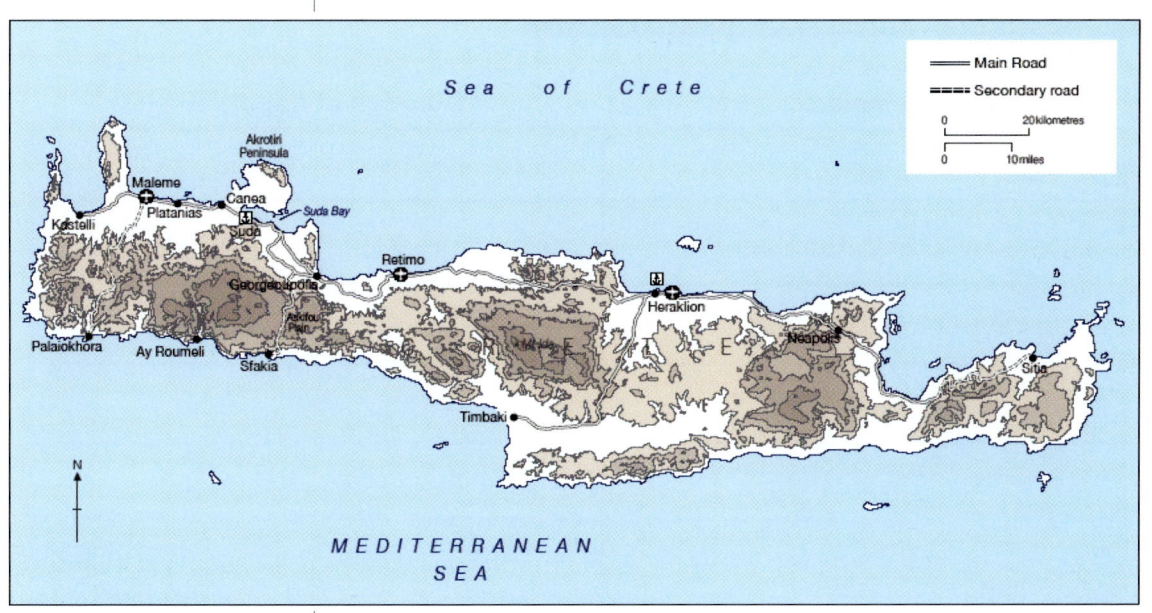

The Island of Crete
Drawn by Keith Mitchell

Yet the absence of formal instruction can never excuse the lack of initiative displayed by a series of British garrison commanders. Implicit in command is the responsibility for the defence of that command; there can be no excuse for the garrison's failure to make basic defensive improvements or undertake contingency planning. Nor did the commanders familiarise themselves with the local Greek troops or encourage the development of a militia. The shifting of blame to higher authority cannot absolve a series of British leaders for allowing time to slip away without making material improvements to their force's readiness.

In fact, between November 1940 and April 1941 the British garrison had ample opportunity to implement significant improvements to Crete's defensive capabilities. However not one of the British commanders possessed the vision or drive to undertake these preparations. Part of the problem lay in the constant turnover of commanders which effectively prevented any continuity of ideas or the development of any plans. In a six-month period there were seven garrison commanders.

> **Lesson 1**
>
> Time lost can never be regained. Commanders cannot afford to be content with the status quo, even in the absence of instructions. Instead they must always seek to examine their positions and implement improvements, which need not be structural. Contingency planning is also a critical necessity that will save valuable time later.

Table 1
British Commanders on Crete

Commanders	Duration of Appointment
Brigadier O. H. Tidbury	November 1940 – 9 January 1941
Major-General M. D. Gambier-Parry	9 January – 7 February 1941
Lieutenant-Colonel C. H. Mather	7 February – 19 February 1941
Brigadier A. Galloway	19 February – 9 March 1941
Brigadier B. H. Chappel	20 March – 22 April 1941
Major-General E. C. Weston	22 April – 30 April 1941
Major-General B. C. Freyberg	30 April – 30 May 1941

I. McD. G. Stewart in *The Struggle for Crete* identified five simple and immediate steps the British garrison could have taken. They could have:

1) improved landing facilities in the southern fishing villages;
2) upgraded roads leading from southern landing points to the north coast;
3) constructed airstrips on the plateaus of the mountain interior;
4) laid mines and prepared to destroy the airfields at Maleme, Retimo and Heraklion; and
5) armed able-bodied males and formed a reserve Cretan Division.

Other achievable measures included the development of defensive plans, the undertaking of hydrographic or beach surveys, the installation of a military communication system, and the construction of aircraft shelters.

The Troops Arrive from Greece

Further complicating the situation was the fact that the hastily organised withdrawal from Greece did not include an evacuation plan that would deliver units to their destinations in combat-ready order. Instead, the priority lay in simply evacuating as many men as possible.

Instead of landing in Egypt, many soldiers found themselves at Suda Bay on Crete. There was no organised unit selection. Some ships stopped at Suda to take on fuel and continued on to Alexandria with their passengers, while others unloaded and returned to Greece to embark more troops. As a result, few units were complete and some were linked to form ad hoc units; for example, 2/2 and 2/3 Australian Battalions were hastily reorganised to become 16 Australian Brigade Composite Battalion.

After disembarking at Suda the troops marched to dispersal areas. The first few nights they slept rough under the olive trees, some with blankets, others sharing with mates. Those staying in one area were able to construct shelters; those marching on spent the nights huddled together sheltering under trees. Rations were short. At times there might be half a herring per man with no biscuit or tea, while at other times there was simply no food at all. Scrounging parties were the order of the day with some men managing to buy food from the local population. Gradually, order returned. The men received issues of razors, blankets and clothing, were reunited with mates and discipline was restored. It is a remarkable feat that an army was reborn as quickly as it was from the detritus of the Greek evacuation.

British, Australia, and New Zealand troops arrive at Suda after evacuation from Greece.
National Library of New Zealand DA-01611

Troops resting in a temporary shelter on Crete.
National Library of New Zealand DA-03179

The only units with their full establishment of men and weapons belonged to the original garrison comprising 14 British Brigade. On 10 May the brigade was joined by the Mobile Naval Base Defence Organisation (MNBDO). This was a Royal Marine organisation whose primary function was base defence. The MNBDO included a number of anti-aircraft, coastal artillery and searchlight batteries, base units and a tented hospital. Most of its units were at full strength, the exception being 23 Light Anti-Aircraft Battery which arrived without its guns.

The Challenges Facing Freyberg

When Major-General Bernard Freyberg, commander of the New Zealand Division, arrived at Suda Bay from Greece he was invited to attend a conference with General Archibald Wavell, the Commander-in-Chief of Middle East Command. His superior's request that he take command of Creforce came as a complete surprise. After all, the island already had a garrison commander—Royal Marine Major-General Eric C. Weston who had arrived on the island with the MNBDO. Freyberg was reluctant to accept the command, but believed he had no choice. He saw it as a temporary appointment, and his priority remained the return of his New Zealand troops to Egypt so that he could rebuild the division. Freyberg then handed command of the division to Brigadier Edward Puttick.

Throughout his tenure on Crete, Freyberg's ability to shape the campaign was hindered by three critical deficiencies, namely:

- a lack of staff officers;
- a primitive and unreliable communication network; and
- a shortage of heavy weapons.

Manpower was never an issue. In fact, there were too many soldiers on the island and Freyberg asked Wavell to take off excess service and support troops.

After the meeting with Wavell broke up, Freyberg proceeded to Headquarters Creforce on the Akrotiri Peninsula just outside of Canea. There he discovered that his predecessor, Weston, had taken almost the entire staff with him back to his original command, the MNBDO. The marine general had drawn on the MNBDO to create the Creforce staff and they now returned from whence they had come. Freyberg could have ordered their return, but chose not to do so. He was alone, accept for an aide, a couple of signallers, and a car.

The staff shortage facing Freyberg could easily have been avoided.

Lieutenant-General Bernard Freyberg, Commander Creforce (photograph taken in 1943).
Australian War Memorial 053498

Only hours earlier, the New Zealand Division's 6 Brigade and divisional staff had departed Suda for Egypt. The British cruiser *Ajax* had not put them ashore because it was forced to sail in accordance with Royal Navy scheduling. Freyberg was now without one of his brigades and his headquarters staff. To make matters worse, 6 Australian Division's headquarters had sailed from Crete the preceding day. The Australian divisional headquarters could have served as a ready source of staff officers but it too had been allowed to sail. Wavell himself must share part of the blame for this critical oversight. At no point did he send out any spare staff officers from Cairo or order the New Zealand Division staff to return to the island. Freyberg had no choice but to raid his two remaining brigades for personnel.

LIEUTENANT-GENERAL SIR BERNARD CYRIL FREYBERG

Born in Richmond, London, on 21 March 1889, Bernard C. Freyberg migrated to New Zealand with his family in 1891. He would serve his adopted country in both world wars, becoming New Zealand's most renowned soldier.

Freyberg's military career began in 1911 when he joined a local unit of the Territorial Force. The following year he made an unsuccessful bid for a commission in the New Zealand Staff Corps.

The outbreak of the First World War found Freyberg in Mexico. He made his way to Britain and joined the Royal Naval Division as a company commander. He saw service at Antwerp, Gallipoli, and on the Western Front. He was awarded the VC during the Battle of the Somme. Freyberg combined coolness in battle with courage and dash which, while resulting in numerous wounds, also marked him as a top tactical-level commander. In addition to the VC, he received the DSO with two bars and was mentioned in dispatches at least five times. He ended the war in command of a brigade.

After the war Freyberg gained a regular commission in the Grenadier Guards and enjoyed a series of command and staff appointments. In 1934 he was promoted to major-general and seemed destined for the highest levels of the British Army. However poor health forced his retirement in 1937.

With the onset of the Second World War Freyberg's military career resumed. His first appointment was in command of the Salisbury Plain area. However, he was soon given command of the 2nd New Zealand Expeditionary Force and its fighting formation the New Zealand Division. Freyberg proved a skilled and determined trainer of men, and the New Zealand Division developed into one of the elite formations of the war. Despite having spent many years amongst professional British soldiers, Freyberg instinctively knew to treat his New Zealanders differently. Saluting and deference to higher authority were not priorities within the formation. Instead of discipline Freyberg emphasised camaraderie and self-respect.

Freyberg led the New Zealand Division through the Greek, North African and Italian campaigns. Crete was the only blemish on an otherwise distinguished military career. In 1942 he was promoted to lieutenant-general. In the war's final days he received a third bar to his DSO.

Freyberg was knighted in 1942 and served as New Zealand's Governor-General from 1946 to 1952. In 1951 he was made Baron Freyberg of Wellington, and in 1953 he was appointed Constable and Lieutenant-General of Windsor Castle. He died at Windsor on 4 July 1963.

FIELD MARSHAL ARCHIBALD WAVELL

Archibald Percival Wavell was born in Colchester on 5 May 1883. The son of a general, his future lay in the army. After school at Winchester he entered Sandhurst, from which he graduated in 1901 at the top of his class.

Wavell joined the Black Watch and saw service in the Boer War and India. In 1909 he attended Staff College at Camberley. At the First Battle of Ypres in World War I, Wavell won an MC but lost his left eye. He spent the rest of the war in a variety of staff positions, finishing with General Edmund Allenby in Palestine. Wavell's experiences on Allenby's staff laid the foundation for his authoritative study *The Palestine Campaign*.

During the interwar years Wavell established himself as a thinking officer whose destiny lay in the army's senior ranks. In 1939 he became Commander-in-Chief Middle East Command, a command second only in importance to India in Britain's hierarchy of overseas commands. Wavell's responsibilities covered a vast area on two continents for whose defence he was never allocated sufficient resources. While the outbreak of war saw his forces heavily outnumbered, he responded with aggressive action against the Italians in Libya which culminated in the enemy's rout and destruction.

Wavell's command in Cairo was marred by his inability to capitalise on his successes and his deteriorating relationship with the Prime Minister, Winston Churchill. His victory in Libya was followed by the break-up of the victorious force, the dispatch of a large proportion of its units to Greece and their subsequent defeat by the Germans. Churchill rightly pushed Wavell hard but appeared to have little understanding of the vast gulf between his subordinate's responsibilities and resources. Moreover, Wavell's blunt objections to the East African campaign permanently marred his relationship with the Prime Minister.

Churchill used the failure of the Battleaxe Offensive of June 1941 to remove Wavell, sending him to India as Commander-in-Chief. The Japanese attack resulted in Wavell's appointment to head American-British-Dutch-Australian (ABDA) Command on Java. The enemy's rapid advance doomed ABDA and Wavell had barely organised his headquarters when he was forced to flee. He returned to his duties in India where he oversaw the retreat from Burma and began to lay the foundation for the British return.

In 1943 Wavell was promoted Field Marshal and was created a Viscount. He was also appointed Viceroy of India, a post he held until 1947 when he became the first Earl Wavell. He died in London in 1950.

General Archibald Wavell, Commander-in-Chief Middle East Command.
Australian War Memorial 007861

Creforce's communication system was even more parlous than its staff situation. The primary link between units was the civilian cable network supplemented by military telephone lines. Neither survived the German aerial bombardment on the morning of the invasion. Creforce's establishment included plenty of signallers but few wireless sets; the units at Retimo, for example, had just four telephones and one wireless. Communication within the area depended on the use of runners, and on the ability of Retimo's commander, Lieutenant-Colonel Ian Campbell, to travel around on his motorcycle. The commander of 19 Australian Brigade, Brigadier George Vasey, had no wireless sets at all. He used the public phone system to speak to his superior, Weston.

Freyberg addresses a party of officers near Suda Bay.
Australian War Memorial 069892

Of Creforce's many equipment deficiencies this was the most significant, and the one that would have been most easily rectified; yet no senior commander, either on Crete, in Cairo or in London made an effort to do so. Instead of trying to change the course of the coming battle by rushing ships laden with heavy weapons through the gauntlet of German bombers to Suda, the British could have more directly improved their chances of victory with the arrival of just one planeload of signals equipment.

The units arriving on Crete lacked almost all of their heavy weapons. After visiting a number of units, Freyberg concluded that the situation was worse than he had feared. He wrote that 'it was not unusual to find that the men had no arms or equipment, no plates, knives, forks, or spoons, and they ate and drank from bully beef or cigarette tins. There was no transport and no tools for most of the B[attalio]ns.' One brigade—10 New Zealand Brigade—had a single truck, and there were only seven motor ambulances on the entire island.

> **Lesson 2**
>
> The importance of communications is so obvious that a formal lesson may seem unnecessary. Yet the consequences for a commander who neglects any of the essential requirements of sound communications may be far-reaching and disastrous. Poor communications can affect the successful conduct of a campaign because they force a commander to:
> - operate in a fog of war that is unnecessarily thick; and
> - operate within a decision cycle that is unnecessarily long.

Requests soon began to arrive in Cairo, but it was simply too late to rectify the damage done by months of neglect. Moreover, Wavell had other more important fronts to worry about, including the growing German threat in Libya. As a result, Crete received cast-offs: weapons that were non-standard or barely serviceable. When 2/3 Australian Field Regiment received its replacement guns, its historian described them as 'high wheeled monstrosities ready for a museum'. In fact, they were Italian 75 and 100mm weapons captured in the Western Desert, and they arrived without sights, range drums or telescopes and with suspect ammunition and fuzes. Home-made sights soon appeared, fashioned from bits of wood and chewing gum. The fundamental problems with these weapons combined with the lack of signals equipment, however, meant that the gunners' ability to fire indirectly was severely compromised. Most gunners aimed by simply peering down the barrel. Wavell also sent out 7 Royal Tank Regiment (RTR) with six Matilda tanks, but the vehicles despatched had not completed their refit. During the Crete campaign they broke down frequently.

Matilda Mark II (infantry tank)

Length:	6 m
Width:	2.6 m
Height:	3.5 m
Weight:	11.1 tonnes
Crew:	four (commander, gunner, loader and driver)
Power plant:	Two 6 cylinder diesels (Leyland or AEC)
Armament:	One 2-pounder gun, one Bren .303-inch or Vickers machine-gun. An anti-aircraft machine-gun could also be fitted and two 4-inch smoke dischargers either side of the turret.
Max. Armour:	14-78 mm
Speed:	25 kph (road)
Range:	80 km

The Matilda Mark II was designed as a heavily armoured vehicle for infantry support and it performed well in this role from the beginning of the Second World War up to mid-1941. However, more powerful German tank and anti-tank guns, particularly the dreaded 88, made it obsolete.

Only nine Matildas of 7 RTR were present on Crete. Six came from workshops in Egypt before necessary repairs had been completed. These quickly broke down from the strain of operational use or were destroyed. Three new tanks arrived as the campaign began and two of them performed well in the retreat.

Rifles and Bren guns were in such short supply that Freyberg had the support and service units stripped of nearly all their small arms. These weapons were then redistributed to the infantry. Other specialist units without their proper equipment found themselves reassigned as infantry, including the New Zealand Division engineers who held a perimeter near Maleme. Ammunition was also limited. At Retimo, the Australians had just 80 rounds for their 3-inch mortars, which also lacked base plates. There was even less ammunition for the 2-inch mortars and just ten belts of ammunition per Vickers machine-gun.

Jointness and Intelligence

Complicating Freyberg's control of the campaign was the fact that he commanded only the army component of the garrison. The British maintained three chains of command on Crete, one for each of the services. Freyberg was the island's senior officer and the commander of the largest British contingent, yet he could not issue orders to the more junior leaders of the much smaller Royal Navy and Royal Air Force elements. Instead, Freyberg's requests to the other services took the form of suggestions, which his colleagues dutifully forwarded up their chains of command for consideration. This procedure made immediate action impossible and obstructed Freyberg's management of the battlespace. Moreover, there was never a guarantee that his air and naval colleagues would acquiesce, and indeed they sometimes refused his requests.

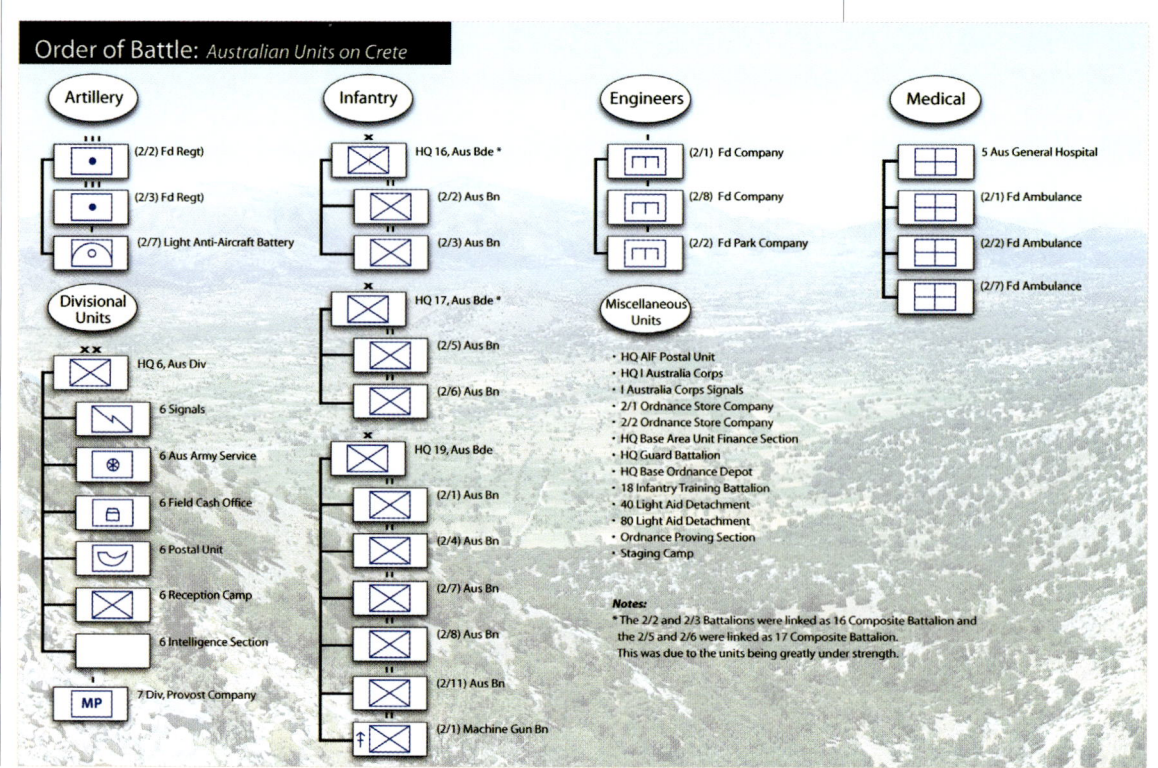

Freyberg also had to take national considerations into account given his position as the New Zealand national commander with direct access to the New Zealand Prime Minister. Vasey, as the senior Australian officer, represented Australian interests on the island. The Order of Battle identifies the Australian units on Crete and indicates all too clearly that combat units were in the minority. Many of the Australian units on the island comprised service and support troops for whom there was little need during the coming battle.

The complexity of Freyberg's chain of command stood in stark contrast to the simplicity enjoyed by Student. The invasion of Crete was an air force show, and Hitler subordinated German naval and army forces participating in the operation to *Luftwaffe* command. There were no parallel chains of command, as indicated by wire diagrams 1, 2, and 3 which illustrate the German and British chains of command.

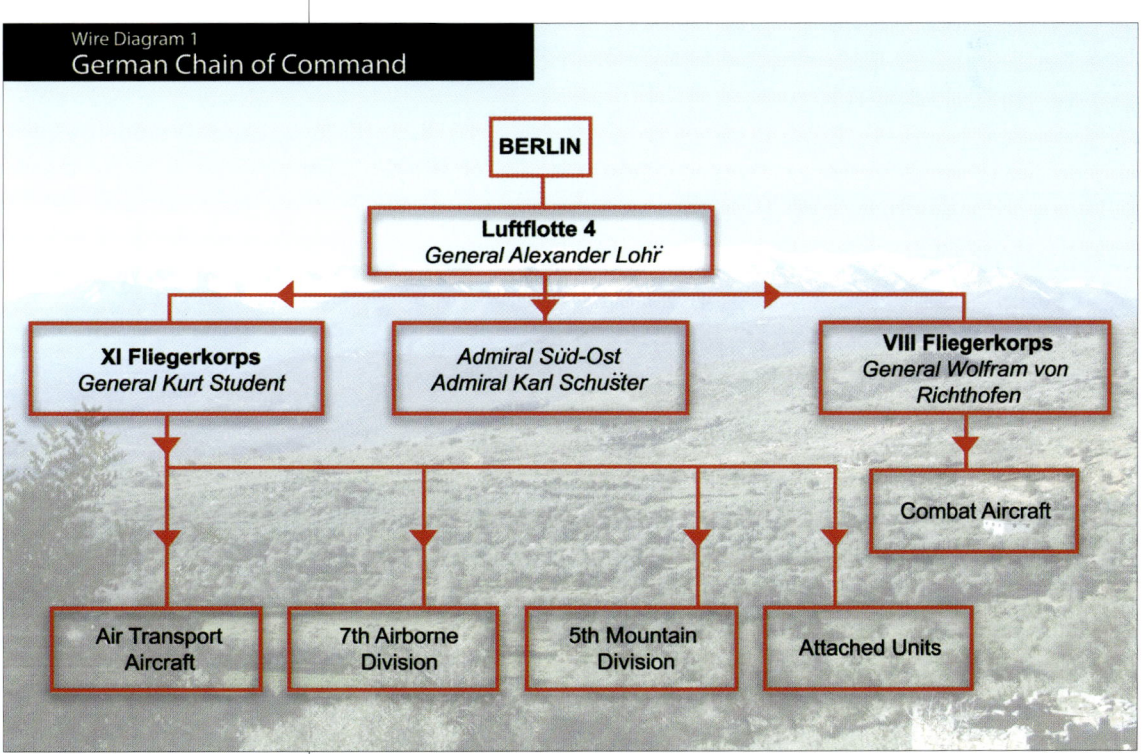

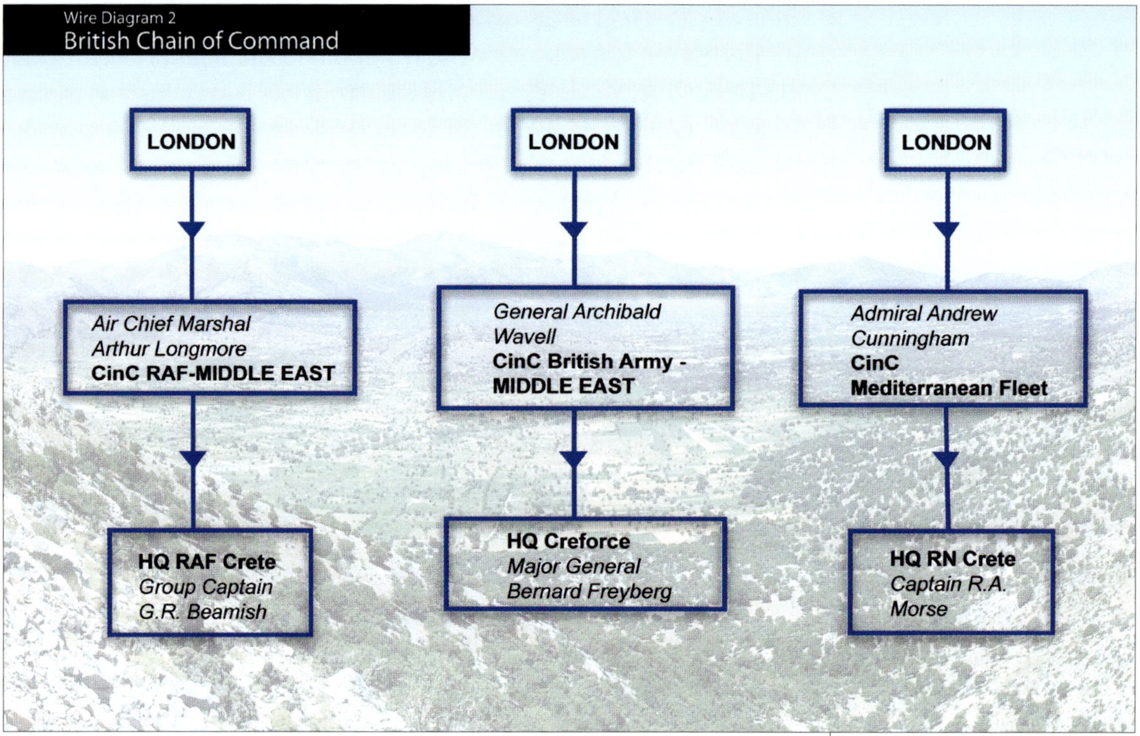

Wire Diagram 2
British Chain of Command

- **LONDON** → Air Chief Marshal Arthur Longmore, **CinC RAF-MIDDLE EAST** → **HQ RAF Crete**, Group Captain G.R. Beamish
- **LONDON** → General Archibald Wavell, **CinC British Army - MIDDLE EAST** → **HQ Creforce**, Major General Bernard Freyberg
- **LONDON** → Admiral Andrew Cunningham, **CinC Mediterranean Fleet** → **HQ RN Crete**, Captain R.A. Morse

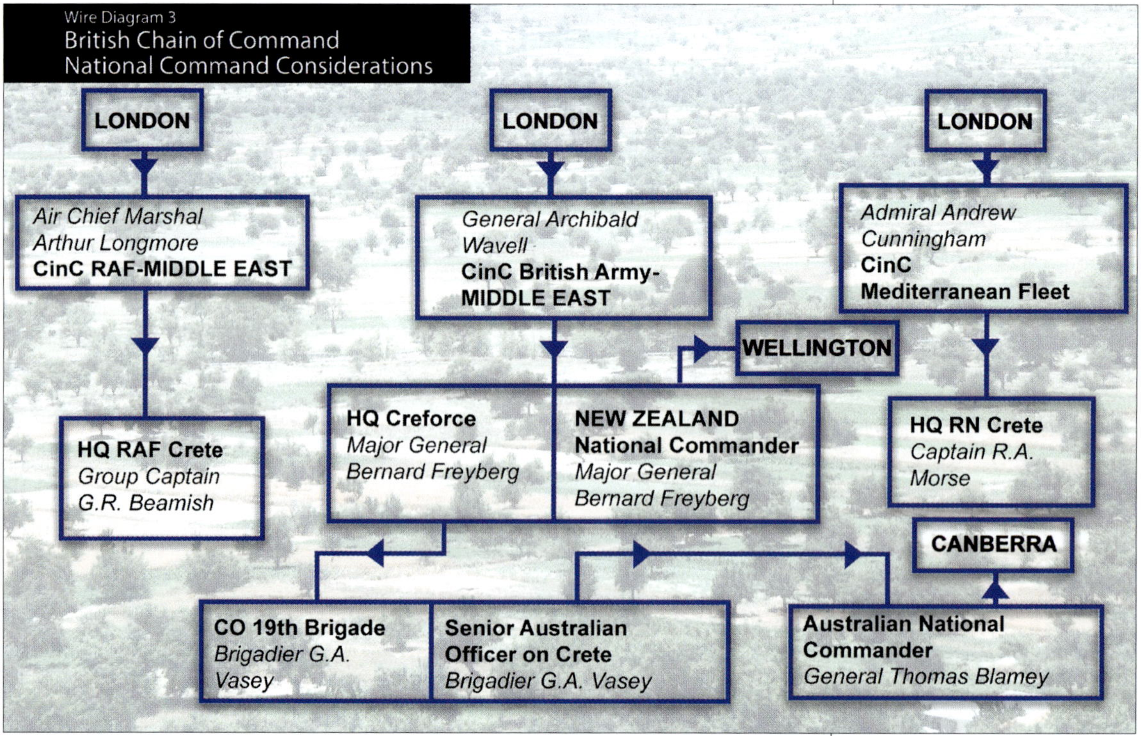

Wire Diagram 3
British Chain of Command
National Command Considerations

- **LONDON** → Air Chief Marshal Arthur Longmore, **CinC RAF-MIDDLE EAST** → **HQ RAF Crete**, Group Captain G.R. Beamish
- **LONDON** → General Archibald Wavell, **CinC British Army-MIDDLE EAST** → **HQ Creforce**, Major General Bernard Freyberg
- **WELLINGTON** → **NEW ZEALAND National Commander**, Major General Bernard Freyberg
- **LONDON** → Admiral Andrew Cunningham, **CinC Mediterranean Fleet** → **HQ RN Crete**, Captain R.A. Morse
- **CANBERRA** → **Australian National Commander**, General Thomas Blamey
- **CO 19th Brigade**, Brigadier G.A. Vasey
- **Senior Australian Officer on Crete**, Brigadier G.A. Vasey

Throughout the lead-up to the invasion the British received valuable intelligence which clearly detailed German intentions. In part this was because the Germans could not hide the build-up of forces in southern Greece. However, of even more significance was the role of Ultra. Since Operation *Merkur* was an air force responsibility, its planners used the *Luftwaffe*'s code for wireless transmissions. British cryptologists had cracked this particular code, providing London with unmatched insight into the German plan.

Through Ultra the British had:

- learned that Student had set the date of the invasion for 17 May;
- discovered the roles intended for *VIII* and *XI Fliegerkorps*;
- found out that *XI Fliegerkorps* had been granted priority for fuel;
- decrypted *XI Fliegerkorps'* order to move to Greek bases; and
- intercepted the request for a detailed air reconnaissance of the island.

Ultra also provided the British with confirmation of the operation's postponement to 20 May.

Intelligence can, however, be a double-edged sword. The code-breakers had also learned of the German intention to support the air assault of Crete with a seaborne landing. Intelligence officers estimated that the Germans would ship about 10,000 troops by sea, more than double the number of parachutes scheduled to land in the first wave. This estimate proved a gross exaggeration. Yet the scale of the seaborne movement convinced Freyberg and his subordinates that the main threat was from the sea rather than the air. Throughout the final pre-invasion days, and even after the Germans had landed, Freyberg and most senior New Zealand officers remained overly focused on the Aegean until it was too late. After the war Freyberg would admit that 'we were mostly preoccupied with sea landings, not the threat of air landings.'

Freyberg's concentration on a seaborne invasion rather than air assault indicates that he had failed to realise the potential of a new form of warfare. Freyberg knew of the existence of paratroopers, but could not conceive of them as the main threat. Instead, he continued to look to the sea, from which he anticipated the decisive blow would come.

ULTRA

During the course of the Second World War, the British, and later the Americans, enjoyed increasing success in decrypting German wireless transmissions. The reason for this was the secret decoding establishment at Bletchley Park in England. Messages decoded by this organisation were given the code-name 'Ultra'.

German coders employed an enciphering machine called 'Enigma' in whose security they had complete faith; they never deduced that the allies were reading their signals. While Bletchley Park staff did not break all German codes, one of the most vulnerable codes was that of the *Luftwaffe*. Since Operation *Merkur* was a *Luftwaffe* operation, Bletchley Park decrypts gave British leaders an unprecedented window on German plans.

To protect Ultra, the British carefully guarded knowledge of its existence. Prior to the Crete campaign, even Freyberg was unaware that Ultra existed. By the war's end the pool of people who knew about Ultra numbered in the thousands, yet not one person revealed the truth during the conflict or afterwards.

The Royal Navy should have allayed Freyberg's concerns over a seaborne assault. Senior ground commanders did not appreciate that there were few places where a seaborne landing was feasible—nor did they realise that the Germans did not have access to landing craft. There was a simple reason these officers had failed to grasp these facts: the Royal Navy had not informed them. Information did not flow freely between the services because each staff was isolated from the other, and there were insufficient points of contact for the ready exchange of intelligence. Other significant details included the fact that the Germans had to rely on fishing boats for their armada. These boats required the shelter of a harbour or a secure beachhead to land reinforcements, particularly armour and heavy weapons. It is unlikely that they could have forced a landing on a hostile shore.

By contrast, the greatest failure of the German campaign rests with the German intelligence service. Student's intelligence officers significantly underestimated the strength of the British forces on Crete. As a result the paratroopers at some landing sites were heavily outnumbered by the defenders and their attacks failed. The German intelligence service also concluded that the Cretan people would welcome the invasion because, as far as Greece was concerned, it would bring the war to an end. Consequently, the troops on the ground were stunned by the violence and tenacity of the Cretan resistance. What the intelligence officers had failed to appreciate was the military ardour of the Cretan people and the island's history of fanatical resistance to invaders.

> **Lesson 3**
>
> It is advantageous for a theatre to have a single commander who commands all forces within that theatre. In lieu of this provision there must be close physical links and a culture of cooperation between the services.

Logistics

Both the British and the Germans had to solve an almost identical logistic problem: the maintenance of their forces across an air-sea gap. The way in which they managed this was ultimately to determine the outcome of the campaign.

The German lines of communication leapt the gap between Crete and mainland Greece by air. The workhorse Ju 52 transport plane was the invasion force's lifeline. However the *Luftwaffe* only had the strength to sustain the deployment by air drop for a short period following the insertion of the paratroopers. It was essential that the paratroopers seize a working airfield at the earliest opportunity in order to permit the air landing of men and supplies. Without an airfield the operation would fail. Student's attempt to reduce the support burden on the air bridge through the movement of men and materials by sea failed when the Royal Navy intercepted his convoys.

	Junkers Ju 52
Type:	transport
Wingspan:	29.5 m
Length:	18.5 m
Engine:	three BWM 132A (485 kW each)
Max Speed:	265 kph (depending on height)
Range:	870 km
Armament:	various weapon configurations were fitted, usually rearward-facing, crew-served MGs

Nicknamed 'Tante Ju' (Auntie Ju) and 'Iron Annie', the Ju 52 proved a successful civil (Lufthansa) passenger aircraft in the 1930s and was the most famous German transport of the war. The Ju 52 had a characteristic corrugated metal fuselage which gave it an unusual boxy appearance. It was slow, lightly armed, and required a fighter escort in order to survive on operations. Consequently, it regularly suffered losses from ground fire and enemy air attack. During the Crete campaign, 151 Ju 52s were lost to allied fire from a total of approximately 500. The Ju 52s played a vital role in the campaign, transporting the German parachute troops to their drop zones and towing the DFS 230 gliders.

For Freyberg the island's lifeline was the sea. British supplies arrived from Alexandria by ship, landing principally at Suda. The area around Suda and Canea was Creforce's administrative area and its warehouses stored the defenders' reserves prior to distribution. Suda was not the island's best port—that was Heraklion—but it was the closest to Freyberg's centre of gravity.

The main problem facing Freyberg was that the throughput of his line of communication was barely sufficient for his daily needs or the build-up of reserves for an intensive campaign. What made his position even worse was that the island was not self-sufficient in food. Freyberg was responsible for the approximately 30,000 men of Creforce, the 10,000 Greek Army troops, the island's 400,000 civilians, and 15,000 Italian prisoners of war. The daily requirement to support this population amounted to some 600 tons of food.

The British line of communication was highly vulnerable to air interdiction. On 15 May the *Luftwaffe* established an aerial blockade over Suda Bay, whose waters were choked by now with the wrecks of sunken ships. Of the 27,000 tons of stores that left Alexandria, only 3,000 made it ashore at Suda. The enemy's dominance in the air made the harbour untenable during daylight hours. This forced the Royal Navy to use small, fast ships that could unload supplies during the brief hours of darkness and race for the relative safety of the waters south of Crete before first light. The most that a destroyer could unload at Suda during the hours of darkness was 100 tons. Freyberg thus faced a downward spiralling supply situation.

Suda Bay after a *Luftwaffe* raid. The photographs shows several ships burning.
Australian War Memorial 007845

The two combatants' supply limitations placed them in a similar situation. Neither could survive a long campaign. The only options were to establish an adequate supply system for their own forces or deny the enemy his own logistic capability. The Germans did both.

Battle Plans

The nature of the campaign was largely dictated by the geography of Crete. A narrow, rocky island, Crete is dominated by mountains that, in many places, march down to the sea. Only a few coastal enclaves of flat, arable land exist and these hold the main population centres. The most important areas for the campaign were the plains around Heraklion, Retimo and Canea. Each of these areas also contained an airfield. Suda Bay was a naval refuelling base and, along with Canea, had become the Creforce's administrative and logistic centre.

Freyberg accepted that each enclave had to be responsible for its own defence. Creforce's lack of transport and the enemy's control of the air meant that it would be extremely difficult for him to shift reserves to a threatened point in a timely manner. Freyberg therefore provided each sector with its own self-sufficient brigade group. Each would have to stand on its own.

XI Fliegerkorps staff planning the invasion of Crete.
Australian War Memorial 072856

Student's plan called for *XI Fliegerkorps* to seize Crete's three airfields (Maleme, Retimo and Heraklion) and the British administrative and logistic areas of Canea and Suda by parachute and glider assault. Having taken the airfield, the Germans would be able to fly in the waiting waves of mountain troops and supplies. The force at Student's disposal comprised:

- *7 Flieger Division*;
- *Luftlande-Sturmregiment*;
- *5 Gebirgs Division*; and
- elements of *6 Gebirgs Division*.

Student divided the assault into three sectors:

- West: objective Maleme airfield;
- Central: objective Suda port and administrative area and Retimo airfield; and
- East: Heraklion port and airfield.

Since the *Luftwaffe* could not provide enough transports to insert the paratroopers in a single lift, he split the attack into morning and afternoon waves. Student allocated Maleme and the Suda area to the first and Heraklion and Retimo to the second.

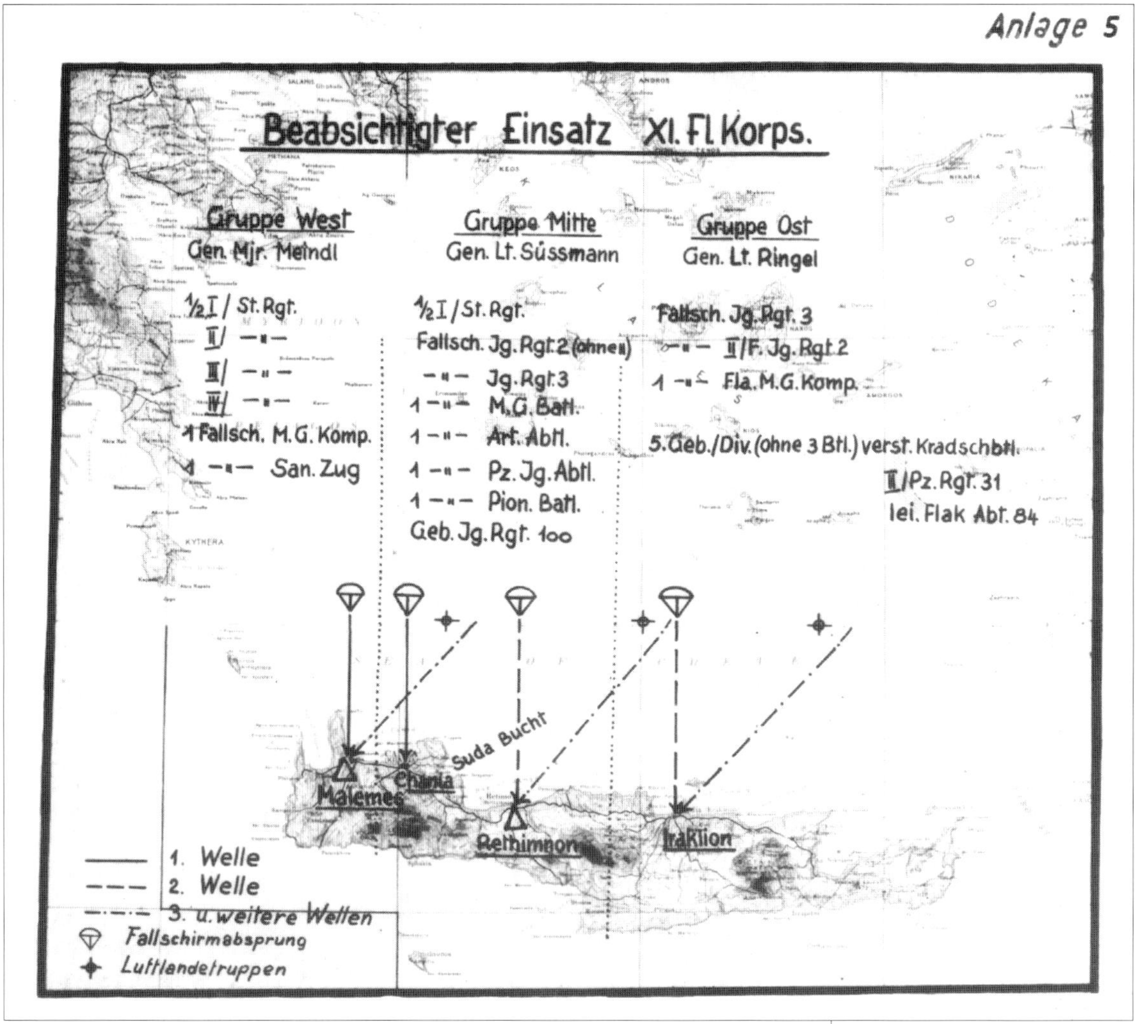

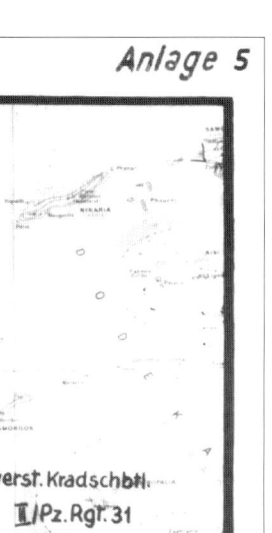

Student's invasion plan.
Australian War Memorial Map Collection

While targeting all of the airfields effectively divided his strength, Student had also allowed himself a margin of error. He needed to succeed at only one airfield in order to fly in reinforcements. By contrast, Freyberg had to be victorious at all of the assault points; defeat at one would inexorably lead to the defeat of all.

AIR ATTACK ON MALEME

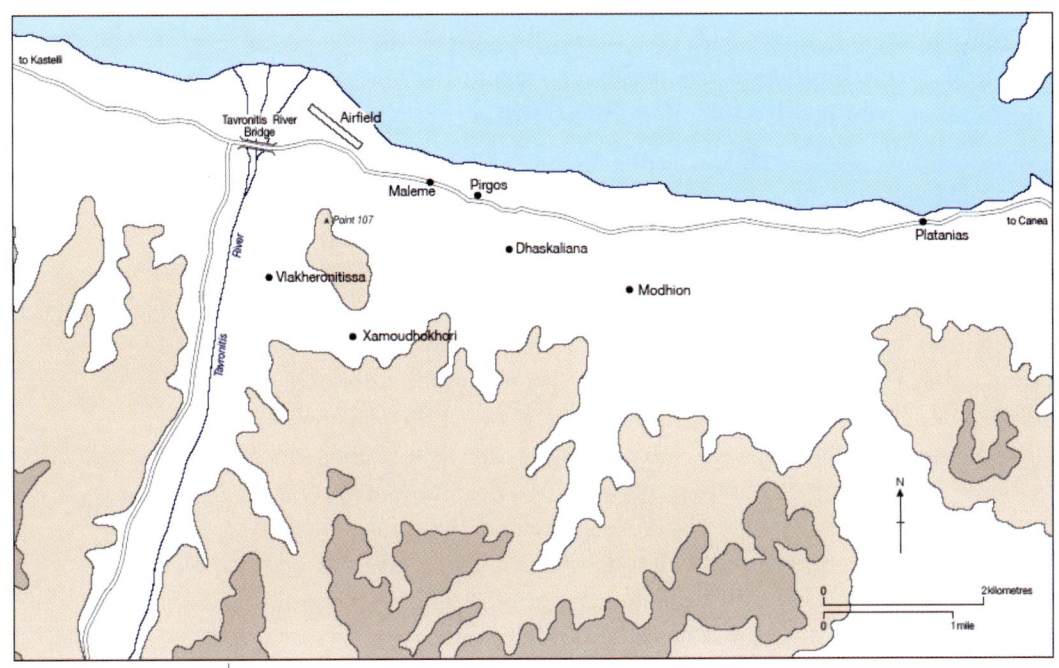

Maleme Sector
Drawn by Keith Mitchell

The New Zealanders at Maleme

The formation responsible for the defence of the Maleme sector was Brigadier James Hargest's 5 New Zealand Brigade. The brigade consisted of four battalions: 21, 22, 23 and 28—a Maori battalion; 1 Greek Regiment; a detachment of engineers fighting as infantry; elements of 27 New Zealand Machine Gun Battalion; and two Matilda Infantry tanks from 7 RTR. There were other units within the brigade's defensive zone, but these were not part of Hargest's command. These units included a dozen British, Australian and Royal Marine anti-aircraft guns, a variety of French, Italian and British field guns, a battery of mountain howitzers, two 4-inch coastal guns, and the New Zealand Division Field Punishment Centre.

While on paper Hargest had a powerful force, his battalions had not made up their losses in Greece, were deficient in heavy weapons, and suffered from poor coordination with the nearby supporting arms. Similarly, the Greek regiment at Kastelli had a strength of approximately 1,000 men but only half these men had rifles. Ammunition was in short supply and the bulk of the guns comprised a motley collection of captured ordnance that the Cairo depot had failed to restore to proper working order. Most critically, the brigade had only a handful of wireless sets and Hargest depended on the Cretan phone system for much of his communications.

The 5th New Zealand Brigade's zone of responsibility ran from the village of Platanias to the Tavronitis River on the western edge of the airfield. The zone itself resembled a narrow rectangle: the sea lay to the north and the southern end was ringed by foothills. The brigade's area of responsibility also included the fishing port of Kastelli.

Even at a casual glance, Hargest's placement of his brigade appeared ill-advised. His headquarters was sited at Platanias on the extreme eastern flank. Platanias was chosen because it was the closest point in the brigade's sector to divisional headquarters. By minimising the distance between the two, Hargest simplified his line of communication with Puttick. Yet, in streamlining his communication with his divisional commander, Hargest effectively complicated communication within his brigade. Two of his battalions where spread along the coast where they combined with the engineers to protect the area against the feared seaborne assault. Only the half-strength 21 New Zealand Battalion was positioned inland in support of 23 New Zealand Battalion. Hargest assigned the Maleme airfield's defence to a single unit—22 New Zealand Battalion. This unit also had the secondary assignment of forming a flank guard for the remainder of the brigade.

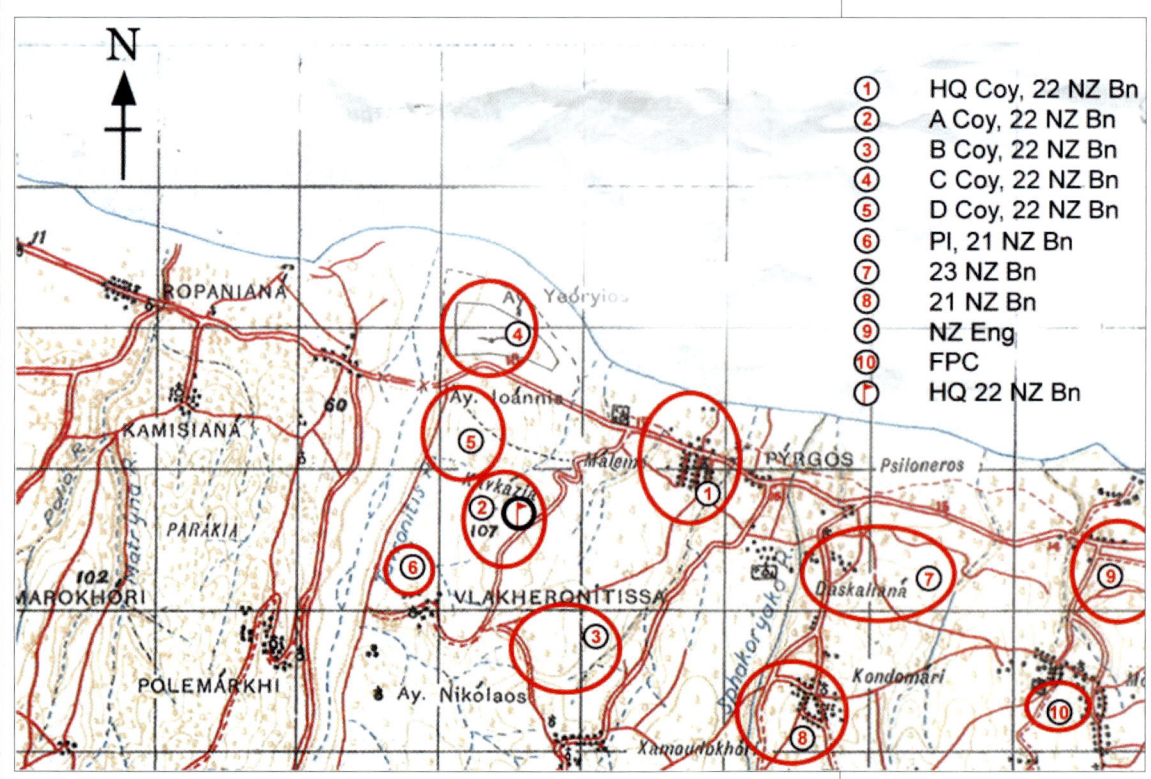

New Zealand Positions at Maleme
Australian War Memorial Map Collection
Modified by Mark Wahlert

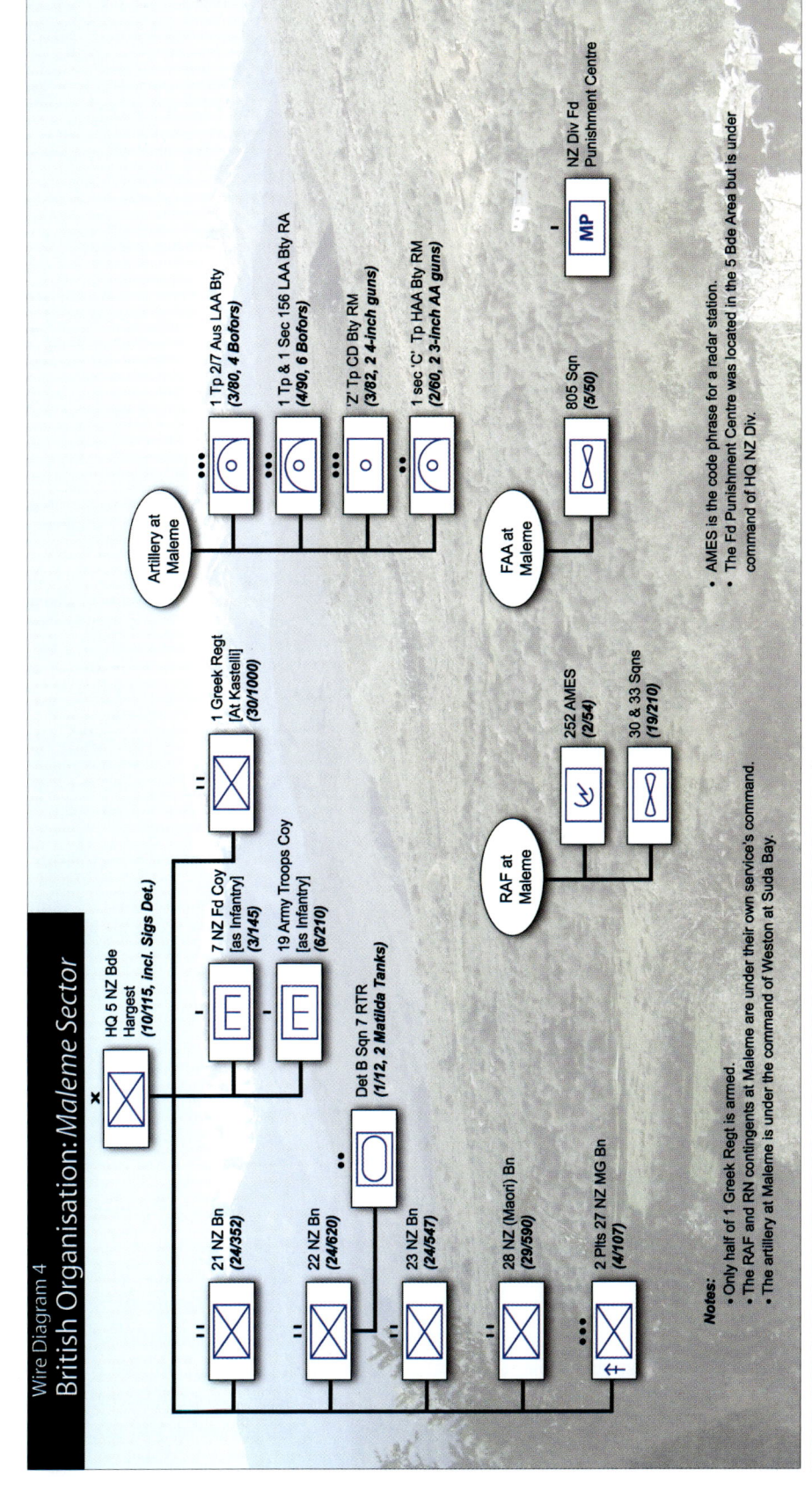

Brigadier P. S. W. D. [James] Hargest
National Library of New Zealand C-095-030

BRIGADIER JAMES HARGEST

James Hargest was born in Gore on 4 September 1891. In 1911 he joined the Territorial Force and was an early volunteer for the New Zealand Expeditionary Force, joining in August 1914. He received a commission in the Otago Mounted Rifles and was wounded at Gallipoli. Having recovered, he served on the Western Front where he rose in rank and, by the end of the war, commanded 2 Battalion, Otago Infantry Regiment. He was considered a fine battalion commander. The DSO was one of his many awards.

After his return to New Zealand, Hargest took up farming in the Invercargill district. He also continued to serve in the Territorial Force and, by 1925, commanded 3 New Zealand Brigade. In 1931 he won a seat in the New Zealand Parliament.

After the start of the Second World War, Hargest again offered his services to New Zealand, seeking a senior appointment in the 2nd New Zealand Expeditionary Force. However a poor medical report saw him declared unfit for overseas service. Hargest used his influence with the acting Prime Minister of New Zealand, Peter Fraser, to secure a brigade command.

Hargest's first campaign was Greece, where he performed creditably in command of 5 New Zealand Brigade. However, his performance during the Crete campaign revealed his unsuitability for high command. Throughout the critical phase of the battle he remained at his headquarters, aloof and unresponsive to the crisis and seemingly unperturbed by the loss of Maleme.

After his evacuation to Egypt, Hargest criticised Freyberg's handling of the battle, going so far as to speak privately to Fraser who happened to be in Cairo. As a result, Hargest escaped blame for the island's loss. Instead he received a bar to his DSO.

During Hargest's next campaign, Operation *Crusader*, German armour overran his brigade headquarters, leading to his capture and imprisonment in Italy. In March 1943 he escaped and made his way to England via Switzerland, France and Spain. This exploit earned him another bar to his DSO. Hargest next served as an observer with 50 Infantry Division in Normandy where he died on 12 August 1944.

Hargest provides a fine example of an officer who was promoted above his level, mainly through his willingness to employ personal contacts to his own advantage. His most enduring legacy is the collection of insightful reports that he wrote on the Normandy campaign.

While 22 New Zealand Battalion was Hargest's strongest, its commander, Lieutenant-Colonel Leslie W. Andrew, had an area of responsibility that was so large that he was forced to spread his men thinly on the ground. The area's key terrain comprised the runway, Hill 107 directly behind it, and the village of Pirgos in the east. The battalion's western boundary—the Tavronitis River—evaporated by the harsh Greek sun, was now little more than a rivulet meandering through a broad bed.

Andrew was conscious of the need for direct protection of the crucial runway, but could spare only C Company for this task. In turn, C Company had only 15 Platoon to allocate to the airfield's western boundary—the section facing the river bed. Watching the sea from its beachfront position was 13 Platoon. D Company guarded the bridge while A Company was on the top of Hill 107. B Company was dug in further back on the hill protecting the battalion's rear. Headquarters Company—fighting as infantry—was sited in Pirgos, most of its members having left their specialist equipment in Greece. Andrew did not have enough men to guard the open ground at the mouth of the Tavronitis River, nor could he allocate a company as a reserve. The battalion entered the battle fully committed.

> **Lesson 4**
>
> It is essential for commanders at every level to possess a dedicated reserve. A reserve provides a commander the flexibility to respond to enemy threats to his position, and the ability to exploit an opponent's weakness which is exposed in the course of battle. The absence of a reserve denies a commander the ability to respond to the unexpected, and the unexpected is the norm in war.

Andrew's men suffered from Creforce's usual shortage of weapons. The grenades hurled by 15 Platoon were home-made—jam tins filled with bits of concrete and gelignite. Those troops positioned near the airfield cannibalised wrecked planes for Browning machine-guns. The only additional weapons Andrew commanded were two clapped-out Matildas belonging to 7 RTR.

Along the perimeter of the airfield were ten Bofors light anti-aircraft guns manned by 2/7 Australian Light Anti-Aircraft Battery and 156 Light Anti-Aircraft Battery, Royal Artillery. The gunners were responsible for the runway's aerial defence. Positioned on the lower slope were two 4-inch coastal defence guns, their barrels pointing out to sea, and near the hill's peak were two 3-inch anti-aircraft guns. Despite being located within 22 Battalion's perimeter, these guns lay outside Andrew's control. They belonged to the MNBDO and took their orders from Weston's gun operations room in Canea.

Andrew had already told Hargest that he believed the gunners' positions were badly exposed; in fact they had not even bothered to dig in. His conclusion was that they 'won't last long.' One Australian of the 2/7th commented that the sandbags around his Bofors' position did not reach his knees. The gunners were also largely without the means to defend themselves—only a handful had rifles. Because of the lack of unified command, the infantry and the anti-aircraft gunners at Maleme never established a coordinated area defence against a ground attack.

Also at Maleme was a party of Fleet Air Arm and Royal Air Force personnel. When the few British aircraft that had survived the *Luftwaffe*'s preliminary raids withdrew to Egypt, the squadrons left behind approximately 300 ground staff. Since they belonged to other services, their chains of command followed lines that were independent of the ground commanders. Freyberg had no authority over these men. Many regarded the absence of aircraft as a chance to enjoy an island holiday, and requests by army officers that they move or at least help prepare for the expected German invasion were largely ignored. Suggestions by 5 New Zealand Brigade to Creforce Headquarters to relocate the airmen's camp did not progress due to the difficulty of liaison across the parallel chains of command.

> **Lesson 5**
>
> Within any battlespace, it is a fundamental requirement that all units, no matter their function or service, be responsive to the commander of that battlespace.

The presence of the airmen's camp had a significant effect on the battle. The camp, on the west side of Hill 107, overlapped part of 22 New Zealand Battalion's perimeter. The battalion's historian observed that the location of the camp made it impossible to link C and D Companies' lines and that 'one good defence line would have run straight through the officers' mess.' Of course, moving the mess was considered 'unthinkable'.

The three elements at Maleme—the infantry, the anti-aircraft gunners and the air personnel—approached the coming battle as if it were an independent affair. One historian has noted that the studied separation of the three bodies reached such absurdities that each maintained a different daily password.

The defence of the area that lay beyond the Tavronitis was not 22 Battalion's responsibility; yet this was the unit that would pay the price for leaving it unsecured. Hargest did have another infantry unit at his disposal—1 Greek Regiment in Kastelli—but this unit was so far away that it was effectively an independent command. Neither Hargest nor Puttick was willing to move it closer. Instead, they chose to leave the western approaches to the airfield unguarded.

The consequence of Hargest's focus on the sea was a lack of manpower to defend the west bank of the Tavronitis River. Even the far side of the bridge spanning the river was left unattended. Hargest's placement of his forces did not create a zone of defence in depth for the airfield's protection against an attack from the west. Andrew's perimeter ran only as far as the weapon pits at the end of the runway. This was a major flaw as it denied the New Zealanders room in which to absorb and dissipate a German thrust, and space within which to manoeuvre their own forces for a counter-attack. Instead, 22 Battalion's positioning offered the enemy the opportunity to gain the runway in the first rush and to consolidate their gains on the vital ground.

Anti-aircraft gun, 40 mm Bofors Mark 1	
Calibre:	40 mm
Weight:	1981 kg
Effective Ceiling:	1524 metres
Maximum Ceiling:	7193 metres
Ground Range:	9875 metres
Ammunition:	high explosive and armour piercing in four-round clips
Shell weight:	.90 kg
Rate of Fire:	60-90 rpm (single shot)

The Bofors anti-aircraft gun was a Swedish design developed in the 1930s. It was widely exported or built overseas under license. Within the British Army it was the standard light anti-aircraft gun. Creforce had 36 Bofors guns deployed in Maleme, Canea-Suda and Heraklion sectors.

A Bofors gun crew from 2/7 Australian LAA Battery on the north side of the airfield. The scene looks across the runway towards the beach. Several wrecked British planes are in the background.

Australian War Memorial P01495.002

> **Lesson 6**
>
> To defend a bridge it is essential to protect both banks. By not defending both banks a commander concedes that he does not intend to use the bridge. In that case, as it will be only of use to the enemy, why leave it standing?

Hargest's battle instructions compounded the isolation of Andrew's men at Maleme. Officially, he had designated Lieutenant-Colonel G. Dittmer's 28 New Zealand (Maori) Battalion as brigade reserve. However, the battalion was not centrally located and its primary mission was beach defence in the Platanias area. In fact, no battalion had sole responsibility for responding to a threat to the airfield if the 22nd gave way. The instructions given to 21 New Zealand Battalion acknowledged the need to support the airfield's defence, but its commander, Lieutenant-Colonel J. M. Allen, had several additional and conflicting tasks. These included the need to defend the unit's own perimeter, move to the Tavronitis in case of attack, and support 23 New Zealand Battalion on the coast if it moved to assist in the defence of the airfield. Andrew made an independent arrangement with the commander of 23 New Zealand Battalion, Lieutenant-Colonel D. F. Leckie, to respond to a call for help, but this unit's first priority remained defence of the coastline in its area.

Hargest exacerbated the situation by failing to provide his subordinates with clear instructions to resolve their competing assignments. Instead, his orders comprised platitudes that the brigade was to destroy any airborne or seaborne attack and that 'the whole essence of the b[riga]de's work is a spirited defence.' In the absence of direction, the brigade's success depended on the ability of Hargest and his subordinates to respond to the German challenge.

The 28th New Zealand (Maori) Battalion performs the Haka on Crete.
Imperial War Museum E3261E

Hargest's dispositions involved a compromise between the two incompatible invasion threats—airborne versus seaborne—that he and his superiors anticipated. However, Hargest's placement of units confirmed that the New Zealanders viewed an invasion from the sea as the greater danger. Most of 5 New Zealand Brigade's troops faced the sea, ready to stop the enemy on the beaches. Airfield defence was a secondary consideration. The result was an ill-considered placement that handicapped the brigade's performance from the very onset of the German attack.

Student's Plan at Maleme

Unfortunately for the New Zealand defenders, Student did not have any plans for a seaborne invasion. He did intend to send some reinforcements by boat, but they were to supplement the aerial invasion; after all, he was a paratrooper general. In 5 New Zealand Brigade's sector the decisive ground was always the airfield.

Student allocated responsibility for the seizure of Maleme to West Group under Generalmajor Eugen Meindl. Meindl commanded the *Luftlande Sturmregiment*, a powerful and experienced formation containing one battalion of glider-borne troops and three battalions of paratroopers. They were:

- *3* and *4 Companies*, *I Battalion*, Major Walter Koch (glider);
- *II Battalion*, Major Edgar Stentzler;
- *III Battalion*, Major Otto Scherber; and
- *IV Battalion* (heavy weapon), Hauptmann Walther Gericke.

Student had allocated two of *I Battalion's* companies to support *7 Flieger Division's* insertion around Canea.

Meindl's plan called for the seizure of two objectives: the airfield and Hill 107 from whose heights the gunners commanded the airfield. He planned to land troops on either side of these objectives and capture them in a converging assault. Following German practice, elements of the *Sturmregiment* would land as close as possible to their objectives and take them before the defenders had a chance to react. Reinforcements from units landing further away would race to the objectives to support the first wave, enlarge the position, and prepare to meet a counter-attack. Similar tactics had brought success against the fortress of Eben Emael, the Maas Bridges and, only a few weeks previously, the bridge over the Corinth Canal in Greece.

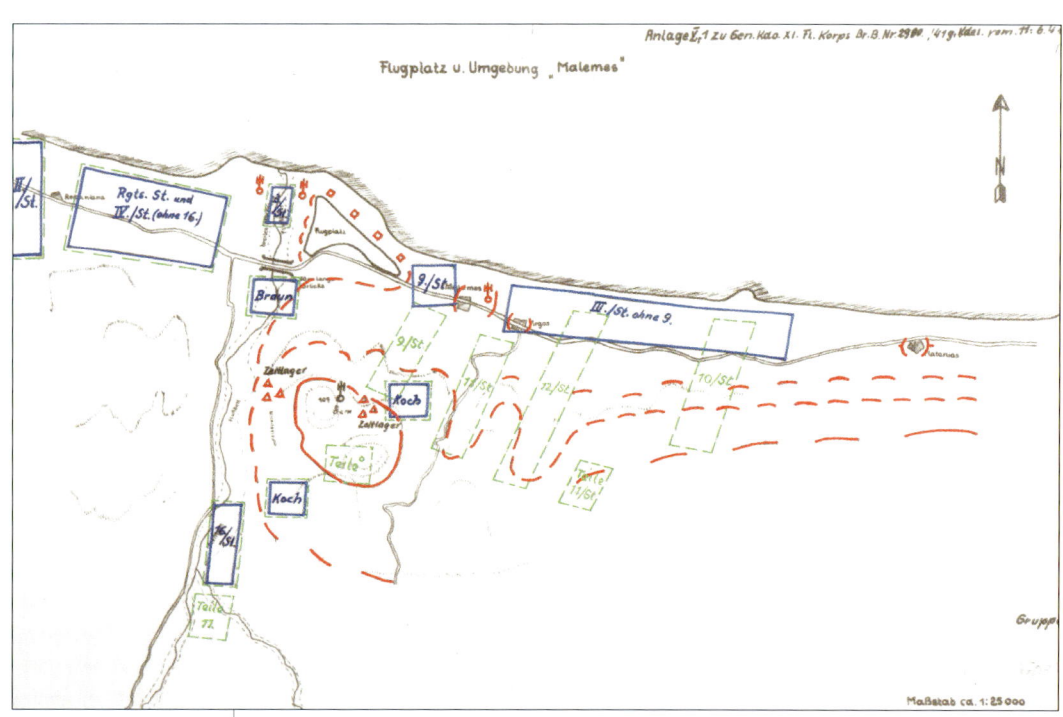

German Planned and Actual Landing Zones at Maleme
Australian War Memorial Map Collection

The landing sites and objectives were:

- *I Battalion*:
- *3 Company* to land at the mouth of the Tavronitis River to destroy hostile anti-aircraft batteries and advance on the airfield.
- *4 Company* (with Koch) to land at two locations on the slope of Hill 107 and to seize the high ground.
- *II Battalion*:
- majority of unit to land near Kolumwari and protect approaches from the west.
- *Muëbe Detachment* to land near Kastelli and seize town and harbour.
- *III Battalion*:
- majority of unit to land east of Maleme. Its objectives were to capture the airfield from the east and to prepare to advance towards Canea in order to make contact with Centre Group.
- *Braun Detachment* (with Meindl and Regimental Headquarters) to land in gliders in Tavronitis River bed to prevent destruction of bridge.

- *IV Battalion* (heavy weapon):
  - *Battalion*, less *16 Company*, to land west of bridge over Tavronitis River.
  - *16 Company* to land in upper Tavronitis River and secure southern approaches from Palaochora.

Confident of rapid success, Meindl had not given most of *II* and *IV Battalions* any objective. They formed his reserve.

The Battle Begins

On the morning of 20 May the *Luftwaffe* began its most intensive bombardment to date, the air filling with fighters, bombers and Stukas. Freyberg, turning to an aide, observed the commencement of the onslaught with the remark, 'dead on time'—a reference to the accuracy of his Ultra intelligence. At 0800 hours, as soon as the hail of bombs ceased, gliders carrying *3 Company*, *I Battalion*, swooped through the clouds of obscuring dust and landed around the mouth of the Tavronitis. Oberleutnant Wulf von Plessen's troops poured out of the gliders and overwhelmed the virtually unarmed anti-aircraft gunners along the east bank of the river. The Germans struck so quickly that few gunners escaped and at least one Bofors was captured before being disabled. The guns at Maleme, as would happen elsewhere on Crete, fell quickly because the gunners narrowly defined their role as anti-aircraft defence and did not entertain the possibility of a threat coming from any direction but the sky.

Having secured the guns, the glider troops pressed onto the airfield itself, but intense fire from 13 and 15 Platoons, and Vickers fire from the slope of Hill 107 forced them to go to ground. Plessen had pulled off a brilliant stroke, although the effort cost him his life. At 0815 hours transports began their drop runs unhindered by anti-aircraft fire.

> **Lesson 7**
>
> Units cannot absolve themselves of the responsibility for their own defence but must be prepared to defend their positions on their own. For commanders the lesson is that all units in the battlespace must have the requisite arms with which to defend themselves.

Most of the *Luftlande Sturmregiment* landed as Meindl had instructed; yet, as the sky filled with canopies, his plan started to unravel. Across the Maleme sector, Vickers, Bren and small arms fire ripped into the JU-52 transports or cut through the air in which the paratroopers floated. The effect on *III Battalion* was devastating. Its companies fell scattered over 21 and 23 New Zealand Battalions and the New Zealand engineers. Leckie shot five paratroopers without leaving his command post, and his adjutant bagged two from his desk. One soldier from 23 New Zealand Battalion compared the morning's work with duck shooting and wrote, 'we blazed away with our rifles and there were not many to reach the ground alive.' The inmates of the Field Punishment Centre spent the morning redeeming themselves, hunting paratroopers amongst the olive trees. On the body of one German officer the Kiwis found a company roll with 126 names. Within a couple of hours they had ticked off 112. One officer commented that 'the Huns were easy shooting.' By midday *III Battalion* had virtually ceased to exist.

The paratroopers were handicapped in that they carried only a pistol, a couple of grenades and a knife. Their rifles, machine pistols, machine-guns and other arms arrived via a weapon container which they had to find in order to arm themselves for the assault. Most never had the chance. Occupying part of Pirgos was *III Battalion's* one success and that lasted only until 22 New Zealand Battalion's Headquarters Company forced the Germans out.

Everywhere, parties of Germans were fighting for their lives. *Group Koch's* gliders fell scattered across Hill 107. Some of the craft broke up as they slammed into rocks, killing or injuring their passengers. As the Germans emerged they came under intense fire from A and B Companies whose pits lay concealed in the area. Koch was wounded as he tried to rally his men. Instead of securing the hill's peak the New Zealanders forced the survivors downwards towards the bridge.

Major Franz Braun commanded the nine gliders that landed in the river bed. They arrived with near perfect accuracy, some of the gliders actually coming to a stop next to their objective—the bridge over the Tavronitis. The structure spanned the nearly dry river bed in an east-west direction. On the Maleme side the bridge ended perpendicular to the lower slope of Hill 107 where it began to rise from the coastal plain. Further on were the structures of the Royal Air Force camp.

Dornier Do 17

Type:	light bomber
Wingspan:	18 m
Length:	15.8 m
Engine:	two Bramo 323P Fafir (750 kW each)
Max Speed:	427kph
Range:	1160km (with combat load)
Armament:	various weapon configurations were fitted, usually up to eight 7.92 mm MG 15 and 1000 kg of bombs

The Dornier Do 17, often referred to as the 'flying pencil', was initially used as a civilian airliner in the 1930s. The *Luftwaffe* was quick to see its potential for use as a fast, light bomber. In the Polish campaign the Do 17 proved capable of outrunning most enemy fighters. However, by the time of the Battle of Britain it was no match for the British Hurricane and Spitfire interceptors. The *Luftwaffe* ceased its production at the end of 1940. During the Crete campaign three groups of Do 17s were used by *VIII Fliegerkorps*.

Light machine-gun, Bren Mark 1	
Calibre:	.303 inch
Operation:	gas, magazine fed, selective fire: semi-automatic and automatic; air-cooled; quick-change barrel, bipod mount
Magazine:	30 rounds (normally filled with 28 rounds)
Weight (empty):	10 kg
Weight (loaded):	11.3 kg
Length:	1155 mm
Sights:	182 to 1646 metres
Effective Range:	548 metres (from the bipod)
Rates of Fire:	Cyclic: 450-550 rpm. Normal: bursts of 4-5 rounds as required. Slow: one magazine per minute. Rapid: four magazines per minute

Originally designed in Czechoslovakia, the Bren was introduced into service in the British Army in 1938 and quickly became the standard infantry section machine-gun. The Bren was among the best light machine-guns ever produced. Extremely accurate, reliable, robust and simple to use, it became the standard light machine-gun used by most Commonwealth nations in the Second World War. It remained in use in the Australian Army until the late 1980s. The Bren could be mounted on a tripod for ground or anti-aircraft use. The usual allocation was one per infantry section, four per anti-aircraft section and 13 per Bren gun carrier platoon.

EQUIPMENT AIR DROP CONTAINER

Length:	1.52 m
Width:	406 mm
Load Weight:	118 kg (maximum), normally loaded at around 90 kg to avoid heavy landings

The *Fallschirmjäger* did not drop with any weapons apart from a pistol and a knife. Instead, the Luftwaffe delivered their arms in equipment containers. The reason for this practice lay in the design of the German parachute. The parachute's rigging pitched its wearer forward and required him to absorb the impact of landing by rolling. Any protruding weapon was likely to injure the paratrooper. In addition, the absence of weapons created a streamlined profile that minimised the risk of fouling the parachute's lines. Some paratroopers did jump with MP40s strapped to their bodies, but only highly trained *fallschirmjäger* could do this safely.

The containers were carried either in the Junkers 52's bomb bay racks or outside underneath the wings. They weighed up to 120 kilos and were colour coded to identify the contents. A platoon required fourteen containers. Different colour parachute canopies and paint markings indicated the contents of each container. Fitted to the bottom of the container was a metal shock absorber to take the force of the landing. Inside was a pair of small wheels and two handles that converted the container into a small cart.

The container delivery system had one fatal weakness: on landing, a paratrooper was virtually helpless until he found his weapons. Many of the paratroopers who landed on Crete died unarmed. Captured containers also provided the enemy with a handy source of equipment. By the end of the first day on Crete the British and Greek soldiers had significantly augmented their arsenals by looting the enemy's containers.

Present-day view along the bridge looking east. Hill 107 begins its rise just beyond the bridge's end. The building in the photo marks the approximate location of the RAF camp. This photo illustrates the camp's role as a battlefield obstruction. Photo courtesy of author.

At this time of the year the river proved no obstacle. Braun urged his men across it towards the hill before he fell dead. The Germans dodged forward using the bridge's pylons for cover. The defenders in this sector were the men of 18 Platoon, D Company. Their task was made more difficult by the Royal Air Force camp whose occupants remained in the area. The camp's structures interdicted the best lines of sight covering the bridge and forced 18 Platoon to take up less favourable positions that offered the Germans dead ground in their approach. The enemy, exploiting this vulnerability, secured the New Zealand end of the bridge. They then pushed towards the airfield driving a wedge between D and C Companies.

Further west, *II* and *IV Battalions* dropped unmolested. Their only losses were some heavy weapons and motorcycles that struck olive trees. On *IV Battalion's* establishment were six 81-mm mortars, two 20-mm Flak 38s, four PaK36 anti-tank guns and four 75-mm recoilless guns.

View of the bridge over the Tavronitis. This is the original bridge and its pylons still bear the scars of the battle. The river is wider today than it was in 1941 because of the construction of a weir just downstream from the bridge.
Photo courtesy of author.

Meindl now arrived and set up his command post by the bridge. He immediately realised that the enemy's resistance was far greater than his intelligence reports had predicted. He sent part of *IV Battalion* across the bridge to support the remnants of the Koch and Braun groups still clinging to the east bank. Together they pressed the attack up the hill using the airmen's camp as cover. The Germans gained the lower slope and the camp proper, but as soon as they emerged into the open, fire from D and A Companies stopped them. The commander of D Company, Captain T. C. Campbell, suggested to the crews of the two 4-inch coastal guns that were behind his position that they fire on the Germans gathering below. He received the reply that this was impossible because the guns had been sited for sea targets only. Both guns would be lost later that afternoon without firing a shot.

While one wing of his command attacked by the bridge, Meindl sent Major E. Stentzler with two companies of *II Battalion* on a flanking move. They were to cross the river below Hill 107 and attack up its slope from the south and south-west. As Stentzler's men crossed the river they ran into a platoon from 21 Battalion which occupied a forward position. They brushed the Kiwis aside but the encounter cost them time and casualties. Then, as they began to climb the hill, they ran into the prepared positions of A and B Companies. By this time the New Zealanders had recovered from the landing of Koch's gliders and had not yet been hard pressed. The Germans made little progress against them.

Leichte Geschutz 40 recoilless gun, 75 mm

Calibre:	75 mm
Operation:	percussion fired, recoilless
Weight:	145.6 kg
Ammunition:	high explosive (weight 5.82 kg)
Maximum Range:	6798 metres.

The Leichte Geschutz 40 was fixed to a small two-wheel mount for manual movement; it was designed for airborne forces and could be broken down into four loads for parachute dropping or air landing by Junkers 52 transport. Crete provided the first operational use for this weapon. Seven of these guns served on the island (four at Maleme and three at Heraklion) as part of the *Fallschirmjäger Regiment* heavy weapon companies. It was soon replaced by a 10.5 cm version.

As the day wore on the German position looked increasingly precarious. They had suffered heavy casualties, and the Kiwis still held most of the runway and nearly all of Hill 107. Officer casualties had also been heavy; Meindl himself was severely wounded, struck in the chest by a burst of fire. As the day drew to a close the Germans had exhausted themselves but had not reached their objectives.

The Struggle at Kastelli

Kastelli was a small fishing village on the Gulf of Kísamos approximately 18 kilometres east of Maleme. Its garrison was 1 Greek Regiment with 1,030 poorly armed and recently recruited soldiers. Attached to the regiment was a party of New Zealand officers acting as advisers.

As the paratroopers descended around Maleme a detachment of 72 men from *6 Company, II Battalion Luftlande Sturmregiment* dropped in two groups near Kastelli. Their commander was Leutnant Peter Müerbe. His mission was to occupy the village if undefended, or establish a blocking position between Kastelli and Maleme if enemy forces were present. German intelligence had not revealed the existence of the Greeks.

The Greek reaction was immediate and violent, stunning and overwhelming the Germans. Within minutes the Greeks killed 44 Germans and captured 28, including 15 wounded. Müerbe was among the dead.

While lacking the trappings of the professional, the raw recruits of 1 Greek Regiment showed what soldiers could do when motivated by the defence of their homeland. Had Puttick or Hargest positioned them along the Tavronitis River, vital ground left undefended, the result at Maleme might have been different. At the very least, the Greeks would have disrupted the invaders at the decisive point instead of garrisoning a distant and strategically unimportant fishing village.

The Greek defenders had rebuffed the paratroopers, but they were to pay a heavy price for the temerity of their success. The Germans wanted the fishing village's small jetty in order to land seaborne reinforcements and supplies. On 24 May a battlegroup built around 95 *Gebirgs Pionier Battalion* from 5 *Gebirgs Division* renewed the assault on Kastelli. Despite determined resistance the heavily armed mountain troops overwhelmed the Greeks and secured the village. The Germans then rounded up 200 of Kastelli's men and shot them in reprisal for the alleged mutilation of the bodies of the parachutists. The massacre was the first in a pattern of German reprisals against Cretans who had resisted the invasion and occupation.

The Greeks, however, continued to resist from the hills overlooking the small harbour. They denied the invaders the use of Kastelli's jetty until 27 May when the Germans were finally able to unload light tanks.

A Time to Die

Over the course of the day the Germans had hammered 22 New Zealand Battalion; 15 Platoon alone suffered 23 casualties out of 25 men before being overrun. But while the Kiwis gave up some ground, at the day's end they retained their grip on the decisive points—part of the airfield and nearly all of Hill 107. However, as darkness fell, the battle was about to enter a new phase, one not of combat but of psychology. The Kiwis were about to transform victory into defeat.

The fog of war was to have a disastrous effect on Andrew. As soon as the battle joined it broke into a number of smaller actions which Andrew was unable to control. His command post, on the rear slope of Hill 107, did not have line of sight to the action below, and he lost all direct communication with his companies when his telephone

> **Lesson 8**
> It is all too easy to underestimate the battle worth of militia or irregular units, especially when they are armed or trained to fight in ways that are different from one's own units. While in many cases scepticism is warranted, the potential value of local troops should not be summarily dismissed. Instead, a commander must evaluate the capabilities of indigenous soldiers in the light of mission objectives, and take into account intangible factors such as patriotism, cultural legacy, and knowledge of the local environment. Without a fair assessment a commander may lose the services of a valuable ally.

cables failed. He could hear the battle raging below him but had little information on its course. His only source of intelligence was provided by runners who risked their lives dashing across fire-swept ground or exposing themselves to the enemy's prowling planes.

By afternoon the pressure had increased. Andrew initiated the assistance arrangement with 23 New Zealand Battalion and fired the agreed-upon signal flares. There was no response. Leckie later explained that he had not seen the signal. At 1700 hours Andrew got through to Hargest by wireless and requested 23 New Zealand Battalion's assistance. His superior replied that the 23rd was fully engaged with the enemy in its own sector, an incorrect statement since only a few paratroopers remained alive within Leckie's area. Hargest did not offer any other support.

BRIGADIER LESLIE WILTON ANDREW

Leslie Wilton Andrew was born in Ashurst on 23 March 1897 and enlisted in the New Zealand Expeditionary Force in late 1915. He joined 2 Battalion Wellington Regiment in time for the September phase of the Battle of the Somme. By the following year he was a corporal in command of a section. On 31 July 1917, Andrew received the VC for eliminating three German machine-gun posts at Passchendaele. He was commissioned in March 1918.

At the end of the war Andrew returned to New Zealand, secured a commission in the New Zealand Staff Corps and became a professional soldier. During the interwar period he held a number of administrative appointments and travelled to India to take up a position with the Indian army as an exchange officer. Andrew had risen to the rank of major by the time the Second World War erupted.

With the commencement of hostilities Andrew joined the 2nd New Zealand Expeditionary Force. He was promoted to lieutenant-colonel and took command of 22 New Zealand Battalion. The disastrous Greek campaign was the unit's baptism of fire. On Crete, Andrew was responsible for the defence of the airfield at Maleme. It was his decision to withdraw that tipped the campaign in the enemy's favour.

Following the evacuation Andrew rebuilt his battalion and served in North Africa. In late 1941 he temporarily commanded 5 New Zealand Brigade following Hargest's capture. By this time, however, Andrew's days of active service were numbered. Freyberg had lost faith in him after the disaster on Crete. In April 1942, Andrew returned to New Zealand and took command of the Wellington Fortress Area. He did not serve in an operational role again.

In 1948 Andrew reached the rank of brigadier. His final position was commander of the Central Military District. He retired from the army in 1952 and died on 8 January 1969 at Palmerston North.

Lieutenant-Colonel Leslie Wilton Andrew, VC
National Library of New Zealand 1/2-043326

Andrew's sense of isolation grew throughout the day. Unable to control his own battle, and unable to obtain support from the brigade, he launched his only reserve into the fray. At 1715 hours two Matilda tanks rumbled from their camouflaged positions and rolled across the runway towards the bridge. The only infantry that could be spared to assist them were twelve men from 14 Platoon and a party of eight British anti-aircraft gunner volunteers. There was hardly time for the three groups to coordinate the advance—not that it mattered, the infantry did not last long as the enemy's converging fire raked the exposed ground. One tank crew discovered that their ammunition would not fit the gun's breech and turned back; the other continued into the riverbed, bellied on a rock and was captured.

After witnessing the failure of the tanks, the commander of C Company, Captain S. H. Johnson, managed to get a message through to Andrew. He informed the battalion commander that he required reinforcements or else C Company would be overwhelmed. He anticipated that he could last until dark.

At about 1800 hours Andrew managed to reach Hargest a second time on his fading wireless and explained the worsening situation around the airfield. He warned his brigade commander that if help did not arrive he would have to withdraw. Hargest's response was singularly unhelpful. He replied, 'If you must, you must.' Shortly afterwards another conversation took place and this time Hargest said he would send Andrew two companies, one from 28 New Zealand (Maori) Battalion and one from 23 New Zealand Battalion.

The communication difficulties served to exacerbate Andrew's confusion. His impression was that these reinforcements would arrive shortly. He was not helped by the fact that Hargest had spent the entire day at his headquarters in Platanias and had not bothered to come forward. Had he done so he could not have missed the contrast between the desperate struggle at Maleme and the relative tranquillity of the rest of his command.

As time passed the reinforcements did not arrive. Andrew had heard nothing from C or D Companies for some time and assumed them destroyed. He had seen the Germans land around his headquarters company at Pirgos but was not aware that the enemy had been defeated. Close to his command post, A and B Companies were still in action against Stentzler's flanking move from the south. From the rest of the brigade Andrew heard nothing.

At approximately 2100 hours Andrew spoke to Hargest for the last time and told him he was taking the battalion back to B Company's position. His wireless then failed, and Hargest's response is not recorded. Andrew sent runners to the positions occupied by C, D and Headquarters Companies to tell any survivors to fall back. None of the runners got through.

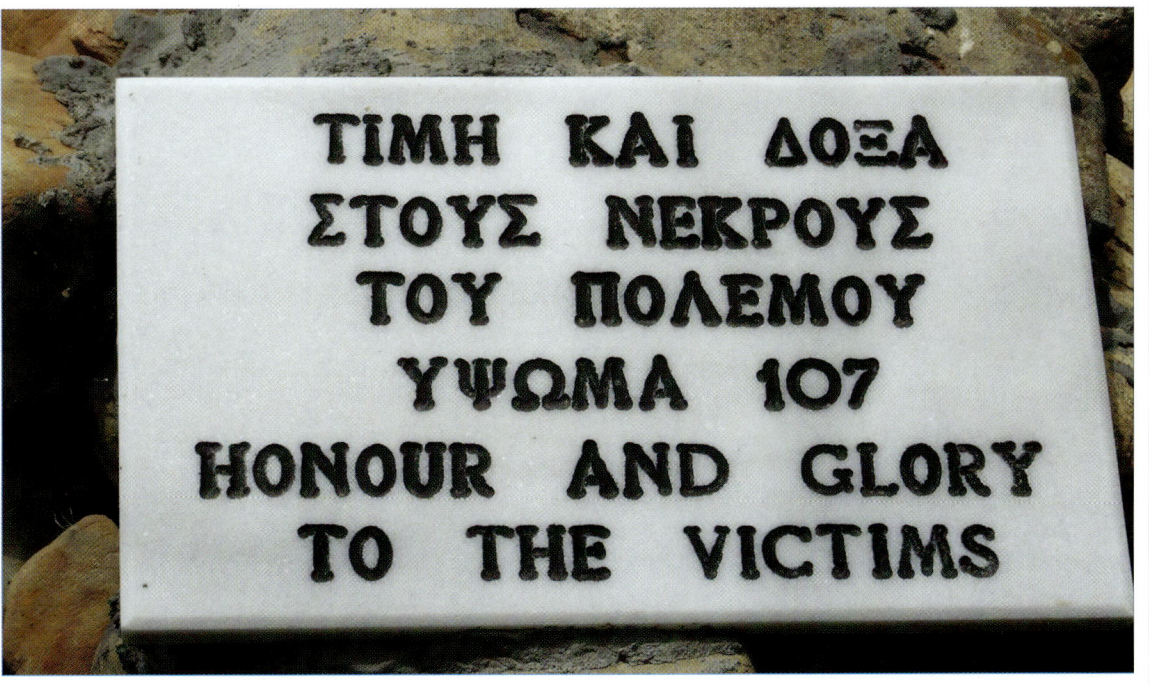

A Cross of Sacrifice located at the top of Hill 107.
Today the hill is heavily covered in olive trees.
Photo courtesy of author.

The inscription from the Cross of Sacrifice.
Photo courtesy of author.

On his new position Andrew had just A and B Companies. It was here that the company from 23 New Zealand Battalion finally arrived. At first, Andrew sent it forward to occupy A Company's old position, but then he rethought his entire situation and concluded that the remnant of his battalion was too exposed to survive the next morning's expected German attack. He decided to withdraw completely. After midnight, Andrew, with A and B Companies, and 23 New Zealand Battalion's men, marched off Hill 107 and headed east.

After the withdrawal, the promised company from 28 New Zealand (Maori) Battalion finally arrived. It probed onto the airfield coming within metres of C Company without making contact. Instead of occupying the position it turned around and marched all the way back to its battalion.

Since Andrew was a winner of the Victoria Cross, it is not possible to fault his courage. However, his decision to abandon the key ground turned the fate of the entire British force on Crete. Andrew was not pushed off, but went willingly. Instead of denying the Germans their objective he handed them the airfield they needed as well as the overlooking high ground. It was a concession of defeat that held ramifications for the entire campaign.

What Andrew did not know was that not only did C and D Companies still live but they continued to cling to most of their original positions. Unquestionably they had taken heavy casualties, but both companies had fought gallantly against the Germans all day and remained undefeated. In Pirgos, Headquarters Company also fought on. Later one of its men would comment that he had received 'no indication that the position was so serious.' In fact, the battalion's fatalities for the entire campaign would number just 62. Now, in the small hours, each of these companies discovered that it had been abandoned and, one by one, they pulled back eastwards.

Once Andrew began the withdrawal he did not stop until he reached the safety of the line held by 21 and 23 New Zealand Battalions, a distance of about two kilometres. In so doing he decided not to make a stand at the strong point of Pirgos but to break all contact with the enemy. He withdrew so far that his men could no longer cover the airfield with small arms or machine-gun fire.

Andrew's actions require some explanation. In mitigation, he was in a difficult position and was hamstrung by Hargest's inactivity and Leckie's reluctance to move from his battalion's position. His communication difficulties only worsened his predicament. Andrew also spent the day under constant threat of attack from the enemy's planes which enjoyed complete freedom of the air. However, this was the campaign's decisive moment. Andrew had been given responsibility for ground that needed to be held at all cost and to the last man. The campaign's outcome hung in the balance.

Andrew made his decision neither in haste nor in immediate danger but upon careful reflection. His action was that of a senior New Zealand officer who shared his division's ethos favouring institutional survival over all other outcomes. When Freyberg took responsibility for Creforce he looked upon it as a temporary measure pending his division's embarkation for Egypt where he could oversee its rebuilding after the losses of Greece. In order to rebuild, the formation had to survive intact. Thus, when Andrew withdrew his battalion he did so in order to save it to fight another day. Unfortunately, for the British to claim victory on Crete, today was the day the battalion had to die.

THE DESCENT AT PRISON VALLEY

The Defence at Canea and Suda

Freyberg and his headquarters were located in a villa on a hill overlooking the Gulf on Canea just east of the city. It was from here that Freyberg attempted to control the battle, although his lack of headquarters staff and the generally poor communications infrastructure made this more difficult than the situation warranted. It is illuminating to compare Freyberg's staff establishment with that enjoyed by Weston at the lesser MNBDO headquarters. By spiriting away all the Creforce Headquarters staff when Wavell replaced him with Freyberg, Weston did the campaign a disservice. Likewise it revealed a character weakness in Freyberg who failed to demand the return of the headquarters staff. Creforce's headquarters organisation is summarised in wire diagram 5.

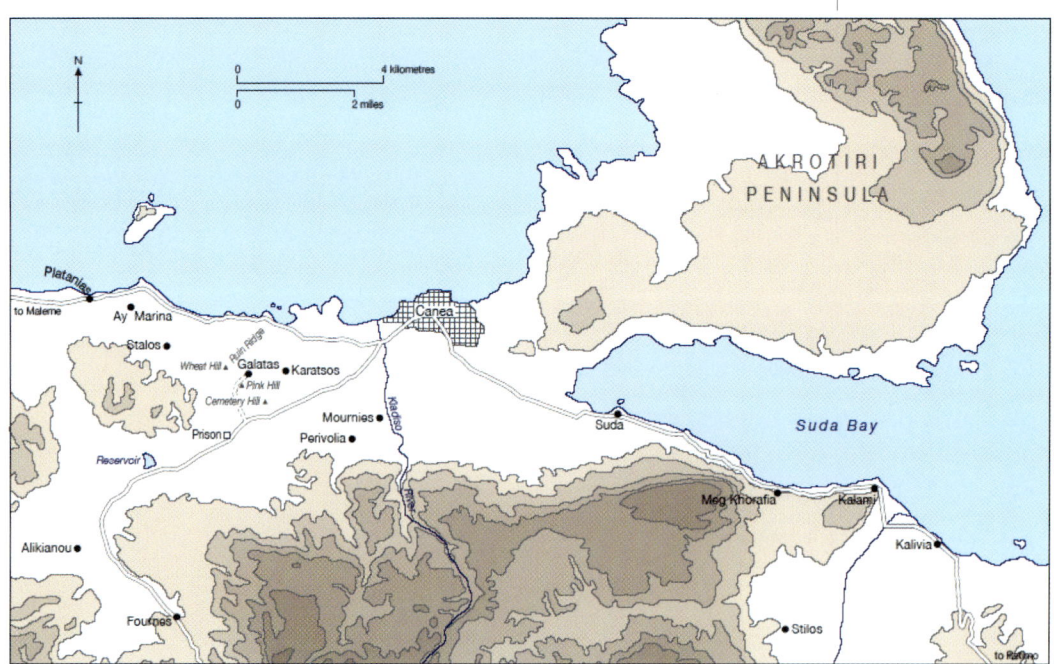

Canea Sector
Drawn by Keith Mitchell

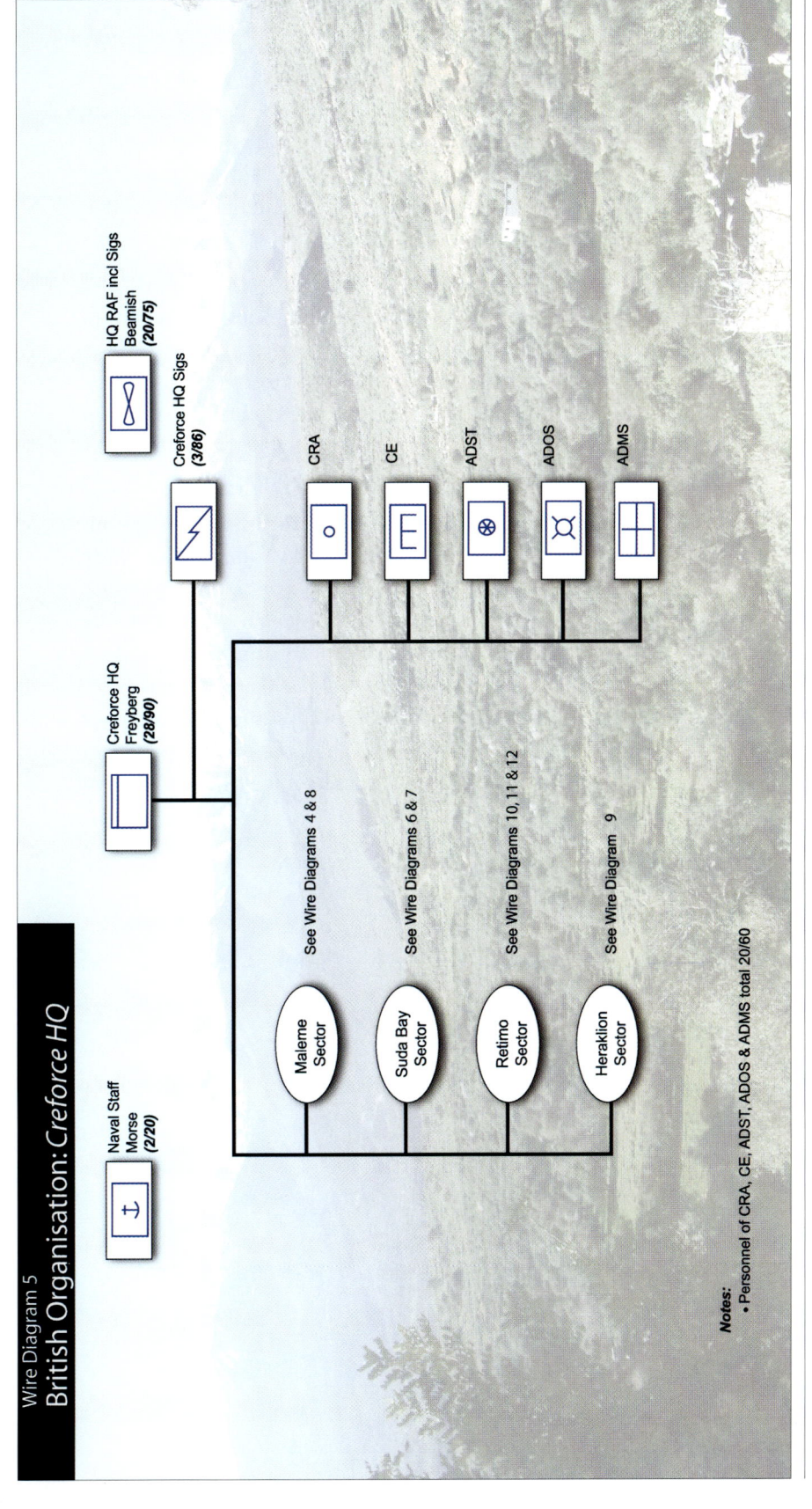

In addition to the MNBDO, Freyberg had given Weston responsibility for the defence of the Suda Sector, an area that contained Creforce's administrative and logistic infrastructure. Weston commanded almost 15,000 soldiers—effectively a division. However the great majority of these comprised labour, transport, depot and administrative units, many of which should have been evacuated since there was little requirement for their skills and most of the men were poorly trained for combat. Wire diagrams 6 and 7 provide an outline of Weston's command.

The real strength of Weston's command lay in its anti-aircraft and coastal guns. These were sited on the heights around Suda Bay in order to protect the port area from aerial bombardment and sea invasion. Weston's order of battle contained a dozen infantry units, although most were indifferently armed ad hoc creations. Many of Weston's soldiers carried the American Springfield rifle and his command was deficient in automatic and heavy weapons.

The bulk of Weston's infantry was incapable of offensive action. For Example, the New Zealand Division Supply Column, was only positioned in the sector because it was awaiting evacuation. Weston's best infantry unit was 1 Welch Battalion which had arrived on the island with the original garrison and was fully equipped and staffed. The Northumberland Hussars (as infantry) and 1 Rangers may have been refugees from Greece but they were exceptional fighting men and possessed good combat qualities. Apart from these three units, the remainder of Weston's infantry was capable of playing a defensive role only.

Part of Weston's command, a Bofors anti-aircraft position overlooking Suda Bay.
Australian War Memorial P02053.013

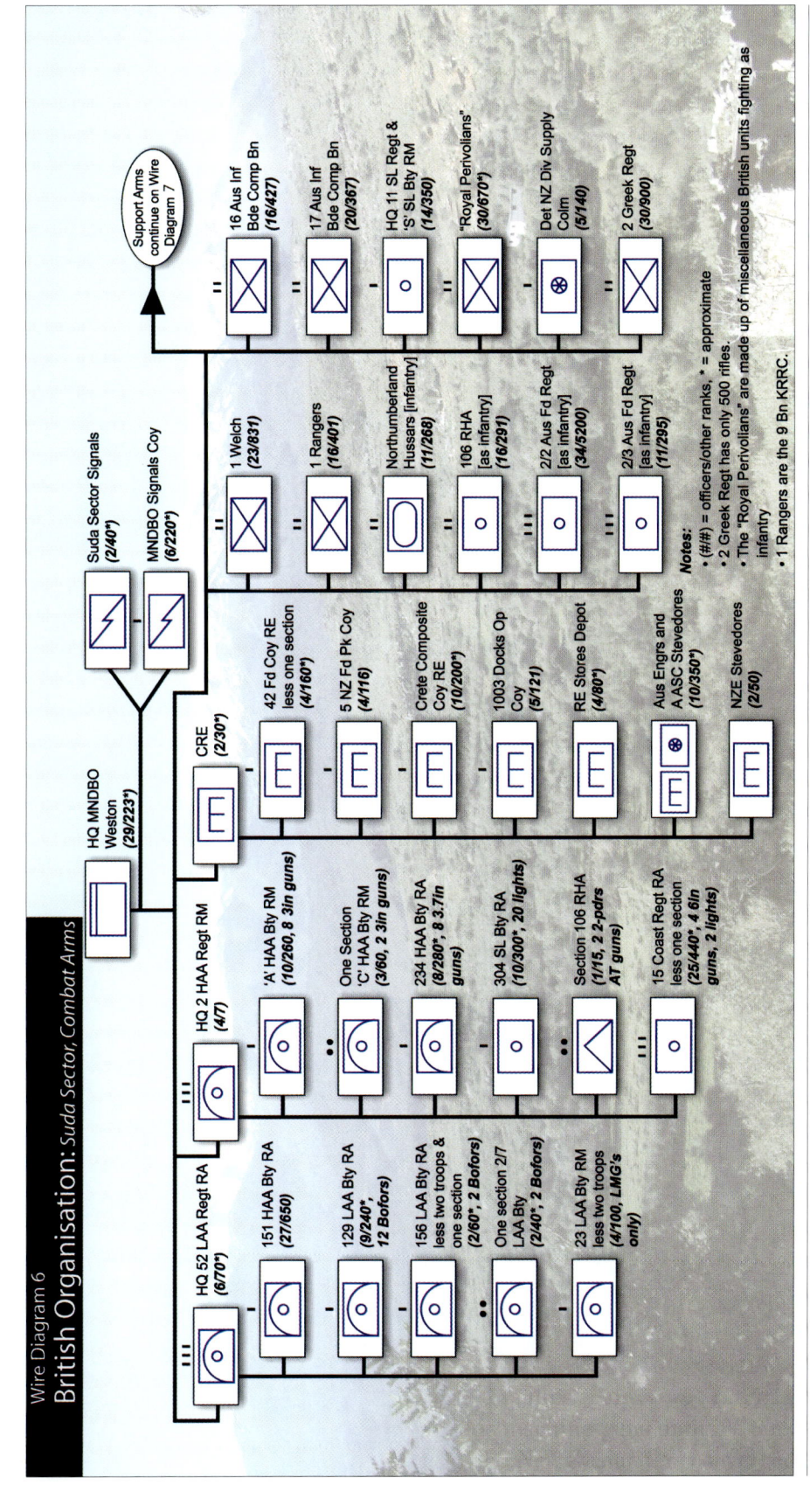

Wire Diagram 7
British Organisation: *Suda Sector, Support Arms*

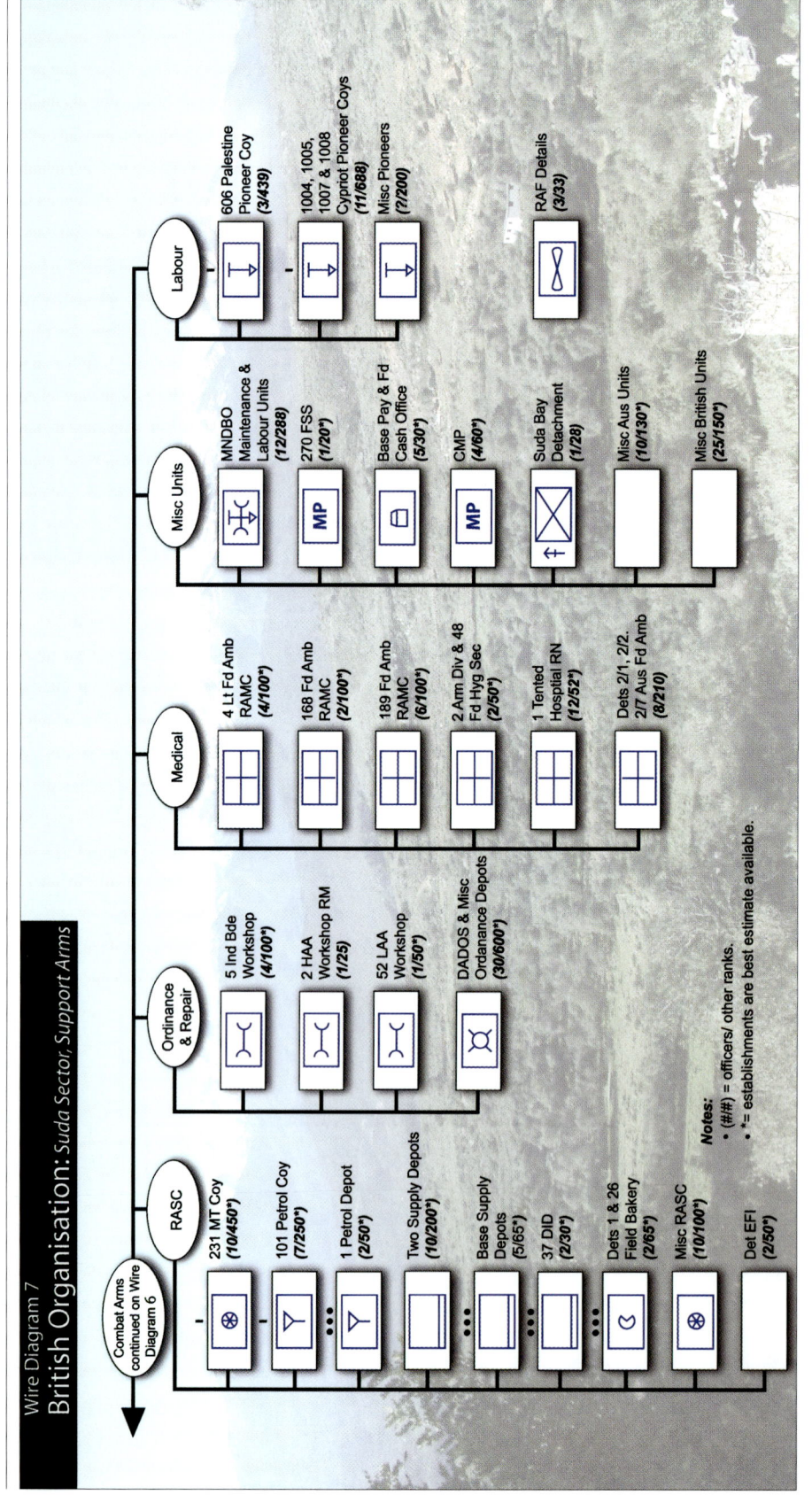

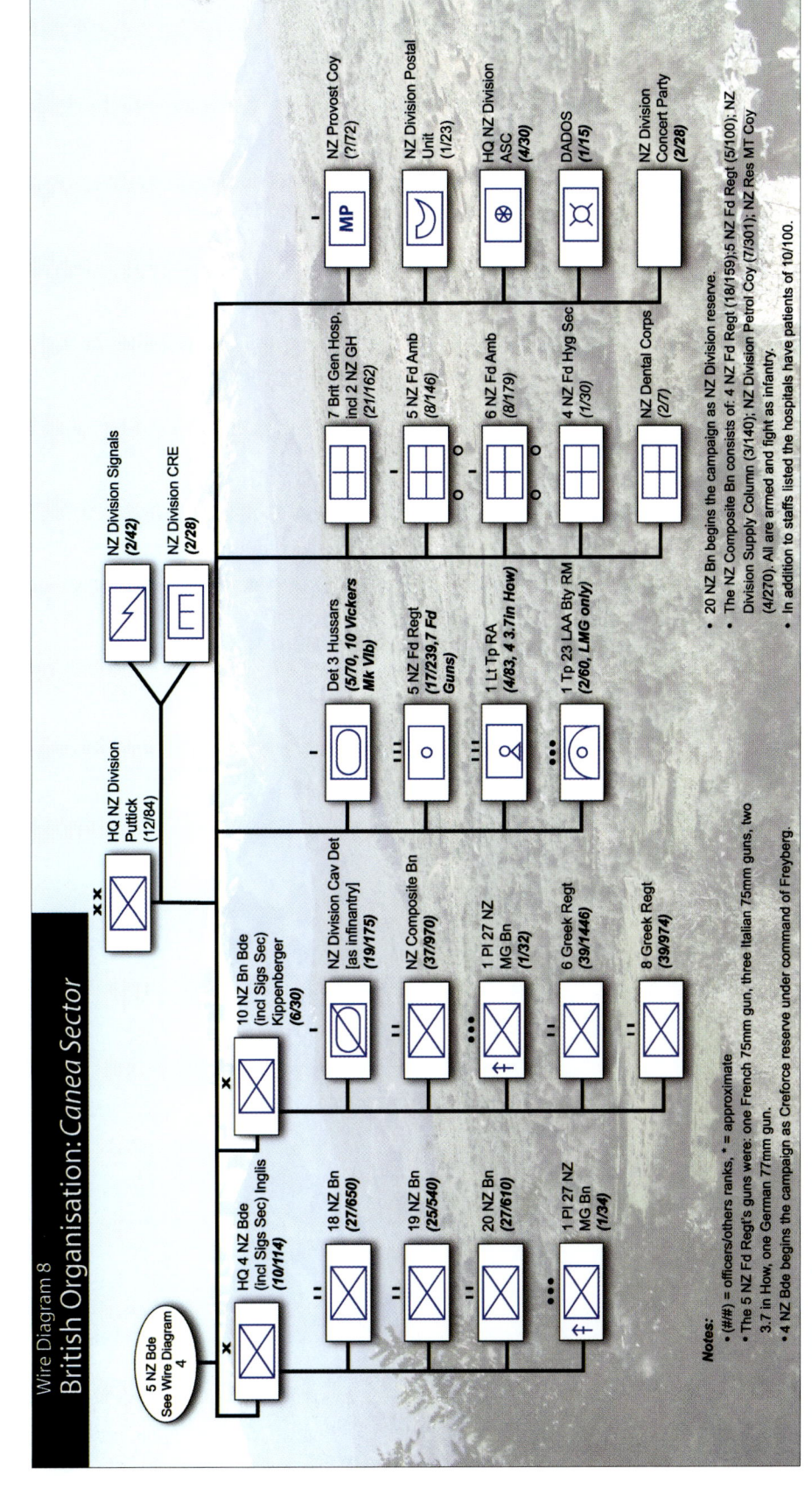

To the west of Weston's force was the New Zealand Division under Puttick. Its zone of responsibility ran along the coast from Canea to Maleme, and south-west towards Alikianou. The battle zone near Alikianou would become known as Prison Valley because of the presence of a Cretan prison which was the valley's dominant structure.

Puttick had two formations available for the defence of Prison Valley and the coast west of Canea: 4 and 10 New Zealand Brigades were commanded by Lieutenant-Colonels Lindsay M. Inglis and Howard K. Kippenberger respectively. Kippenberger's Brigade was newly formed and represented an attempt to provide the division with the customary three brigade structure in the absence of 6 New Zealand Brigade which had been sent to Egypt. Wire diagram 8 illustrates Puttick's organisation.

The positions assigned to the two brigades provide a further indication that the New Zealanders perceived the German threat as coming primarily from the sea. Puttick sited two of 4 New Zealand Brigade's battalions on the coast just west of Canea. The third occupied a ridge to their rear. The brigade's role was two-fold: to protect the city from a seaborne invasion and to act as the Creforce reserve. The brigade entered the battle under Freyberg's direct control.

A contemporary view of Prison Valley from the top of Cemetery Hill looking southwards across the valley to the foothills on the other side. This area comprised the narrows that Kippenberger expected 6 Greek Regiment to hold.
Photo courtesy of author.

The 10th New Zealand Brigade consisted of a Composite Battalion comprising troops drawn from the division's artillery regiments and support units, and two Greek infantry regiments. Part of the Composite Battalion's position lay on the coast adjacent to 4 New Zealand Brigade. The rest of the battalion occupied a series of hills overlooking the Alikianou Valley.

Looking east, a contemporary view from the New Zealand position on top of the ridgeline near Galatas. The Germans would repeatedly assault up these slopes. In the distance is Signal Hill, the feature guarded by the New Zealand Divisional Cavalry Squadron.
Photo courtesy of author.

It is worth examining Kippenberger's dispositions in detail since 10 New Zealand Brigade's positions would prove to be critical in the coming battle. Like the neck of a bottle, Prison Valley narrowed as it neared Canea. At its most constricted point the valley floor measured less than a kilometre in width, and movement could be interdicted by fire from the overlooking high ground. Kippenberger placed the Composite Battalion on a series of hills outside Galatas. Each of its companies occupied a separate hill running in an arc from the sea moving inland to overlook the valley. Their positions were:

- Divisional Transport – overlooking the coast;
- 4 Field Regiment – Red Hill;
- Divisional Supply – Ruin Hill;
- 5 Field Regiment – Wheat Hill; and
- Petrol Company – Pink Hill.

Lieutenant-Colonel Howard K. Kippenberger
National Library of New Zealand 017467

MAJOR-GENERAL SIR HOWARD KARL KIPPENBERGER

Howard Karl Kippenberger was born on 28 January 1897 at Ladbrooks, near Christchurch. He enlisted in the New Zealand Expeditionary Force in 1916 and arrived in France to take part in the September phase of the Battle of the Somme. In November he received a serious arm wound from a piece of shrapnel and doctors were unsure whether he would recover use of the limb. While it did heal, it left him no longer fit for service in the trenches and he was invalided home. Kippenberger's First World War experience had lasted only two months.

In New Zealand Kippenberger studied law and qualified as a solicitor and later as a barrister. Once in practice he renewed his military interests, joining the Territorial Force in 1924 as a second lieutenant. An avid reader of military history, he educated himself in the art of war. When the Second World War broke out Kippenberger was a lieutenant-colonel and was given command of 20 Canterbury-Otago Battalion.

Kippenberger's first campaign was Greece, immediately followed by Crete. On Crete he commanded 10 New Zealand Brigade, an ad hoc formation of Greek and composite New Zealand units. He was the only senior New Zealand officer to distinguish himself during the campaign. Unlike his peers, Kippenberger kept himself well forward, sought out information, was quick thinking and not afraid to attack. He was awarded a DSO for his actions.

In North Africa, Kippenberger led his men from the relief of Tobruk to the surrender of the *Afrika Korps* in Tunisia. Continuing to display an extraordinary talent, he was confirmed in the rank of brigadier and received a bar to his DSO.

With Freyberg's promotion to corps commander during the Italian campaign, Kippenberger was appointed commander of the New Zealand Division. On 2 March 1944, during the Battle for Casino, Kippenberger stepped on a mine and lost both feet. He recuperated in England, was fitted with artificial feet, and his temporary rank of major-general was made permanent. However, his career as a field officer was at an end.

During his time in London the New Zealand government appointed him to command the organisation responsible for the repatriation of New Zealand prisoners of war. He served in this post from 1944 to 1946 before returning home.

Once back in New Zealand, Kippenberger wrote his memoirs, *Infantry Brigadier*, one of the finest written accounts of middle-level command. Kippenberger was knighted in 1948 and died suddenly on 4 May 1957 in Wellington.

Within the battalion's sector there was a further ridge that rose just outside the New Zealanders' perimeter in front of Pink Hill and jutted into the valley. From its peak an observer would have a line of sight into the valley in three directions: north-east towards Canea, south-west towards the prison, and south towards the hills on the opposite side of the valley. It was easily the best position from which to control movement below, but it was exposed and the New Zealanders had delayed incorporating it into their defences until it was too late, despite having fairly precise knowledge of the date of the German assault. On its bald summit was the cemetery to which it owed its name: Cemetery Hill.

On the Composite Battalion's left, continuing along the ridgeline towards Canea, was 4 New Zealand Brigade's 19 Battalion, positioned in front of Karatsos.

The only other New Zealand unit in Kippenberger's brigade was the Divisional Cavalry Squadron. As these men were without their vehicles they fought as infantry. Kippenberger placed them on the lower slope of Signal Hill near a reservoir named Lake Aghya.

Kippenberger's command included almost 2,500 Greek soldiers organised into two regiments. The 8th Greek Regiment occupied a hill on the valley's southern face covering a front of about three kilometres from near the reservoir to Alikianou. Its mission was to protect the open ground in the valley's upper end. The 6th Greek Regiment guarded the opposite end of the valley and was sited in its neck. Its position ran from the summit of Cemetery Hill down across the valley to the high ground on the southern side, almost as far as the positions of 2 Greek Regiment in Weston's Suda Sector. The regiment's role served as a cork in a bottle, trapping any Germans who landed in the valley where they could be destroyed by fire from the surrounding heights. The weak point in Kippenberger's dispositions was 6 Greek Regiment. He had little confidence in the unit, yet despite his qualms he placed it in an exposed position and gave it an important task. It would fail him on all counts.

There was one other unit on the valley floor—1 Light Troop, Royal Artillery, with four 3.7-inch howitzers. It occupied a position alongside the main road to Canea just behind 6 Greek Regiment. From this site it could either fire down the valley towards the prison in support of 10 New Zealand Brigade, or shell the beaches near Canea in support of 4 New Zealand Brigade. This was an economical arrangement, but one that left 1 Light Troop in an exposed position well outside the perimeter of the brigades it was tasked to support. For close protection it had just one section of infantry from 19 New Zealand Battalion which had arrived the day before the invasion.

Most of Prison Valley lay within Puttick's sector—but not all of it. Freyberg drew the boundary between the New Zealanders and the MNBDO at the mouth of the valley where the hills receded and the low ground spread out near Canea. While Puttick controlled the critical heights on the north side, Weston was responsible for the valley's exit, the hills on the south side and the environs of Canea. Since he had allocated the task of the city's close defence to the Welch, Weston had to assign lower quality units to the protection of his landward approaches. If the Kiwis gave way on the heights, all that barred the German path to Canea and Suda was the Royal Perivolians, an amalgamation of various British units acting as infantry, and the occupants of the transit camp including the New Zealand Division Supply Column that was awaiting evacuation.

Student's Plan of Attack

Under Student's plan the Centre Group was assigned three objectives: the administrative centre of Canea, the port facilities of Suda and the airfield at Retimo. The Centre Group was commanded by Generalleutnant Wilhelm Süssmann of *7 Flieger Division*.

Paratroopers in the sky near Suda. A Junkers 52 has been hit.
Australian War Memorial P00433.009

Süssmann allocated a mix of units to the landing in Prison Valley:

- *Headquarters 7 Flieger Division;*
- *3 Fallschirmjäger Regiment;*
- *1* and *2 Companies, Fallschirmpionier Battalion;*
- *4 Company, Fallschirmflak Battalion;*
- *3 Company, Fallschirmmaschinengewehr Battalion;* and
- two companies of *I Battalion, Luftlande Sturmregiment.*

The landing sites and objectives comprised:

- *I* and *II Battalions, 3 Fallschirmjäger Regiment, 3 Company Fallschirmflak Battalion, 3 Company, Fallschirmmaschinengewehr Battalion*: land south and west of the prison and advance on Suda.
- *III Battalion, 3 Fallschirmjäger Regiment*: land east of Galatas and advance on Canea.
- *Fallschirmpionier Battalion* with *13* and *14 Companies, 3 Fallschirmjäger Regiment*: land north of Alikianou and protect the rear of *3 Fallschirmjäger Regiment*.
- *1 Company, I Battalion, Luftlande Sturmregiment* (glider): land south of Canea and capture enemy anti-aircraft positions.
- *2 Company, I Battalion Luftlande Sturmregiment* (glider): land on Akrotiri Peninsula and capture anti-aircraft positions.

Süssmann did not survive the flight from Greece. Soon after takeoff his glider was caught in the slipstream of a passing Heinkel 111. The glider lost its wings, the tug cable parted, and it plunged from the sky to crash on the island of Aegina killing all on board. The rest of the divisional staff fared better, but only marginally. The four remaining divisional headquarters gliders came down right on target in a field near the reservoir in Prison Valley that had been selected through photographic interpretation. What German intelligence had not revealed, however, was the row after row of bare grapevine stumps that covered the field. As the gliders came in to land the pilots were helpless to avoid these deadly obstacles. The gliders slid across the ground, ripped through lines of stumps, and disintegrated. Only a handful of troops emerged from the wreckage. Control of the battle for Prison Valley passed to the commander of *3 Fallschirmjäger Regiment*, Oberst Richard Heidrich.

What Student could not have known was that when the paratroopers landed in Prison Valley the axis of their attack towards Canea and Suda lay at the junction of three British commands: Puttick's New Zealand Division, Weston's Suda Sector force, and Freyberg's Creforce reserve. By simultaneously assaulting the Prison Valley and Maleme, Student forced the New Zealand Division to fight on two fronts, facing two directions. Puttick was not up to the task, nor would he be materially helped by Freyberg and Hargest.

Brigadier Edward Puttick, Acting Commander
New Zealand Division
National Library of New Zealand PAColl-5547-015

The Gliders Arrive

The first invaders arrived in the gliders of the *Lufltande Sturmregiment*'s *1* and *2 Companies*. As at Maleme they swooped down as the *Luftwaffe*'s bombing ended. The objectives for both groups were British heavy anti-aircraft positions.

Hauptmann Gustav Altman's *2 Company*'s objective was a battery of heavy anti-aircraft guns on the Akrotiri Peninsula. As Altman's fifteen gliders crossed the coast they lost cohesion. Once the tows parted, the gliders scattered, coming down over a large area; several broke up on the rocky ground, killing or injuring their passengers. Altman's command was too widely spread for him to control and each glider team had to make its own way to the objective.

LIEUTENANT-GENERAL EDWARD PUTTICK

Born in Timaru on 26 June 1890, Edward Puttick would become New Zealand's first native-born son to reach the rank of lieutenant-general. In 1911 he joined the Territorial Force and, with the outbreak of the First World War, Puttick was an early volunteer. His first service was with the New Zealand expedition to Samoa.

Puttick arrived in Egypt in early 1916 as a company commander in the New Zealand Rifle Brigade. Following operations in Libya against the Senussi he moved to the Western Front where he served in 2 New Zealand Brigade. He was promoted lieutenant-colonel at Passchendaele and appointed commander of 3 New Zealand Battalion. Puttick commanded the battalion until wounded in 1918 when he was evacuated to England. There he commanded a rifle depot until his return to New Zealand in late 1918.

With the war over, Puttick decided to pursue a military career and joined the New Zealand Staff Corps in 1919. Over the next twenty years he enjoyed a series of staff and administrative appointments at which he excelled. The outbreak of the Second World War saw him in command of the Central Military District where he was instrumental in raising the 2nd New Zealand Expeditionary Force. When the force sailed he took command of 4 New Zealand Brigade.

Puttick's first campaign was Greece where he commanded the brigade during the retreat. Arriving in Crete he was given temporary command of the New Zealand Division after Freyberg's appointment as Commander Creforce.

Puttick's performance during the Crete campaign was poor, and he demonstrated that his true calling was military administration rather than field command. He recoiled from the notion of attack, allowed the paratroopers to become established in Prison Valley and failed to push Hargest to retake Maleme. An air of defeatism surrounded him throughout the campaign.

Following his evacuation to Egypt, Puttick was promoted and appointed Chief of the New Zealand General Staff, returning to Wellington to take up his appointment. By 1942 he was a lieutenant-general and also served as Chairman of the Chief of Staff Committee. Following Japan's entry into the war, it was Puttick's task to prepare New Zealand to meet this new threat while also sustaining New Zealand forces in the European theatre. He performed admirably in fulfilling both tasks.

Puttick retired from the army in September 1946. He died on 25 July 1976.

The Gliders Land – gouache on board, 2005.
Artist – Jeff Isaacs, OAM

The Akrotiri was garrisoned by the Northumberland Hussars. These men responded vigorously to the German incursion, methodically killing or capturing Altman's men. One British soldier described the German landing, 'suddenly we heard a swishing noise and above our heads appeared a glider. [It] landed immediately in front of our position on the road-block, about 50 yds away. We opened fire the moment the glider landed. The occupants didn't have much chance to return fire; some were killed, others wounded, until eventually the survivors put up a white flag. We were amazed to see how well they were armed and equipped. The folding bicycle in the glider had been hit by an anti-tank rifle bullet, so it was in a bit of a mess'.

The entire German force was either killed or captured and Altman spent the rest of the war as a prisoner. The few Germans who reached the objective discovered it to be a dummy position.

Heavy anti-aircraft gun, 3.7-inch

Calibre:	3.7 inch
Ammunition:	high explosive, shrapnel, armour piercing
Shell weight:	12.7 kg
Effective Ceiling:	9753 metres
Rate of Fire:	25 rpm

The 3.7-inch heavy anti-aircraft gun entered production in 1938. Throughout the war it served the British well as a high-level anti-aircraft weapon. It was produced in both static and four-wheeled carriage models. Unlike its German rival the 88, the British gun was designed solely for an anti-aircraft role and was not used to attack ground targets. The British had sixteen of these weapons on Crete.

Oberleutnant Alfred Genz and his *1 Company* fared better. Genz's command was also scattered as it crossed the coast, but most of his gliders landed safely near to their objective—four 3.7-inch heavy anti-aircraft guns belonging to 234 Heavy Anti-Aircraft Battery, Royal Artillery. The lightly armed defenders were no match for the automatic weapons of the glider troops. Genz's men stormed the position and took it.

Genz did not have the strength to move against his secondary target, a wireless station, so he attempted to hold the battery position. Later that day he observed the approach of a relief force of Royal Marines supported by Bren Gun Carriers of 1 Welch Battalion. Realising that he now faced serious resistance, Genz disabled the guns and the Germans slipped away to the west towards the drop zone of *3 Fallschirmjäger Regiment*.

When the relief column reached the battery it found near total destruction. Of the approximately 180 gunners assigned to the position only seven remained alive. What happened during the battle is not entirely clear. The New Zealand official historian of the Crete Campaign, D. M. Davin, credits the large number of casualties to the resistance of the gunners whom he suggests fought stubbornly until overwhelmed by the Germans. Davin is almost certainly too kind. The gunners had little in the way of weapons with which to mount a determined defence, and man for man they were no match for the elite paratroopers. The most likely explanation is that the British gunners surrendered when confronted by the hail of German fire. Later, as the relief column approached, Genz had the prisoners executed as he was unable to take them along.

Sub-machine gun, MP40

Calibre:	9 mm
Operation:	blowback, automatic fire
Magazine:	32 rounds
Weight:	4.03 kg (empty), 4.7 kg (loaded)
Length:	833 mm (stock extended), 630 mm (stock folded)
Effective Range:	100 metres
Rate of Fire:	500 rpm (cyclic)

Maschinenpistole (machine pistols) Model 40—the Schmeisser—represented an innovation in the design and construction of sub-machine guns. It was made wholly of welded and stamped assemblies, making it suitable for mass production, contained no wooden components, and had a folding stock. The first model in this series, the MP38, was adopted by the Wehrmacht prior to the war. The improved MP40 quickly became a hallmark weapon of the German army. During the Crete campaign, the MP40 was issued to officers and non-commissioned officers of the *Fallschirmjäger*.

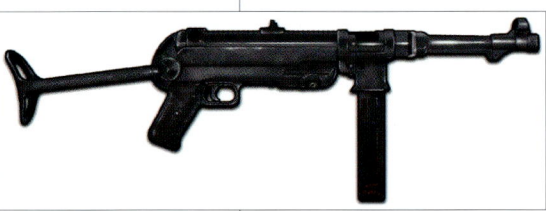

> Lesson 9
>
> The complete destruction of a support echelon unit reinforces the point of two lessons. First it reiterates the necessity for all units to have the means to provide for their own defence, no matter their position or role in the battlespace. Second, and more importantly, it highlights the folly of trying to identify a front line in an era of high operational mobility. In contemporary warfare any point in a theatre may suddenly become the front line. Therefore, it is essential that all units look to their own defence.

The Descent into Prison Valley

At around 0830 hours, Junkers 52 transports began their drop runs and the sky filled with the parachutes of *3 Fallschirmjäger Regiment*. It was the luckless *III Battalion* that felt the full fury of the New Zealand defence. Its companies were scattered widely and most landed outside their drop zones. While the troops' dispersal made it impossible for the unit to march on its objective, Canea, it also saved many members of the battalion from immediate destruction. The two companies that landed closest to the planned landing zone were almost wiped out. Heavy casualties were inflicted on *10 Company* which came down under intense fire on the coastal plain between 18 and 19 New Zealand Battalions. Battalion headquarters, along with *9 Company*, landed on top of 19 New Zealand Battalion, as well as downslope from the Composite Battalion. It, too, suffered heavily. A party of paratroopers captured 7 General Hospital before it, in turn, had to surrender to Kiwi reinforcements.

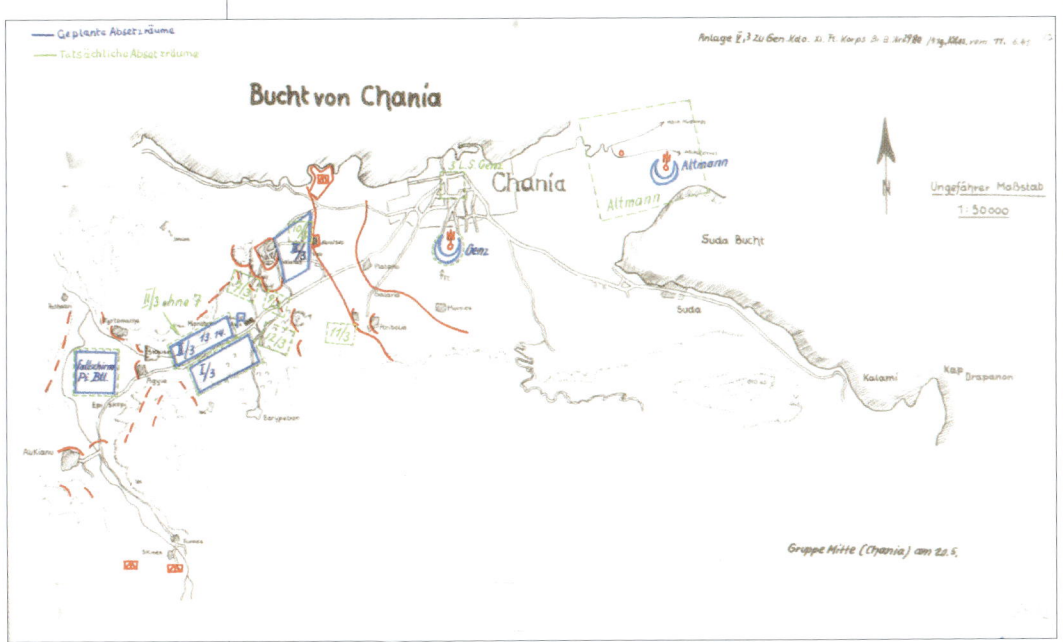

German Intended and Actual Landing Zones around Canea
Australian War Memorial Map Collection

Remains of a paratrooper. He had been a member of the party that captured the hospital.
National Library of New Zealand DA-01108

Other units fared better: *I* and *II Battalions*, less *7 Company*, landed largely intact in the environs of the prison, an area that was undefended except for enfilading fire from the hills. However, *7 Company* drifted onto the slope in front of the Composite Battalion. Its commander, Leutnant Neuhof, rallied his men and led them up Pink Hill towards the Petrol Company. The New Zealanders were not particularly well armed: their only automatic weapons were two Brens, an ancient Lewis gun and some Tommy guns. Yet the Petrol Company stood firm and subjected the paratroopers to such intense fire that it broke the impetuous attack and destroyed the German company as an effective force. Neuhof died on the slope amongst his men.

Light machine-gun, .303-inch Lewis Mark 1	
Calibre:	.303 inch
Operation:	gas; automatic fire; air-cooled; magazine fed; bipod mount
Magazine:	47 rounds
Weight:	13.7 kg (empty), 14.9 kg (loaded)
Length:	1282 mm
Sights:	1737 metres
Effective Range:	548 metres
Maximum Range:	9144 metres
Rates of Fire:	cyclic: 450 rpm. Normal: bursts of 4-5 rounds as required. Rapid: 120 rpm.

The Lewis gun entered service during the First World War. By the onset of the Second World War it was obsolete and had been replaced by the Bren gun. Shortages of automatic weapons on Crete saw the Lewis gun again pressed into action. During the Crete campaign it was generally allocated to support and service units with the Bren gun reserved for the infantry. The Lewis gun was carried and fired by one man, but required at least two men to carry its ammunition.

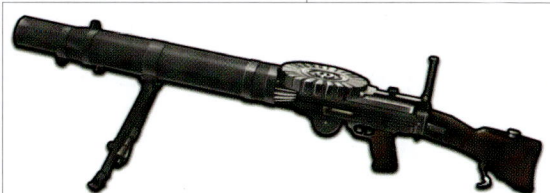

The *Pioneers*, along with the machine-guns and anti-tank guns of *13* and *14 Companies*, came down as planned in the open ground between Alikianou and the reservoir. Throughout their landing zone, small but deadly actions were fought between the invaders and 8 Greek Regiment. The Germans also had to contend with Cretan civilians who stalked the paratroopers through the fields and olive groves. By midday, however, the Germans had gained the upper hand and 8 Greek Regiment retired to a blocking position in the foothills south of the reservoir from which they continued to snipe at the enemy.

On the northern side of the *Pioneers*' landing zone the New Zealand Division Cavalry Squadron commander, Major J. T. Russell, attempted to report the situation to Kippenberger, but discovered that his phone line was no longer working. He did not have a wireless. Assessing his odds against the much more numerous and better armed Germans he decided, as had been agreed in advance, to withdraw around Signal Hill to the main 10 New Zealand Brigade position.

The ill-positioned 6 Greek Regiment was also to feel the German wrath. From his command post near Pink Hill, Kippenberger watched the drama unfold in the valley below. With paratroopers landing on and around them, the men panicked and fled, the unit dissolving under the pressure. In defence of these men, they faced the German assault at a desperate disadvantage as their commander refused to issue ammunition and they went into battle with only three rounds each. Many also soon rallied, joining the New Zealanders on the heights where they fought well, or linked up with 2 Greek Regiment on the valley's southern side. However, as a unit, 6 Greek Regiment had ceased to exist.

The rout of 6 Greek Regiment left Cemetery Hill undefended. The Germans quickly placed observers on its summit and mortar bombs began to rain down on the Composite Battalion's position.

Behind the Greeks, the gunners of 1 Light Troop, Royal Artillery, fared little better. The Germans overwhelmed the battery by sheer force of numbers with the tiny infantry detachment unable to stem the onslaught. As the Germans closed in, the surviving gunners disabled their pieces and scrambled up the heights following the remnants of the infantry section. It is not clear whether the gunners fired even a single round before being forced to flee. The Germans repaired one of the howitzers and were soon using it to fire on the Kiwis. Within minutes of landing the Germans had secured the valley floor.

The Battle for the Heights

Dominating the valley was the prison. It was the focal point of the drop zones for *I* and *II Battalions* and the regimental headquarters. When Heidrich arrived he made it his base of operations. From behind its walls he scanned the surrounding heights and came to the conclusion that the planners had made a serious error in the selection of his regiment's drop zone. Intelligence officers had identified the sector as a plateau. Instead, Heidrich found himself in a valley, surrounded by hills from which fire poured down onto his men. He saw that his command had inadvertently landed in a trap and that to remain in the valley would only lead to death and defeat. Heidrich decided that the key to the position lay in occupation of the heights and he directed his men towards the high ground.

> **Lesson 10**
>
> In selecting the position of their units, commanders must have a clear understanding of their own capabilities as well as those of the enemy. As the art of war evolves, commanders must anticipate the novel and prepare to confront non-traditional methods of waging war, otherwise the battle will be lost before it begins.

A contemporary view of the prison from the top of Cemetery Hill. The prison was less than two kilometres from the New Zealanders' position on the Galatas Heights. If the New Zealanders had had a battery of 25-pounder guns, or even the lost 3.7-inch howitzers, they could have reduced the German headquarters to a charnel-house.
Photo courtesy of author.

At about 1000 hours Heidrich sent *5 Company*, supported by *9* and *12 Companies*, up the road running from the prison to Galatas. Their objective was Pink Hill and the Petrol Company. As the Germans moved up the slope the Petrol Company's commander, Captain W. G. McDonagh, commented as he moved amongst his men, 'This'll be a good shoot.' [and] 'The duck season's a bit late boys, but it's good shooting now.'

Supported by a mortar barrage, the Germans stormed up the road and made good progress despite strong resistance from the Petrol Company. The defenders began to give way as the Germans pushed troops into the gap left in the New Zealand line by 6 Greek Regiment's collapse. At this point every officer in the Petrol Company was either dead or wounded and command had passed to the company sergeant-major. McDonagh did not survive the German attack.

Two New Zealand soldiers near a parachute hung up in an olive tree near Galatas.
National Library of New Zealand DA-00470

The Germans were on the verge of success when suddenly, and quite unexpectedly, their fortunes changed. A party of several hundred Greek soldiers and civilians who had been rallied by a British officer, Captain Michael Forrester, interceded in the battle. Forrester led a mad charge down the hill into the midst of the Germans. Stunned by this unexpected assault the Germans wavered and broke. The second German attack on Pink Hill had failed.

While Heidrich organised the attack on the heights, *I Battalion* moved towards its objective—Suda. Ignoring the fire from the heights, Hauptmann von der Heydte pushed the battalion up the road. En route they gathered up *11 Company, III Battalion*, from its incorrect landing site. The paratroopers pushed past Perivolia and out of the valley's neck almost to Mournies before increasing resistance brought them to a halt. Pushed into a salient with pressure increasing on three sides, von der Heydte fell back to Perivolia and dug in.

Having failed twice to take Pink Hill, Heidrich took a more deliberate approach. For the rest of the day he subjected the hill's defenders to a bombardment of shells and mortar bombs while *Luftwaffe* planes ranged about unmolested. At about 1600 hours the Germans tried again, but this attack did not have the same strength behind it as the earlier assault. The Germans did not get far before being forced to go to ground.

At the day's end Heidrich's situation looked grim. Canea and Suda remained in enemy hands and Freyberg had brought up 2/8 Australian Battalion to strengthen the valley's exit around Perivolia. From the surrounding heights the New Zealanders continued to torment him while from the hills near Alikianou, 8 Greek Regiment threatened his rear. The day's fighting had almost spent his command. The battalions had fared badly: *III Battalion* had been destroyed, *II Battalion* had taken heavy casualties, *I Battalion* had been forced to dig in, and the *Pioneers* had closed up on the main position in order to establish an all-around defence. Heidrich now awaited the enemy's counter-attack which he knew when it came must surely destroy him.

THE LANDINGS AT HERAKLION

The Defence of Heraklion

Heraklion was Crete's major city. It was home to the island's largest population and its most developed port. Since Suda Bay was a finer natural harbour, however, the Royal Navy selected it as the fleet's main anchorage and refuelling point. Canea rather than Heraklion became the centre of the British presence on the island. To the Germans, on the other hand, it was not the harbour that was important; rather it was the airfield a few kilometres east of the city that made it a target.

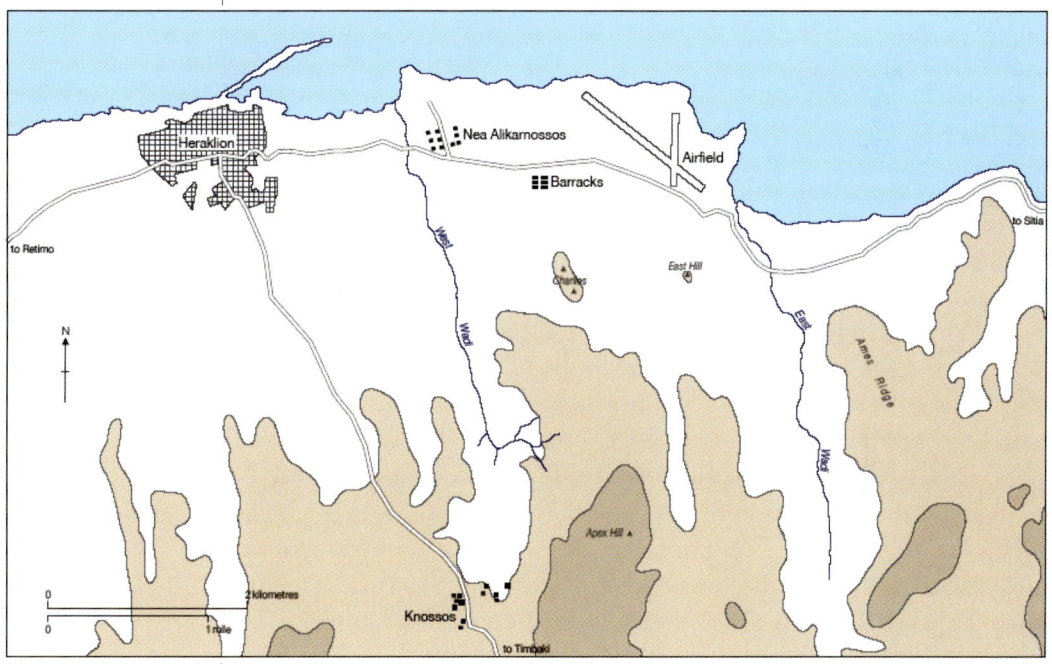

Heraklion Sector
Drawn By Keith Mitchell

Heraklion was separated from Canea by approximately 140 kilometres of winding and mountainous road. The distance between the two forced the British to treat the Heraklion sector as virtually an independent command. Freyberg and his predecessor Weston accepted that it would be impossible to reinforce the garrison within the time-frame of the campaign, especially in light of Creforce's acute shortage of motor vehicles. Consequently, of the island's five sectors, Heraklion had the strongest garrison: 14 Brigade less 1 Welch Battalion.

View of the coastal plain near Heraklion from the Australian position.
Australian War Memorial 130913

As the island's original garrison, 14 Brigade's units were at full strength and fully equipped; for example, its battalions had their Bren Gun Carriers, and their mortars had their base plates. The formation's commander was Brigadier B. H. Chappel. Unusually for Creforce, the brigade also had transport—enough trucks to lift a battalion. Although Chappel did not have as many anti-aircraft guns as Suda Sector, he did possess a reasonable air defence capability. He had fourteen anti-aircraft guns: ten Bofors and four 3-inch guns. Chappel also had three Greek infantry units and six light tanks from the 3rd Hussars under his command. The formation's only deficiency lay in field artillery. Like the other sectors, Chappel had to make do with captured Italian and French ordnance of dubious quality and efficiency. Wire diagram 9 outlines Chappel's command.

While he accepted Weston's dispatch of 14 Brigade to Heraklion, Freyberg believed that the sector's isolation made it critical to further boost the brigade's strength. As a consequence, Freyberg sent Chappel 2/4 Australian Battalion and part of 7 Medium Regiment, Royal Artillery (as infantry). He also requested more men from Wavell, who sent out 2 Argyll and Sutherland Battalion and three more Matilda tanks from 7 RTR. These tanks were not the workshop cast-offs that had arrived earlier, but new machines recently landed in Egypt. The Scotsmen and the tanks landed at Tymbaki on the south coast on 19 May, although they did not reach the city until after the start of the invasion.

Wire Diagram 9
British Organisation: *Heraklion Sector*

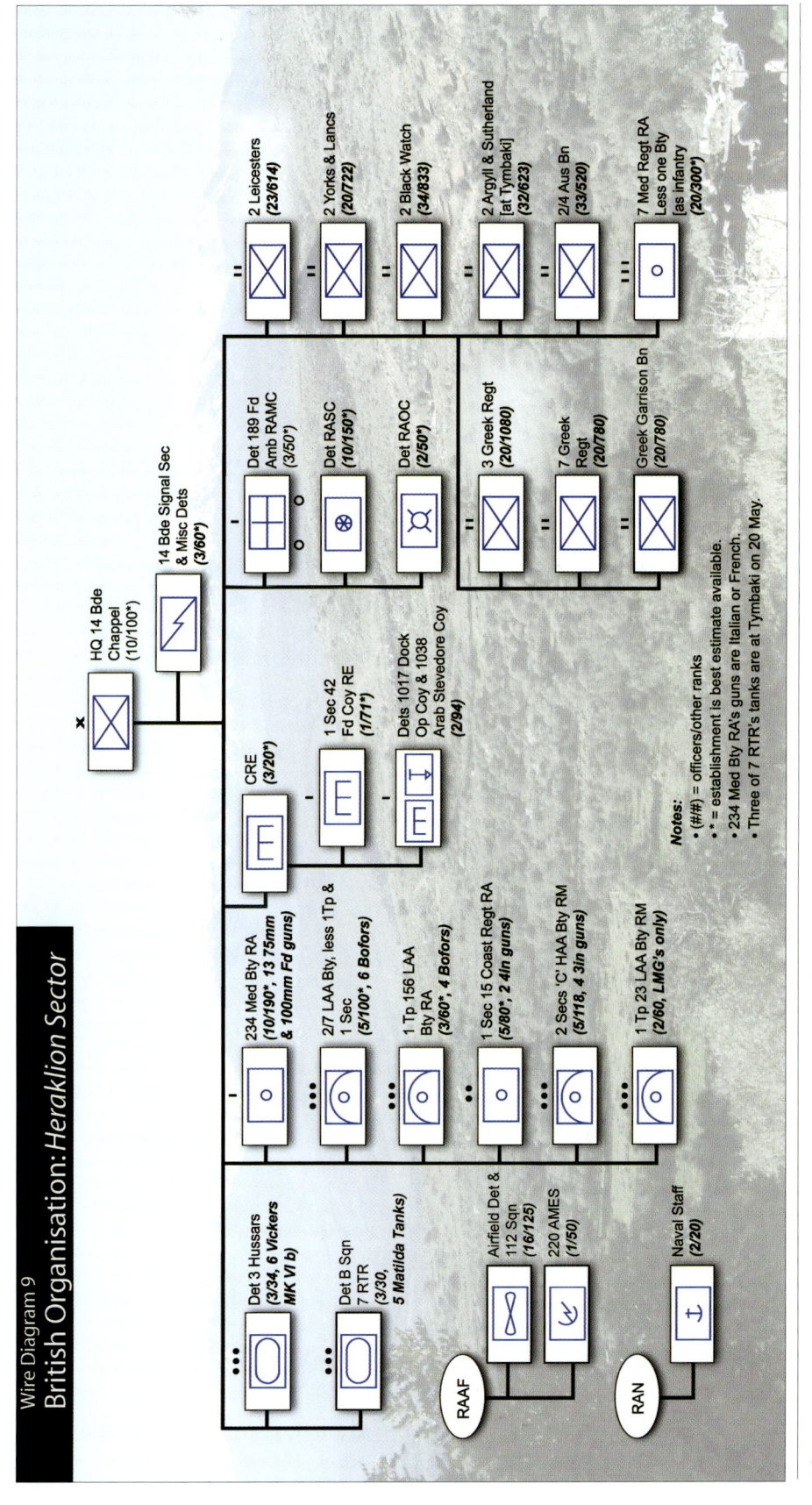

Mortar, 3-inch	
Calibre:	3 inch [76 mm]
Weight:	56 kg (complete): barrel – 19 kg, bipod – 20.4 kg, base plate – 16.8 kg
Ammunition:	high explosive and smoke. Weight of bomb: 4.5 kg
Rates of Fire:	12 rpm
Range:	274 to 1463 metres

The Mark 1 3-inch mortar was an evolution of the First World War Stokes 3-inch mortar. The Mark 1 had a smooth bore, fired a fin-stabilised bomb and was generally cheap to make and reliable. A crew-served weapon, it required a minimum crew of three for its operation, although additional men were needed to carry ammunition. The British establishment was six tubes per battalion but few units on Crete had their correct allocation. Moreover, some mortar crews, such as the Australians at Retimo, did not even have base plates for their weapons.

Chappel faced the easiest operational situation of the Creforce sectors. His critical points were the city of Heraklion, its harbour and the airfield. Located close to one another, the three features fitted into a compact area the defence of which was well within the ability of the available forces. Also of benefit to Chappel was the convergence between the locales which he had to hold and those that his German opponent, Oberst Bruno Bräuer, had to seize. The garrison occupied the precise positions that the invaders wanted, allowing 14 Brigade the luxury of a concentrated and efficient disposition of strength. Moreover, unlike in the Maleme, Canea and Suda sectors, Chappel did not distract himself with the threat of seaborne invasion. He kept his focus on the real danger—the paratroopers and their need for an airfield.

Chappel placed his units in a tight perimeter around the airfield. Their locations were:

- 2 Black Watch Battalion: A, B, and Headquarters Companies on East Hill; C and D Companies near the runway;
- 2/4 Australian Battalion: A Company on the two Charlies, B Company overlooking West Wadi, C and D Companies near the barracks adjacent to the airfield in support of 2 Black Watch Battalion;
- 2 Leicester Battalion: Chappel's reserve, in and around West Wadi in the middle of the brigade's perimeter;
- 2 Yorks and Lancaster Battalion: open ground between West Wadi and Heraklion;
- 7 Medium Regiment: coastal zone overlooking the harbour west of the airfield; and
- Greek battalions: garrison Heraklion and the western and south-western approaches to the city.

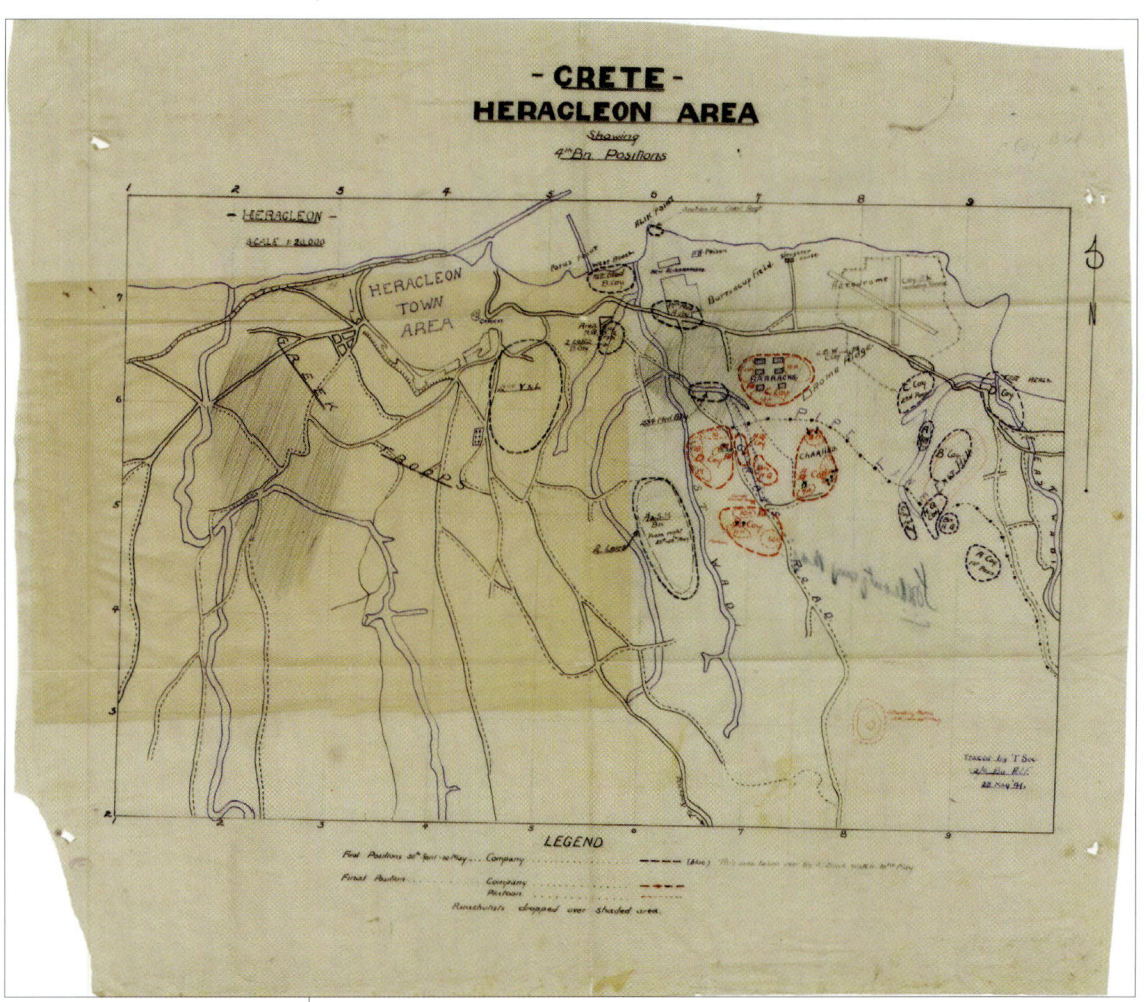

British Positions at time of Invasion. The 2/4th Australian Battalion is shown in red. Shaded areas show the German drop areas. 2/4 Aus Bn War Diary, AWM52, 8/3/4, May 1941, page 13.

East Hill was a low rise whose modest height was magnified by the wadis on three of its sides. The effect of this was to create a highly defensive, steep-sided, rocky rampart that was ideally placed to guard the airfield from the east. Protecting the rear of the Scotsmen was 2/4 Australian Battalion on the two Charlies. The sharply sided Charlies—two matching pinnacles—towered over the surrounding plain. They were the high points within the British perimeter and gave the Australians a line of sight over the airfield, the eastern approaches and westward to the gates of Heraklion. Even today, an observer is rewarded with a panoramic view of the entire coastal plain. The hills were the key to the sector; even if the Germans captured the airfield they would have to clear the Charlies before aircraft could land. Further west the ground flattened, but Chappel had the luxury of greater depth which added to the airfield's security. The Leicesters and the Yorks and Lancasters held the open ground between the two Charlies and the Venetian era ramparts that surrounded Heraklion.

Air Assault on Crete – gouache on board, 2005
artist – Jeff Isaacs, OAM

The German Plan

Süssmann allocated four battalions of paratroopers to the Heraklion operation. The paratroopers were commanded by Oberst Bruno Bräuer of *1 Fallschirmjäger Regiment*. Bräuer's force consisted of:

- *I, II, III Battalions, 1 Fallschirmjäger Regiment;*
- *II Battalion, 2 Fallschirmjäger Regiment;* and
- *1 Company, Fallschirmflak Battalion.*

Student's orders to Bräuer were direct: seize the airfield, clear it, and prepare for the landing of mountain troops.

GENERAL-MAJOR BRUNO BRÄUER

Bruno Bräuer was born in Berlin on 4 February 1893. During the First World War he served as a non-commissioned officer and was awarded the Iron Cross (2nd Class).

Following Germany's defeat Bräuer joined the Prussian security police. With Hitler's rise to power, Bräuer's career accelerated. He was promoted to battalion commander in the *Herman Göring Regiment*.

In July 1938 Bräuer was among the first to join the *Reichswehr*'s paratrooper force, and was given command of *1 Fallschirmjäger Regiment* of the newly formed *7 Flieger Division*. He received the Knight's Cross for his regiment's role in the campaign in Holland in 1940. During the Battle for Crete, Bräuer commanded the German forces at Heraklion.

In early 1943, after a period on the Eastern Front, Bräuer returned to Crete as garrison commander. Unlike his predecessors, he strove to rule gently, if firmly, despite ongoing partisan activity. As a result Bräuer is regarded as the fairest of the island's commanders.

In late 1944 Bräuer took command of the newly raised *9 Flieger Division* in Germany. The division participated in the defence of Berlin where it was virtually annihilated by the Soviet Army. The war's end found Bräuer a prisoner of the British. He was returned to Greece at the request of the Greek government to face charges of war crimes. Despite being the least culpable of Crete's commandants, the court found Bräuer guilty. He received the death sentence and was executed by the Greek government on the sixth anniversary of the island's invasion.

Bräuer gave the key role in the assault to Hauptmann Burckhardt's *II Battalion, 1 Fallschirmjäger Regiment*. The infantry were supported by the 20mm guns of the *Fallschirmflak Battalion*. The paratroopers formed two battlegroups to be dropped on either side of the airfield which they would capture in a simultaneous converging assault. *III Battalion, 1 Fallschirmjäger Regiment*, equipped with the regiment's heavy weapons, was to drop west and south-west of Heraklion, storm the city and take the harbour. Bräuer and the regimental headquarters would arrive with *I Battalion, 1 Fallschirmjäger Regiment*, near Gurnes. This battalion's mission was to seize a nearby wireless station and establish a blocking position from the east. Bräuer's remaining battalion, *II Battalion, 2 Fallschirmjäger Regiment*, was to drop west of the city and set up a blocking position to prevent a British counter-attack from Retimo.

Paratroopers ready to board their Junkers 52 to participate in the invasion of Crete.
Australian War Memorial P00057.032

Prior to the landing, aircraft from *VIII Fleigerkorps* were to bomb the British positions intensively, paying particular attention to the anti-aircraft guns in order to safeguard the vulnerable transports. Once the landing began, the fighters and fighter bombers were to provide the paratroopers with close air support.

The Paratroopers Arrive

The *XI Fliegerkorps* operation plan recognised that the success of the assault at Heraklion 'depended on the concentrated landing of all formations in their target area at 1615 hrs.' This was an optimistic, if not arrogant, expectation, and to meet it planners ignored the possibility of error, delay, the fog of war, and the enemy's interference with their arrangements. The reality was that failure to drop the invasion force on target, in close formation, and at the designated time would be paid for with the parachutists' lives.

Flak 38 anti-aircraft gun, 20 mm

Calibre:	20 mm
Operation:	magazine fed, recoil operation, automatic or semi-automatic fire
Magazine:	20 rounds
Ammunition:	high explosive; armour piercing.
Effective Ceiling:	1066 metres
Ground Range:	4782 metres
Rate of Fire:	180-220 rpm

The Flak 38 entered service in 1940 and became the standard German light anti-aircraft weapon of the Second World War. It came in single and quad mounts, although the *Fallschirmjäger* on Crete only used the single tube variant. The weapon was also effective against ground forces. The Flak 38 was light enough to be air dropped with cluster parachutes. Once on the ground it was towed by the Ketten-Krad half-track motorcycle.

From a logistical perspective, the Heraklion and Retimo landings were always going to be more difficult than those at Maleme and around Canea. When the Junkers 52s returned to their airfields on the mainland after their morning missions, ground crews struggled to turn them around in time for the afternoon attack. Refuelling was one of the choke points. None of the airfields had mechanical facilities for the job. Instead, the aircraft were refuelled by hand with a pump from the fuel drums—which themselves were in short supply. It was a time-consuming procedure that put the entire second wave behind schedule. Adding to the delay, as the aircraft took off they threw up great clouds of dust that completely obscured visibility for the next plane in line. The following pilots had to wait until the dust settled before roaring down the runway themselves. Furthermore, the airfields lacked holding areas, and loaded planes could not circle overhead for too long without requiring more fuel. Lastly, there was so little spare capacity in the movement plan that the morning's transport losses translated into a lack of aircraft for about three companies of paratroopers. This necessitated last minute changes in the loading profile. The cumulative effect of these problems was a delay of such magnitude that it ensured the essential synchronised parachute drop at precisely 1615 hours would not take place. Instead, the Heraklion invasion was marked by the progressive arrival of small groups of planes for a period that extended for more than two hours.

In addition to these problems, there was no element of surprise to assist the paratroopers. The defenders knew about the morning landings and were further alerted by the commencement of an intensive aerial attack by the planes of *VIII Fleigerkorps*. Communication problems with *VIII Fleigerkorps* had prevented *XI Fleigerkorps* staff from informing the bomber squadrons of the need to push back the strike time. Instead, the bombers attacked as scheduled at 1600 hours.

Lesson 11

Victory in war involves danger and risk. When planning operations however, commanders and staff officers have an obligation to be realistic about what is possible. They also have a responsibility to temper operational objectives with logistic capabilities. It must be remembered that the price of ignoring logistics is all too often paid in lives.

The *Luftwaffe* bombardment of Heraklion.
Australian War Memorial P02434.001

Observers on the ground remarked not only on the scale of the raid but also on its ineffectiveness. The ground quaked as the *Luftwaffe* bombed and machine-gunned the whole area; but within 2/4 Australian Battalion's perimeter there was not a single casualty amongst the well dug-in defenders. After dropping their loads the bombers turned for home and the anti-aircraft gunners stood by their guns to await the transports that they knew could not be too far off.

At about 1700 hours the first transports began to arrive. The Bofors and the 3-inch heavy anti-aircraft guns of the Royal Marines filled the sky with explosions. As the Junkers came closer the Vickers and Brens joined in and, once in range, soldiers added their rifle and Thompson sub-machine-gun fire to the fray. One plane caught fire and, as the paratroopers hurled themselves into space their parachutes deployed and then disappeared, one after the other, in a puff of smoke. The men dropped like stones. Other planes exploded, hit by anti-aircraft fire, and fell to earth. Fifteen transports crashed while others were raked by fire as they disgorged their passengers.

Heinkel He 111	
Type:	medium bomber
Wingspan:	22.6 m
Length:	16.6 m
Engine:	two Daimler-Benz DB 601 or two Junkers Jumo 211 (1540 kW each)
Max Speed:	440 kph
Range:	2150 km (with combat load)
Armament:	three machine-guns and 2000 kg of bombs

A variation of a civilian aircraft, the He 111 became Germany's primary medium bomber in the early stages of the Second World War. However, the Battle of Britain demonstrated that it was too vulnerable in this role without air supremacy. During the Crete campaign the *Luftwaffe* enjoyed complete control of the air, allowing the Germans to employ a group of He 111s effectively as bombers.

Sub-machine-gun, Thomson M1928A1	
Calibre:	.45 inch
Operation:	delayed blowback; selective fire
Magazine:	20 round box magazine, and 50 round drum magazine
Weight:	10.75 lb/4.8 kg (empty)
Weight:	5.4 kg: 20 round magazine; and 7.1 kg: 50 round drum
Length:	857 mm
Effective Range:	up to 914 metres
Rate of Fire:	600-725 rpm (cyclic)

The Thomson, nicknamed the Tommy gun, was first issued to US Marines in 1928. At the outbreak of the Second World War both Britain and France placed orders with the United States to increase their own stores of sub-machine-guns. Although heavy, complicated and costly to produce, it had a high rate of fire. The Thomson was commonly used by Australian infantry on Crete where it was issued on the basis of one per rifle section.

As the paratroopers landed, Chappel's men emerged from their dugouts and weapon pits and attacked, in many cases before the Germans had the chance to find their weapons containers. One transport crashed near C Company, 2/4 Australian Battalion. Not waiting for the Germans to emerge, two Australians raced up, tossed grenades in and emptied their weapons. No-one got out. Near the airfield a party of Germans took cover in a field covered with crops. The Australians set it on fire and shot the paratroopers as the flames flushed them out. The tanks also entered the action. Several drove into groups of paratroopers, grinding them under their tracks or slaughtering them with their guns.

The unit on which the German attack depended was the *Burckhardt Battlegroup*. The delay in the batttlegroup's departure destroyed the synchronisation so vital to the landing. Instead, Burchhardt's men arrived in waves, each greeted in turn by the defenders. West Group was destroyed, its five survivors only escaping by swimming eastward along the coast until they rejoined their lines. East Group fared somewhat better. That night Bruchardt rounded up about sixty men and escaped east, but his battalion had disappeared as a fighting force.

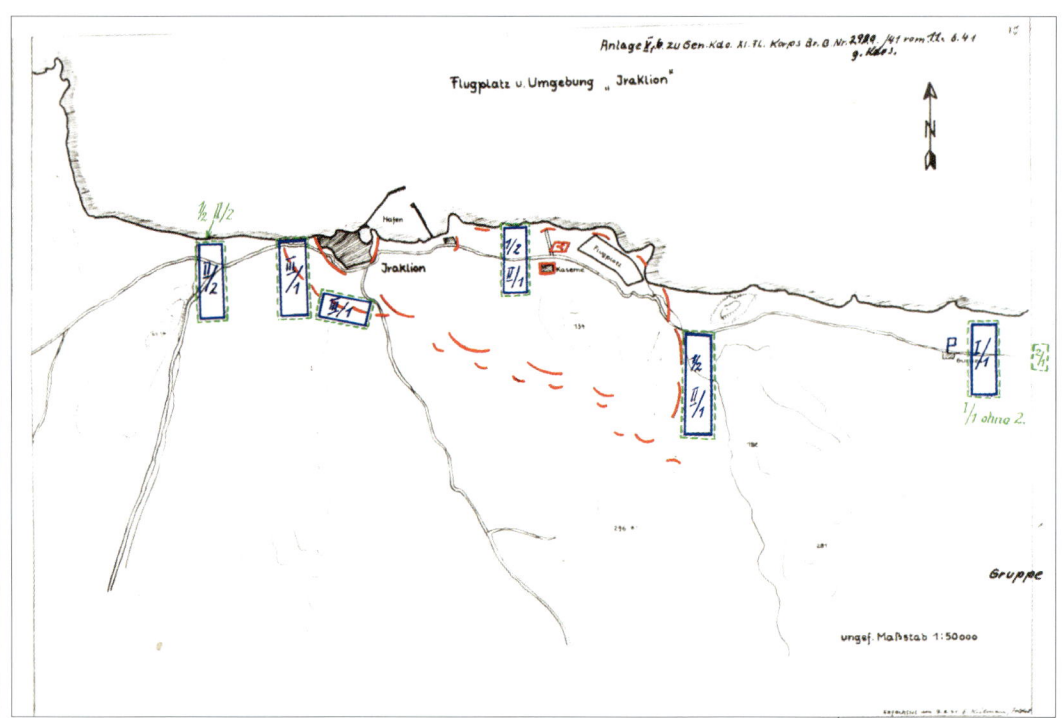

German Planned and Actual Drop Zones.
Australian War Memorial Map Collection

As one Australian described the situation, 'about 10 troop carriers came in and dropped their loads of paratroopers right over some of our men who were concealed just north of where I was & the slaughter was terrific, many of them killed while floating down & few escaped. Then in came another batch to reinforce the first lot & were dealt with the same way.' The next day the Australians were bothered only by the occasional sniper; around them the German dead lay thick on the ground.

As it landed south-west of Heraklion carrying the regiment's crucial heavy weapons, *III Battalion, 1 Fallschirmjäger Regiment*, also suffered heavy casualties. Some of the paratroopers managed to infiltrate the city and the sounds of street fighting filled the air into the night. It was a fierce battle with no quarter asked or given, fought at close range in the narrow streets. Only a few paratroopers were still alive in the morning. Chappel sent the York and Lancasters across the open ground outside Heraklion supported by the carriers of the Leicesters, forcing the Germans to withdraw to a ridgeline to the west.

On the western side of the sector, *II Battalion, 2 Fallschirmjäger Regiment*, arrived as planned and established its blocking position without opposition.

View from the Australian position into one of the wadis. Scores of Germans were killed on the valley floor.
Australian War Memorial 130918

37 mm Panzerabwehrkanone (PaK) 36 anti-tank gun

Calibre:	37 mm
Weight:	432 kg
Ammunition:	high explosive, armour piercing
Maximum Range:	4023 metres
Effective Range:	137 metres (against moving targets)

The PaK 36 was the standard German anti-tank gun at the start of the Second World War. It first saw combat during the Spanish Civil War and, by 1940, had become obsolete due to the increasing thickness of tank armour. For the *Fallschirmjäger*, however, there was really no other anti-tank gun option as the more powerful weapons were too heavy to be air dropped. On Crete the PaK 36 served in the *Fallschirmjäger Regiment* heavy weapon companies. It was mounted on a two-wheel carriage for towing.

When Bräuer landed near Gurnes he did not know of the slaughter that had befallen the units landing around the airfield. His arrival, while late, was at least without opposition. Major Walther, commander of *I Battalion, 1 Fallschirmjäger Regiment*, seized the wireless station as planned, and Bräuer organised a force to link up with the main landing party which by now, he presumed, held the runway. Bräuer's only hint of trouble was when Walther sent a platoon into the hills outside of Gurnes to set up a defensive perimeter. The platoon's bodies were found the next day, victims of local Greeks.

THE AUSTRALIANS DEFEND RETIMO

Vasey's Command

Geography divided Brigadier George Vasey's command into two separate zones, united only by the formation he commanded: 19 Australian Brigade. One zone covered the Georgeoupolis beach, a potential landing site for a German seaborne assault. The formation's other responsibility was the defence of the coastal plain around the harbour city of Retimo and its nearby airfield. Vasey sited his headquarters at Georgeoupolis since it was closer to Canea. Wire diagram 10 illustrates the organisation of Vasey's formation.

At Georgeoupolis, Vasey's task was to prevent an enemy landing on the beach. This was an immense job for what was effectively half a brigade. The beach was almost ten kilometres long with the coast road running parallel to it. A few kilometres to the south the hills began their rise, isolating the coastal zone from the rugged interior. Vasey positioned his two battalions and supporting arms at the western end of the beach near Georgeoupolis. Behind their positions rose a towering mass of rock that ran down into the water, sealing the beach's exit to the west. Through separate gaps ran two roads leading to Canea, one via Vamos and the other through Vrises. Vasey accepted that he could not prevent a landing. Instead he would hold the exits and await reinforcements.

Neither of Vasey's battalions was at full strength and almost all of his units suffered from obsolete equipment and a lack of mobility. Vasey had no anti-aircraft guns and 2/3 Australian Field Regiment had received Cairo's cast-offs. The guns were so old that when Lieutenant Michael Clark conducted a trial shoot of one particular gun he took the precaution of using an extra long lanyard out of fear that the barrel might rupture. Communication to Creforce Headquarters was, again, via the local phone exchange. The only unit with its proper establishment of equipment was the Royal Marine coastal gun detachment. Its guns pointed out to sea and would play no role in the battle.

On the morning of 20 May the Georgeoupolis garrison witnessed the arrival of the German air armada and heard the sounds of battle coming from the west. Throughout the day German planes prowled above, but no paratroopers landed. At about noon Vasey received orders to send 2/8 Australian Battalion to Mournies near Canea. The battalion was needed to help block the exit from Prison Valley.

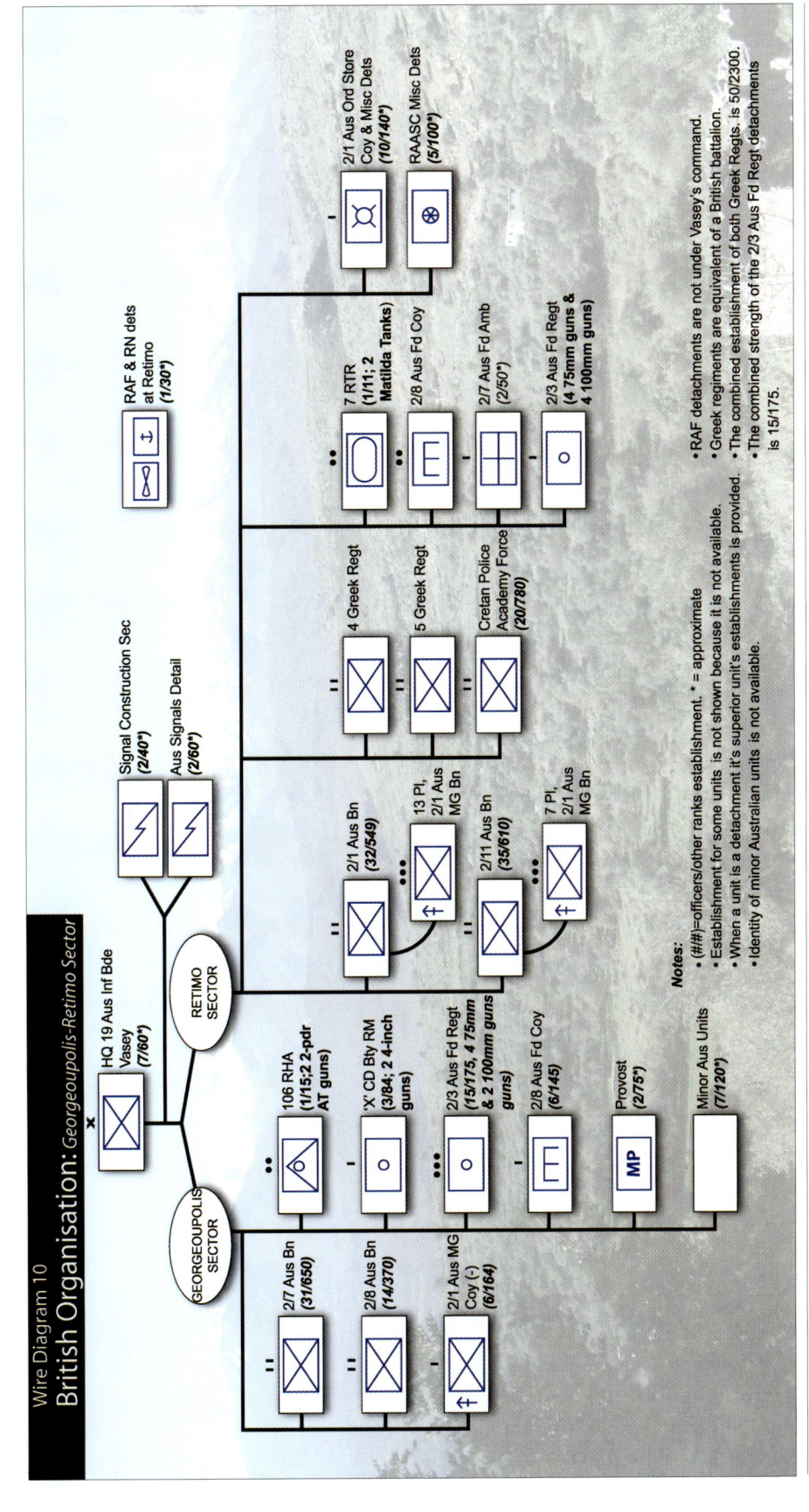

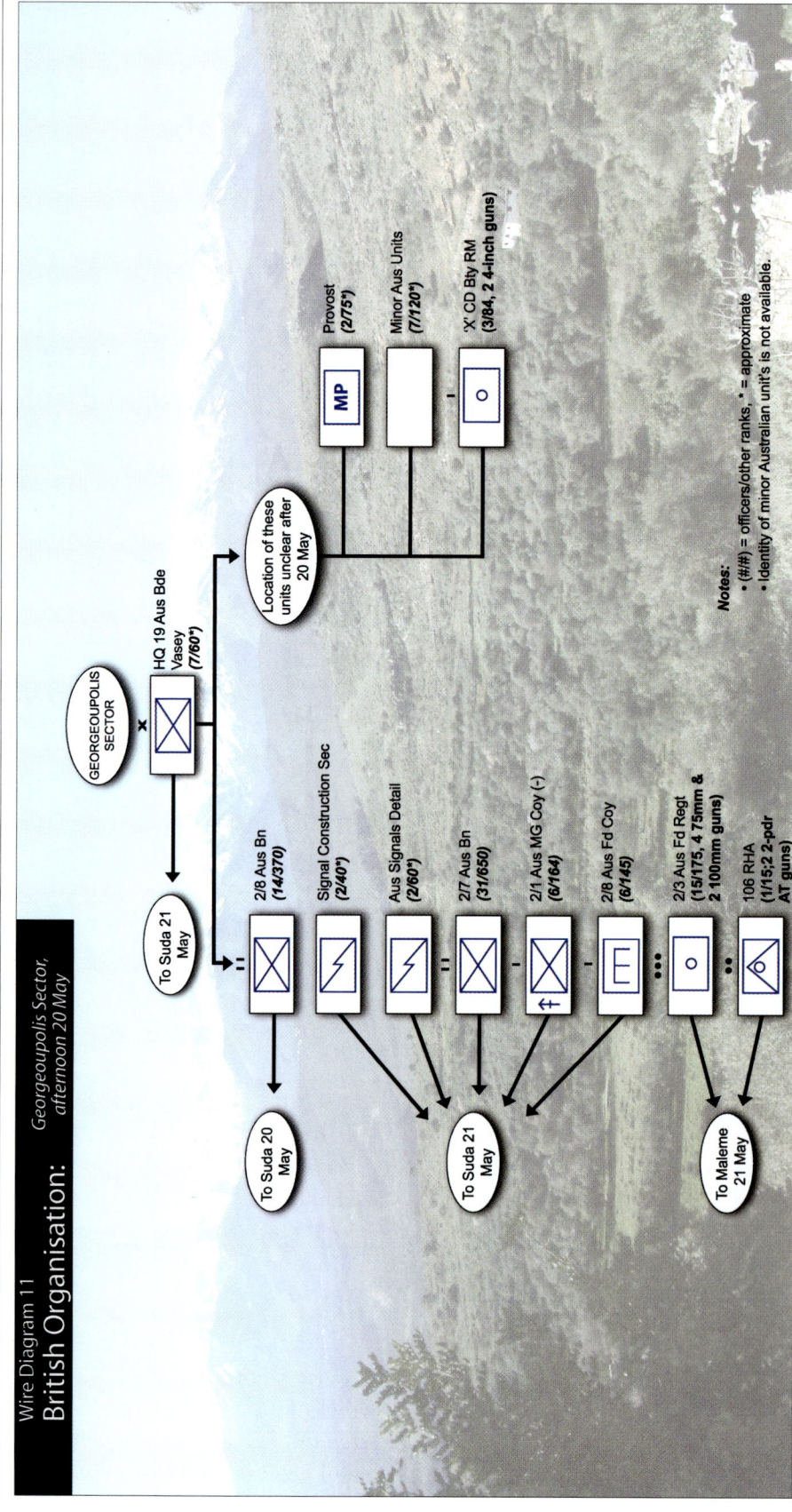

Wire Diagram 11
British Organisation: *Georgeoupolis Sector, afternoon 20 May*

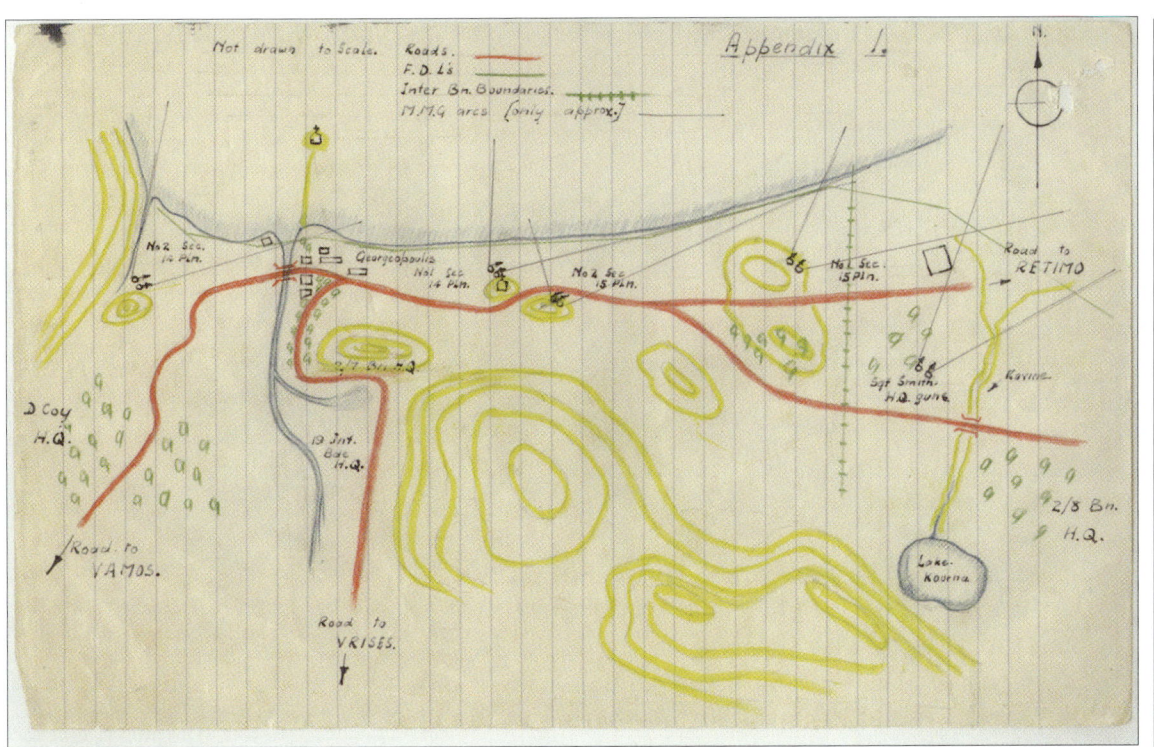

Vasey's Defence of Georgeoupolis. This map was prepared by 2/1 Australian Machine Gun Battalion. It shows the fields of fire of its machine-gun sections, and the headquarters of other units. The roads to Canea, via Vamos and Vrises, are also indicated.
2/1 Aus MG Bn War Diary, AWM52, 8/5/1, page 56.

Later that afternoon more Germans landed at Retimo and Heraklion, but Vasey's position around Georgeoupolis remained unassailed. The next day he received orders to move the remainder of his force west to help the New Zealanders in Prison Valley and around Maleme. Wire diagram 11 illustrates the redeployment of Vasey's force.

The Defence at Retimo

The senior officer at Retimo was Lieutenant-Colonel Ian Campbell, the commander of 2/1 Australian Battalion. Up to the commencement of the battle he was subordinate to Vasey. However when the attack began the *Luftwaffe* severed the phone link between the two 19 Australian Brigade zones. At that point Campbell took command of forces at Retimo in addition to his own 2/1st Battalion.

This modification to the command structure was not without difficulty. Campbell had to lead a brigade-size force without a brigade staff. There were no spare officers in the area, and to create a staff would mean depleting units of officers just as the battle began. Campbell opted to command the area through his existing battalion headquarters, although it consisted of just him and four others.

Vasey allocated the larger share of his command to the Retimo defence. Campbell had two Australian battalions—2/1 and 2/11—supported by two platoons of 2/1 Australian Machine Gun Battalion, the artillery of 2/3 Australian Field Regiment and the engineers of 2/8 Australian Field Company. He also had two clapped-out Matildas. The battalions lacked most of their heavy weapons and ammunition was in short supply. The Vickers crews had only ten belts for each gun, there were no base plates for the 3-inch mortars and no 2-inch mortars at all. There were a few Boys anti-tank guns on hand with several rounds apiece. The 4th and 5th Greek Regiments were raw recruits, virtually untrained and indifferently armed. Of all the Greek forces at his disposal, Campbell could only rely on the police academy cadets. Wire diagram 12 describes the defending force at Retimo.

Despite being assigned airfield defence as his primary task, Campbell had no anti-aircraft guns—nor did he possess secure communications. To cover the entire zone he had four field phones. Campbell did have a wireless to reach Creforce Headquarters but no code book. Communication with Canea, therefore, was infrequent and couched in vague terms to disguise its true meaning.

Like Georgeoupolis, the Retimo zone was a narrow coastal plain that fronted the sea behind a long beach. Blocking the exits at either end were mountains that ended at the sea. A short distance to the south the plain gave way to hills. The city of Retimo sat at the western end of the zone, guarded by a Venetian era fortress that stood on a headland overlooking the city. Its small harbour could accept nothing larger than fishing boats.

MAJOR-GENERAL GEORGE ALAN VASEY

Born on 29 March 1895 at East Malvern, Victoria, George A. Vasey was destined for a military career. In 1913 he entered the Royal Military College, Duntroon. The outbreak of the First World War saw his course accelerated and, in 1915, he graduated as a lieutenant in the Permanent Military Forces. Vasey arrived in France in March 1916 and served mostly in staff positions, although for a brief period he also commanded a field battery. He ended the war as the brigade major of 11 Australian Brigade. Vasey was awarded the DSO and twice mentioned in dispatches.

The return to peacetime soldiering saw him revert in rank to lieutenant. The interwar years were a frustrating time. Promotion was extremely slow and service mandated a series of caretaker appointments in militia units. Vasey did not regain the rank of major until 1935.

Vasey's Second World War career began with his appointment as Assistant Adjutant and Quartermaster-General of 6 Australian Division. In this position he excelled as a logistics planner. In March 1941 he assumed command of 19 Australian Brigade in time for the Greek campaign. Although this mission was clearly doomed, his brigade fought well in the retreat to the evacuation ports. On Crete, Vasey found himself the senior Australian officer on the island, thereby adding to his command responsibilities the need to represent Australia's national interests. That so many soldiers escaped from Crete was largely the result of his efforts with the rearguard in the retreat to Sfakia. For his work in Greece and Crete, Vasey received a bar to his DSO.

Vasey returned to Australia and was promoted major-general. Following a brief period at Army headquarters he was appointed to command 6 Australian Division in Papua. Shortly afterwards he commanded 7 Australian Division, then mired in its fight against the Japanese on the Kokoda Track. This was followed by the battles for the Papuan beachheads. The division's success brought Vasey to the attention of the Americans who awarded him a Distinguished Service Cross.

Vasey also led 7 Australian Division through its next campaign in the Markham-Ramu Valleys. His insistence on speed and his use of aerial insertion and support provide textbook examples of the use of infantry mobility. The campaign took its toll on his health however, and Vasey was invalided home in early 1944. He was not fit for active duty until 1945 when he was again appointed to command 6 Australian Division, then at Wewak. On 5 March 1945 Vasey was killed when the plane transporting him to take up his new command crashed into the sea near Cairns.

Wire Diagram 12 *Retimo Sector,*
British Organisation: Afternoon 20 May

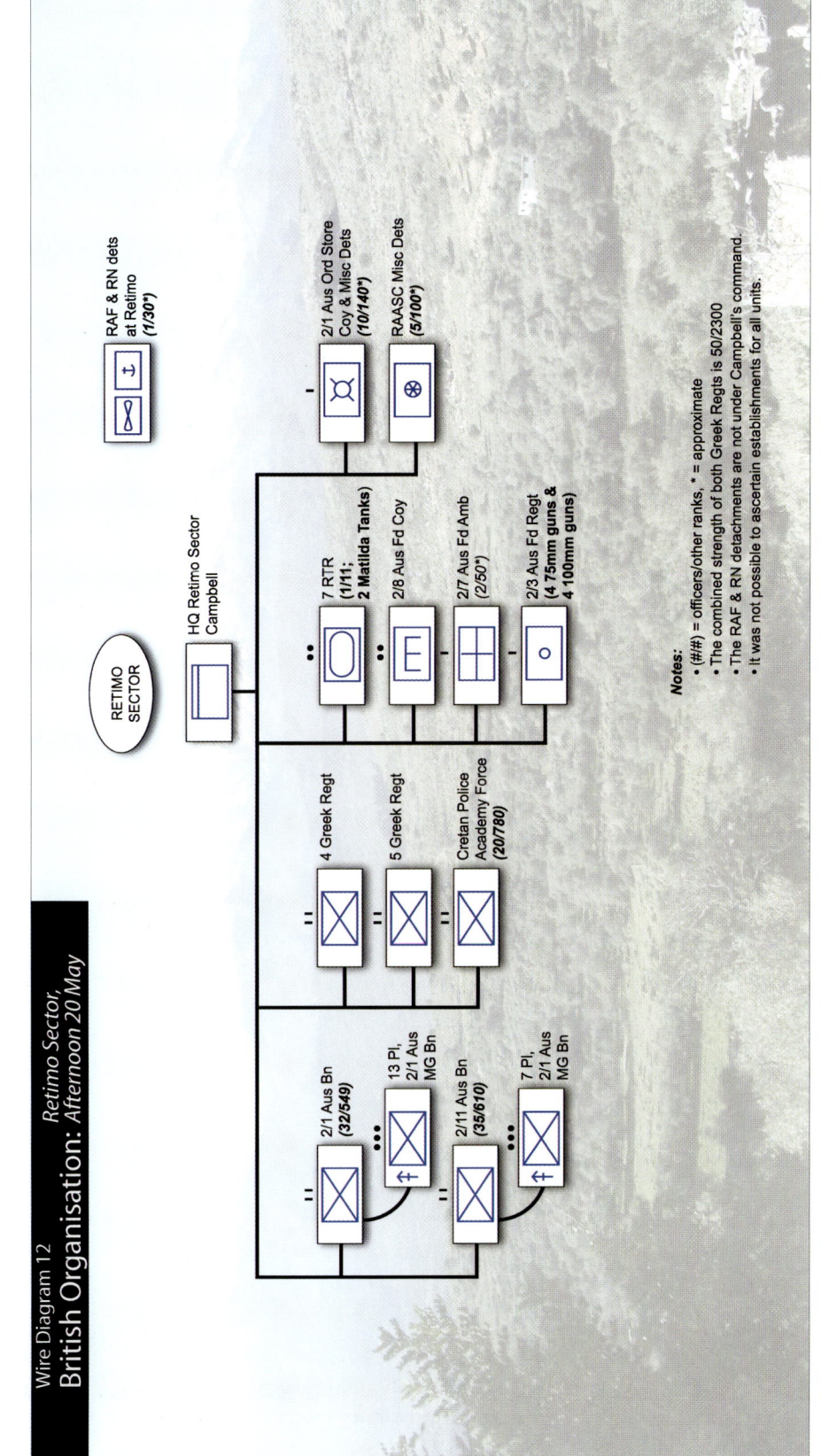

The Paras Descend – gouache on board, 2005
artist – Jeff Isaacs, OAM

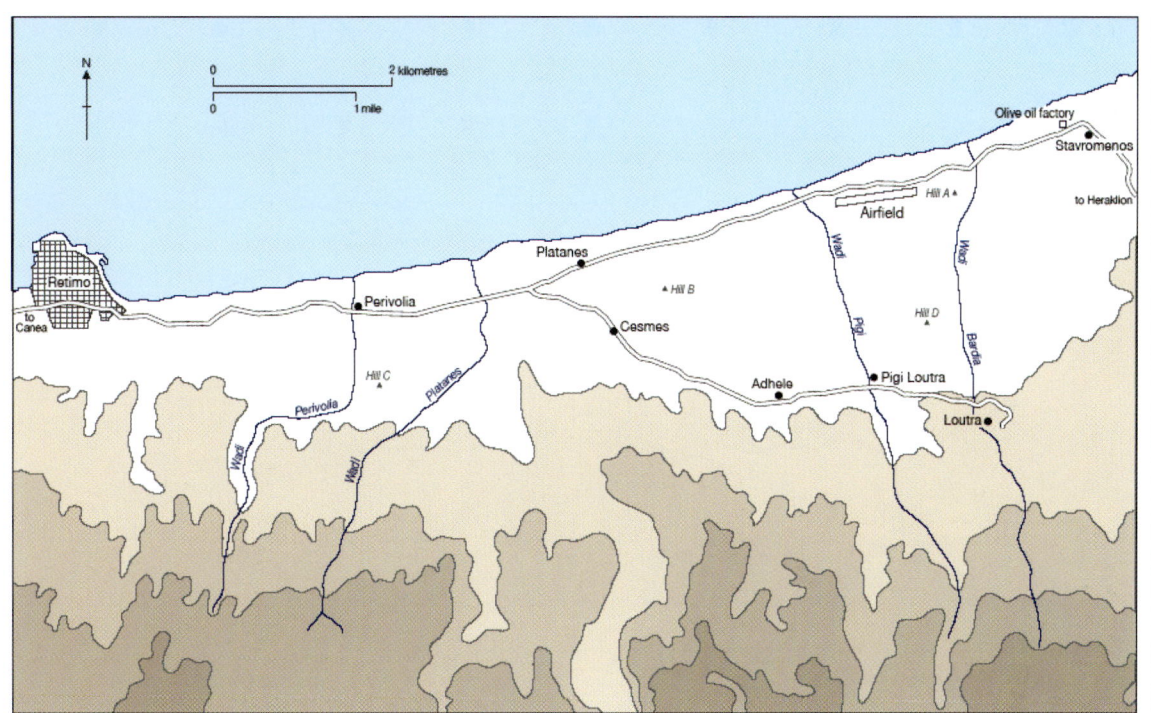

The Retimo Sector
Drawn by Keith Mitchell

The airfield was on the eastern side of the zone, and it was here that the Australians made their preparations. Running parallel to the coast from Perivolia to Stavromenos was a series of low hills, each separated by a wadi. From west to east the Australians labelled them C, D, B, and A. The plain was so narrow that Hill D was no more than a few hundred metres from the runway. Hill A, the eastern end of the feature, jutted forward almost to the water. From its crest the Australians looked westward along the coast, giving them a cone of fire that ran the length of the runway. From the other hills smaller cones of fire cut perpendicular arcs across the runway. The hills and the flat ground were covered with olives and vines. Some parts of the hills were terraced, giving them the appearance of a series of steps.

Campbell planned to dominate the airfield with fire from the overlooking hills. Even if the Germans occupied the flat ground the Australians would still control the zone. He positioned most of his guns on Hill A from which they could enfilade the coastal plain. Campbell had his men dig their weapon pits beneath the olive trees and grapevines where they could not be seen by the enemy's reconnaissance planes. This was not an easy task because at Retimo, as elsewhere, the defenders had few shovels. One digger commented that there was 'not one pick or shovel in the whole company.' In desperation the Australians used their bayonets and tin hats to dig their positions.

The Retimo airfield seen from the headquarters of 2/1 Australian Battalion on Hill D.
Australian War Memorial 131063

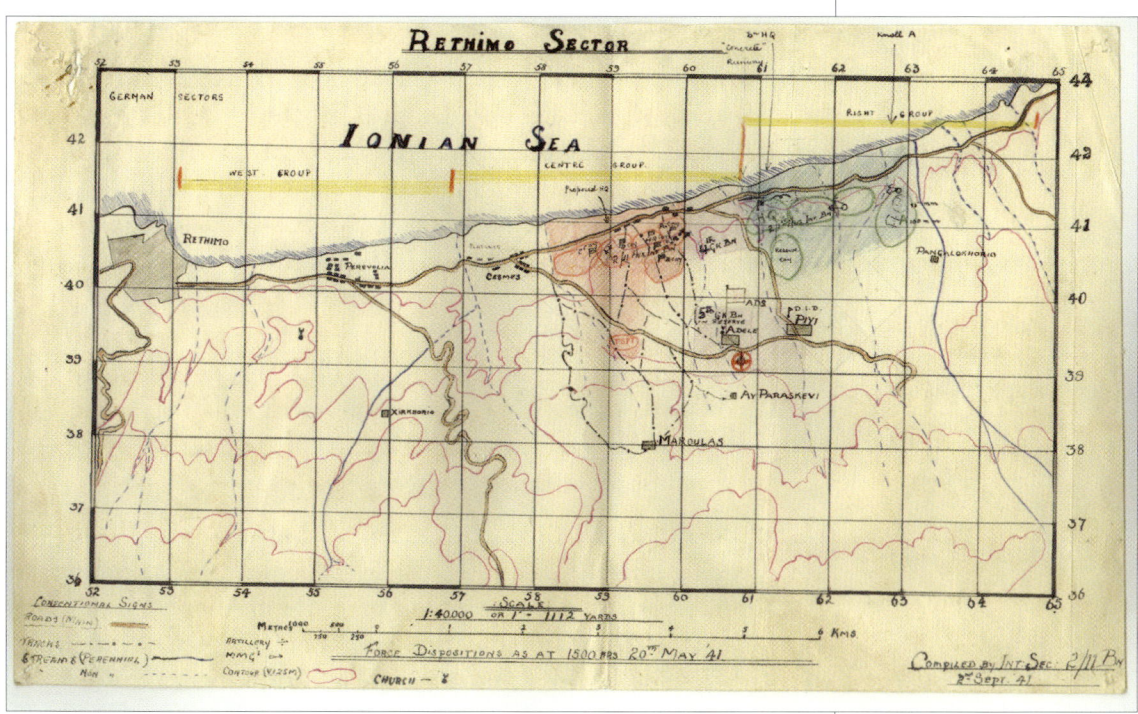

Campbell's Map of the Retimo Area showing the Location of his Units.
2/11 Aus Bn War Diary, AWM52, 8/3/11, page 97.

Anti-tank rifle, Boys Mark 1

Calibre:	.55 inch
Operation:	Bolt action, magazine fed
Magazine:	five rounds
Weight:	16.5 kg
Length:	1625 mm
Effective Range:	up to 457 metres
Rate of Fire:	up to 9 rpm

Firing a steel-cored bullet that travelled at nearly 1000 metres per second, the Boys anti-tank rifle could penetrate any existing armour when it first entered service in 1937. However, with a ferocious recoil and over 16 kg in weight, it was cumbersome for one man to carry and was basically ineffective against the German armour of 1941. While most of Creforce's Boys anti-tank rifles had been left behind in Greece, a small number was available on Crete with a limited supply of ammunition. The Boys rifle was normally issued on the basis of one per rifle platoon.

To deceive the enemy further, Campbell had his men prepare a few First World War style trenches out in the open. He hoped to suggest to the Germans that the sector's defenders were poorly led Greeks, not battle-hardened veterans.

The shortage of digging tools was an endemic problem for Creforce and hampered preparations in all sectors. Freyberg had dispatched requests to Cairo for shovels but none arrived in time. Ironically, the towns and villages of Crete contained a ready supply of digging tools that the Creforce soldiers could have used. Crete's primary economic activity was farming and the island's inhabitants possessed all the equipment the British needed. However, to buy or hire these tools required commanders to act outside their normal supply channels. This they failed to do and Creforce Headquarters continued to send requisitions to Cairo while their soldiers made do with whatever came to hand.

While the lack of shovels may appear a trivial point, it is symbolic of the malaise that gripped the British on Crete. Almost three days after the battle's commencement, Creforce Headquarters was still unable to galvanise itself into action. Instead, on 23 May, Freyberg again resorted to a requisition to Wavell to obtain the shovels he required.

The *Luftwaffe* reconnaissance convinced Student that he need not expect an effective opposition. Hence Retimo was the smallest of the four landings: *I* and *III Battalions, 2 Fallschirmjäger Regiment*, supported by *2 Company, Fallschirmmaschinengewehr Battalion*, and regimental headquarters. Its commander was Oberst Alfred Sturm.

Sturm divided his force into three groups:

- East Group: two companies of *I Battalion, 2 Fallschirmjäger Regiment* (Major Hans Kroh), and machine-gunners to land east of the airfield and capture it.

- Centre Group: regimental headquarters with two parachute companies to land near Platanes and form a reserve.

- West Group: *III Battalion, 2 Fallschirmjäger Regiment* (Hauptmann Wiedemann) with the regiment's heavy weapons companies to land near Perivolia and capture Retimo.

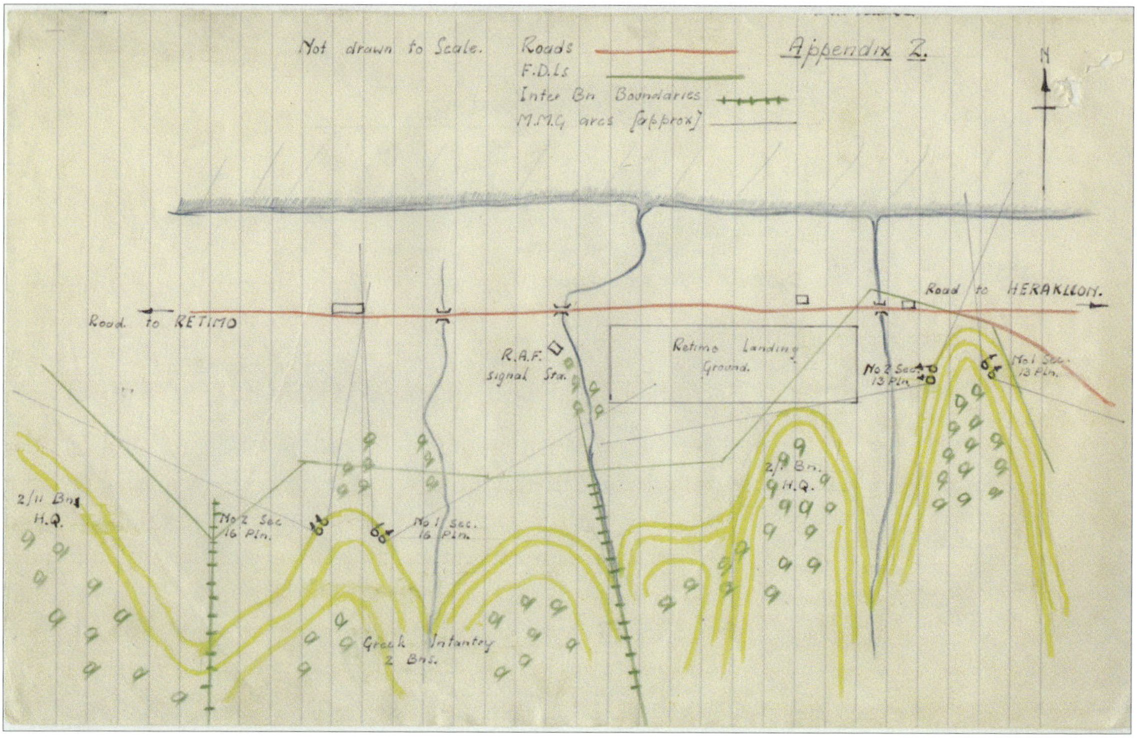

Map of Australian Defences around the Airfield. The map shows the location of the hills and the cones of fire of 2/1 Australian Machine Gun Battalion's machine-gun sections. In particular, it highlights the ability of the defenders on Hill A to sweep the length of the runway with fire. 2/1 Aus MG Bn War Diary, AWM52, 8/5/1, page 57.

View of Hill A from a wadi.
Australian War Memorial 131044

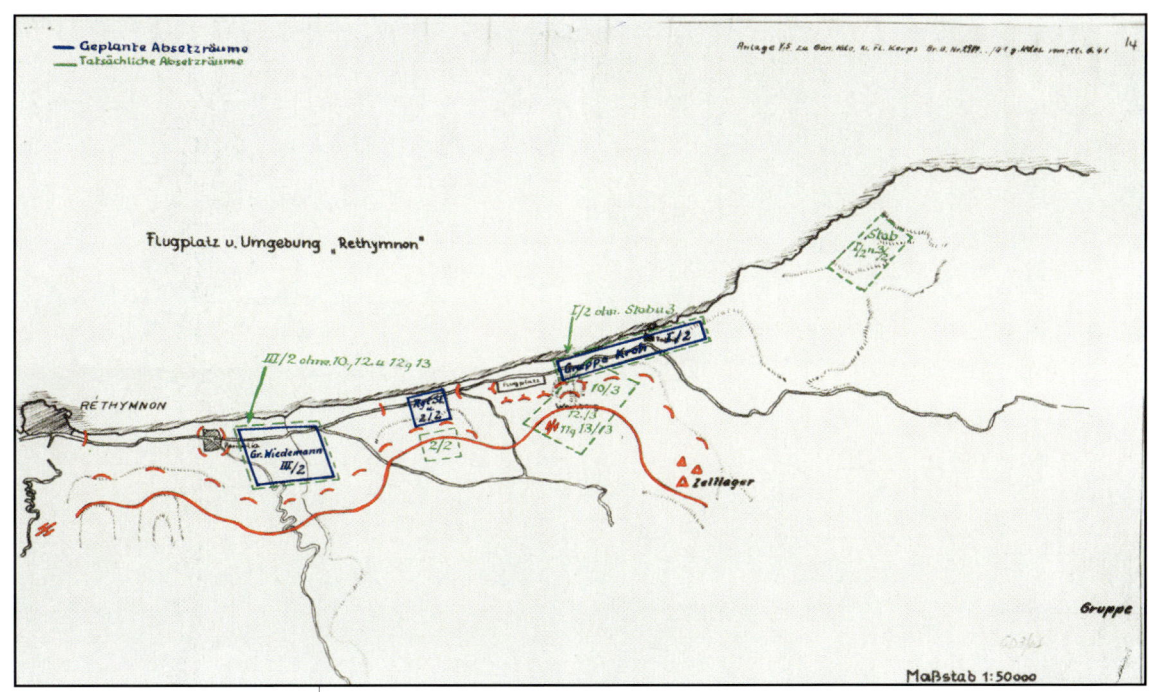

German Planned and Actual Drop Zones.
Australian War Memorial Map Collection

Student's plan called for the landings to commence at 1615 hours, just as the softening-up by the *Luftwaffe*'s bombers finished. As at Heraklion this proved unrealistic. Because of congestion at the airfields on the mainland the transports arrived at Retimo an hour behind schedule and in several waves. By this time the supporting bombers had already finished their work. The Junkers 52s approached the drop zones low from the east over the coastal plain and parallel to the Australians on the ridgeline. The narrowness of the target area meant that some transports were fewer than 200 metres from the hilltop defenders, and at almost the same altitude. The Australians could not miss. At 1715 hours the slaughter began.

> **Lesson 12**
>
> While protocols have their place, when the situation demands bold action, commanders must have the flexibility to act outside normal channels. A slavish devotion to procedure is a poor excuse for defeat.

The Australian greeting was fierce and, for the Germans, unexpected. As the slow-moving transports flew across the face of the defenders' weapons the Australians raked them with fire. At least ten, possibly twelve, were shot down by machine-gun and small arms fire. William Nagle, a Bren gunner, remembered emptying his weapon into the door of a transport. He knocked the lead paratrooper back into the plane and no-one else got out. Once on the ground the paratroopers were caught in overlapping zones of fire. One digger described it as 'Empire Day, with everyone firing.' As some of the Junkers struggled back out to sea the Australian saw them dumping bodies.

97

The Battle of Retimo
Artist - Vernon Jones
Australian War Memorial ART27776

Only half of West Group dropped around Perivolia as planned. Two of its companies landed with East Group by mistake. Wiedemann gathered his men and struck for Retimo. Waiting for the paratroopers behind the thick walls of the city's houses was the Cretan Police Academy Battalion. Unlike the other Greek units at Retimo, these men were well armed, trained and disciplined. The Germans broke into the eastern part of the city but made little headway through its narrow streets. A Greek counter-attack from the south-west forced Wiedemann to retreat into Perivolia where he organised an all-around defence.

Centre Group landed under heavy fire and suffered enormous casualties. About half the group dropped among 2/11 Australian Battalion on Hill B and were annihilated. The rest, including Sturm, landed on the sand and the Australians pinned them with fire from the hill. Campbell's two Matilda tanks made an appearance but both bogged before reaching the enemy. The next afternoon, C Company, 2/11 Australian Battalion, executed a converging assault, cleared the position and captured fifty Germans. Later a patrol eliminated another enemy pocket. Among their captives was Sturm. By the end of the day the Australians had retaken the beachfront and airfield areas.

On the eastern end of the sector part of Kroh's group came down directly onto Hill A. The defenders comprised A Company, 2/1 Australian Battalion, two sections of machine-guns, and six guns manned by 2/3 Australian Field Regiment. One Australian described the scene: 'It [fire] was hesitant at first but swiftly rose to an angry torrent. Paratroopers swinging on their lines knifed in macabre mid-air death dances. The sky was now raining dead.'

Machine-gun, Vickers, Mark 1

Calibre:	.303 inch
Operation:	recoil with gas boost from muzzle booster; belt-fed; automatic fire; water-cooled
Belt Capacity:	250 rounds in cloth belt (weight in box 9.9 kg)
Weight:	41.3 kg unloaded gun mounted on tripod, with water jacket filled
Length:	1448 mm gun mounted on tripod; 1092 mm gun only; 864 mm tripod folded for transportation
Sights:	up to 2652 metres, dial sight up to 4115 metres
Effective Range:	up to 1828 metres, with a maximum range for harassing fire of up to 4115 metres
Rates of Fire:	cyclic: 450-500 rpm, normal: 250 rpm, rapid: 500 rpm

The Vickers medium machine-gun came into service with the British Army in 1912. It was the standard British and Australian medium machine-gun throughout both World Wars, Korea and into the 1960s. While highly reliable, it was heavy and cumbersome to transport. With the introduction of the universal carrier, however, the Vickers gained a form of mobility.

The standard allocation to an Australian machine-gun battalion was 48. However, along with almost everything else on Crete, the Vickers was in short supply. As a crew-served weapon it required a team of at least three men sustain it in action, with additional men to carry ammunition and water.

Those paratroopers who survived the descent had to find their weapon containers scattered amongst the olive trees. It was a fanatical, close action fight. As the Germans landed all around the guns, the poorly armed gunners were particularly hard pressed. An officer shot three paratroopers with his pistol while other gunners raced to arm themselves with the enemy's weapons. One German bounded towards a gun pit. The defenders traversed the gun and, at a range of three yards, pulled the lanyard. The paratrooper disappeared in a mist of blood and gore.

As the Germans armed themselves, their superior weapons and ammunition supply took its toll. Reinforcements also arrived from other drop areas. A Company could not hold the Germans back and gave ground. The Australian machine-gunners kept to their Vickers for nearly two hours, but with their last belts gone they too fell back, as had the gunners. By nightfall the Australians held just the lower southern and western slopes.

That evening Campbell knew that the outcome at Retimo hung in the balance. If the Germans established themselves on Hill A, they could use their greater firepower to roll up the ridgeline and clear the airfield. Campbell moved quickly to organise a counter-attack.

At 0530 hours a company of 2/1 Australian Battalion moved off to retake Hill A. Almost immediately the diggers ran into an enemy mortar barrage followed by intense machine-gun fire. The Germans had launched their own attack, intent on clearing the rest of the hill. As the two sides collided the Australians were overwhelmed and had to fall back, this time abandoning the entire hill. Campbell had asked the Greek regiments to help but they did not appear.

Machine-gun, MG34	
Calibre:	7.92 mm
Operation:	belt fed, recoil; selective fire
Belt Capacity:	50 rounds or 50 round drum magazine for a belt, or 75 round saddle drum magazine with no belt
Weight:	12 kg
Length:	1219 mm
Sights:	200 to 2000 metres, telescopic sight to 3500 metres
Effective Range:	550 metres (bipod), up to 3500 metres from tripod mount
Rate of Fire:	800-900 rpm (cyclic)

Campbell knew that to accept the situation would condemn his command to gradual defeat. He had to dislodge the Germans from the decisive ground before they tightened their grip or reinforcements arrived. Unlike Puttick or Hargest at Canea and Maleme, Campbell realised that this was the time for decisive action, and that his reserve could no longer be held for some possible future task. He had to either win the battle now or accept defeat. Within a few hours he had thinned out 2/1 Australian Battalion's companies on Hill D, gathered up the pioneer and carrier platoons, and put every spare man into the effort. The attack began at 0900 hours. By 1015 hours Hill A was back in Australian hands, and the Germans were in retreat eastward towards Stavromenos.

The Maschinengewehr 34 was an air-cooled weapon with a quick-change barrel. It could be used as an infantry squad light machine-gun when mounted on the integral bipod, a medium machine-gun when mounted on a tripod, and an anti-aircraft machine-gun when fitted with a saddle-drum magazine. It could also be fitted to armoured vehicles and motorcycle side-cars. The MG34 was reliable, accurate and, because it was belt-fed, could sustain high volumes of fire. In 1942 the German army introduced an upgraded model known as the MG42. Despite this, the MG34 remained in service until the war's end.

Remains of a German plane on the beach near the Retimo airfield.
Australian War Memorial 131059

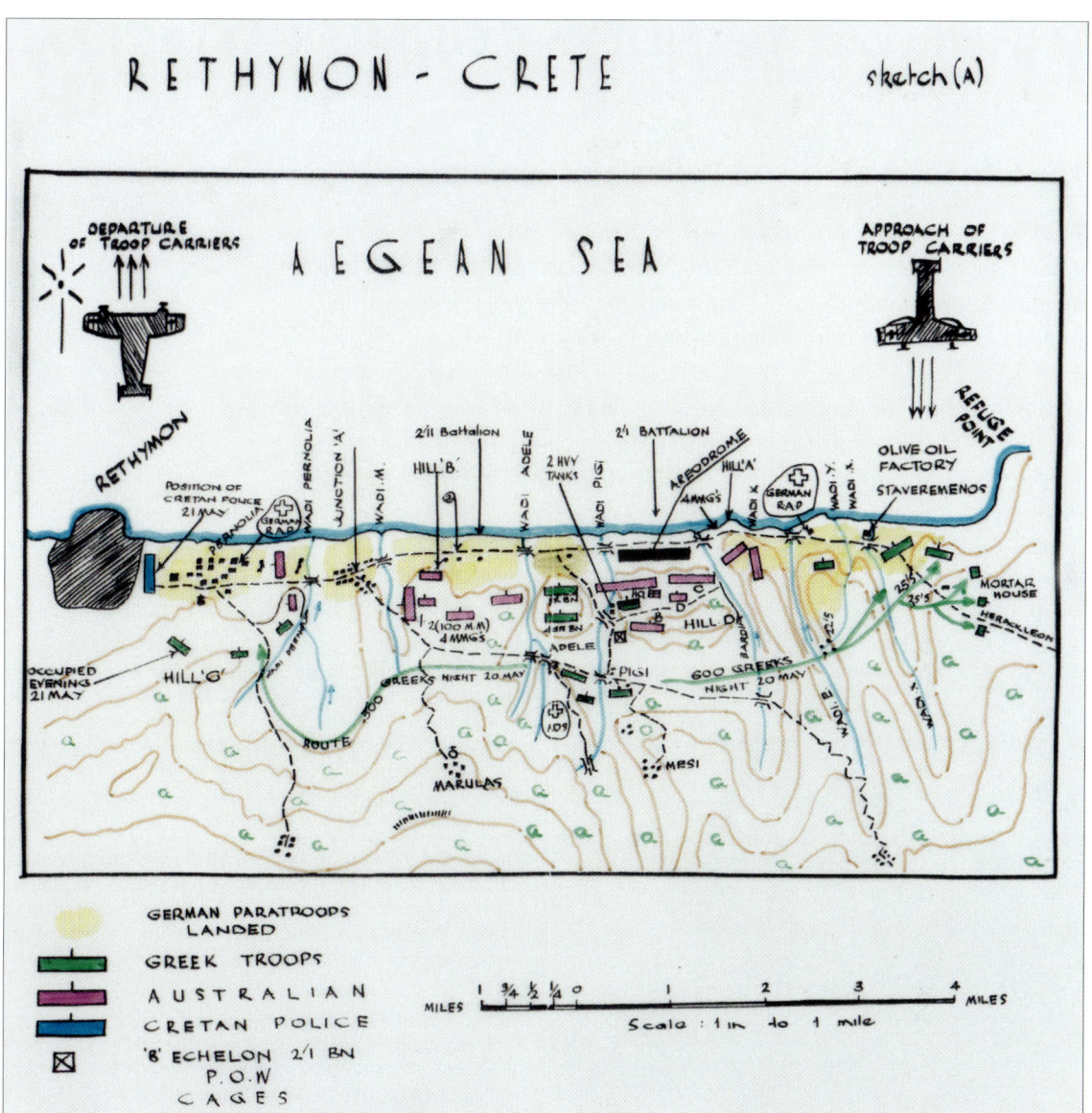

Map showing the German Approach Route and the Australian and Greek Positions.
Australian War Memorial Map Collection

By regaining Hill A, Campbell assured the German failure at Retimo. Without the airfield the enemy could not land reinforcements. Moreover, the Germans were leaderless and split into two isolated groups with over half either dead or captured. The remaining Germans fought on, not for victory but for survival.

THE NEW ZEALANDERS COUNTER-ATTACK

The Situation at Prison Valley and Maleme

Throughout the day of the landing at Prison Valley the Germans made repeated attempts to push the New Zealanders off the Galatas heights. Kippenberger was not content to merely repel these assaults. Instead he sought reinforcements from Puttick with which to strike into the valley to destroy the Germans before more paratroopers arrived. Inglis, commander of 4 New Zealand Brigade, made similar overtures. However Puttick consistently refused these requests, seemingly determined to hold on to 4 New Zealand Brigade for some future use.

Lieutenant-Colonel Lindsay Inglis. This photo was taken in 1943 when Inglis was a brigadier. He is talking to the New Zealand Minister for Defence, Frederick Jones.
National Library of New Zealand DA-02985

MAJOR-GENERAL LINDSAY MERRITT INGLIS

Lindsay M. Inglis was born on 16 May 1894 at Mosgiel in Otago. In 1915, after completing his law degree at the University of Otago, he enlisted in the New Zealand Expeditionary Force. Inglis served on the Western Front in the New Zealand Rifle Brigade and was awarded the MC on 15 September during the Somme Offensive. In 1917 he transferred to the New Zealand Machine Gun Corps where he commanded a company.

Between the wars Inglis continued his military career in the Territorial Force, eventually commanding a brigade. He resigned his commission in 1936, but when the Second World War erupted Inglis immediately volunteered his services. His first command was 27 Machine Gun Battalion.

At the time of the Crete operation Inglis was commander of 4 Brigade. Despite the fact that he blamed Freyberg for the island's loss, he continued to serve under his superior in North Africa and then Italy. His record in North Africa is mixed. The highlights of his campaign contribution included the relief of Tobruk for which Inglis received a DSO, and his leadership of the division during the breakout from Minqar Qaim for which he was awarded a bar to his DSO.

Throughout the remainder of the war, Inglis continued to harbour resentment towards Freyberg. In particular, he felt aggrieved whenever he was passed over for the temporary command of the New Zealand Division in Freyberg's absence. In 1944, Inglis was overlooked again and sent Freyberg an insulting letter. Inglis was promptly sent home.

After the victory over Germany the New Zealand government appointed Inglis to the Allied Control Commission for Europe where he served as president of the military court in the British Zone. In 1947 he was made Chief Judge of the court, a position that came with the nominal military rank of major-general. Inglis returned to New Zealand in 1950. He died on 17 March 1966.

Late on the evening of 20 May, Puttick finally allocated some troops for a counter-attack. Instead of the entire 4 New Zealand Brigade, or even a battalion, he provided just two companies of 19 New Zealand Battalion supported by three light tanks from 3 Hussars. They were to strike from Galatas down the road towards the enemy's strong point at the prison. Despite suffering heavy casualties, the Germans had landed four battalions. Clearly, Puttick's commitment of just two companies was overly optimistic.

Vickers Mark VI tank

Length:	4 m
Width:	2 m
Height:	2.9 m
Weight:	5.3 tonnes
Crew:	three (commander/gunner, loader/radio operator and driver)
Power plant:	Meadows 6 cylinder, water-cooled, in-line petrol engine
Armament:	one .5-inch Vickers and one .303 Bren machine-gun
Max Armour:	14 mm
Speed:	56 kph (road)
Range:	205 km

The Mark VI Vickers was a development of an earlier Vickers design that was introduced into the British Army in 1929. By the start of the Second World War the Vickers tank was too lightly armoured and armed to be effective in anything other than a reconnaissance role. About sixteen Vickers Mark VI from 3 Hussars arrived on Crete shortly before the German invasion. Like the Matildas, they were nearing the end of their operational utility. With the shortage of armour and the close terrain on the island, the British used them primarily as an infantry support weapon.

The organisation of the attack revealed serious weaknesses in the New Zealand Division's command control arrangements and highlighted the communication difficulties under which Creforce operated. Kippenberger was not informed of the attack, even though the assigned companies would form up in his sector and advance over the ground on which he had supervised the day's battle. It was not until zero hour—2030 hours—that he received a message informing him that 19 New Zealand Battalion had been transferred to his command. As Kippenberger went to liaise with the company commanders, the sound of battle told him that he was too late. In his report Kippenberger wrote that, although he was the forward commander, he was 'unable to assist or direct the attack in any way and it was consequently abortive.'

As they moved through the darkened countryside, the infantry and armour immediately lost touch with each other and advanced independently. The tanks charged ahead, spraying Vickers fire at unseen enemies on both sides of the road until it petered out. The infantry moved out, but without knowledge of the ground or the enemy's positions, the troops did not venture far before deciding to stop. The next morning Kippenberger found the infantry 200 metres in front of the Composite Battalion's position and ordered them to return.

The Germans Move First

After pulling off Hill 107 above the airfield at Maleme, Andrew had withdrawn 22 New Zealand Battalion to the safety of 23 New Zealand Battalion's perimeter. At 0300 hours on 21 May a conference took place among the nearby battalion commanders. The conference was attended by Andrew, Allen (21 New Zealand Battalion) and Leckie (23 New Zealand Battalion). The brigade commander, Hargest, remained at his headquarters at Platanias. All the battalion commanders—particularly Andrew—were exhausted, which perhaps explains why none was eager to return to Maleme and reoccupy the evacuated positions. Hill 107, the key to Crete, was left undefended. Instead of a decision to take action, the 21 New Zealand Battalion's war diary records the meeting's conclusion: 'decided to hold our position next day, 22 Battalion to reorganise.'

The paras in action on Crete.
Australian War Memorial 106490

Since Hargest had remained at his headquarters, Andrew made his way there to meet him. The brigade commander conceded that a counter-attack was necessary, but displayed little urgency in planning such an attack. He had two relatively fresh battalions within a few kilometres of the vital ground—the 21st and 23rd—but decided nothing could be done because the *Luftwaffe* would reappear with the approaching dawn.

In stark contrast to the inertia of the New Zealanders, Student spent an uneasy night in Athens at *Headquarters XI Flieger Korps* planning his next move. So far, the battle had not gone well, none of the landings had achieved its objectives, and the cost in casualties had been high. With Retimo and Heraklion firmly in the enemy's hands, Student decided to focus on Maleme which now represented his only chance to gain an airfield. It was towards Maleme, therefore, that he directed his reserves. If the reinforced *Luftlande Sturmregiment* could seize the airfield then the transports could deliver 5 *Gebirgs Division* and salvage the campaign. Without Maleme, Student knew he had lost.

It was not until first light on 21 May that the paratroopers of the *Luftlande Sturmregiment* discovered that the New Zealanders had pulled back from Maleme. Cautiously, Gericke led one group east across the runway, securing the airfield. At the same time Stentzler led the remnants of his companies up Hill 107. After tasting near defeat the Germans had been handed the means of victory.

As the Germans probed slowly eastwards both groups reported contacts and incoming fire. The source of this fire is unclear, as there were no New Zealand units left in the area. It was most likely that Cretan civilians were sniping at the paratroopers. After the trauma of the previous day the Germans exaggerated the strength of the opposition. They even reported driving off a non-existent counter-attack. Unwilling to expose themselves to further risk, they dug in just east of the runway and along the lower eastern slope of the hill.

Student did not know of the airfield's capture and pressed ahead with his priorities: the resupply and reinforcement of the Maleme group and obtaining a firsthand assessment of the situation. In the morning a transport plane managed to land on the stony beach at the mouth of the Tavronitis and delivered urgently needed ammunition. Later, a second plane forced a landing at the airfield. Amongst its cargo was one of Student's aides. Both planes managed to take off, despite sustaining damage from long-range interdiction fire. Amongst the wounded evacuated to Greece was the German commander Meindl.

From reports and the review of casualties, Student concluded that the enemy had held the airfield in far greater numbers than originally thought. He also believed that when the New Zealanders fell back they retreated only a short distance and now held the villages of Pirgos and Maleme in strength. He therefore concluded that the area around Platanias was thinly held. In fact Student was wrong on all counts, demonstrating the fallible nature of intelligence and the hazards of commanders making decisions from a distance.

Student decided to push the Kiwis back further in order to protect the landing of the mountain troops who would arrive later in the afternoon. In order to do this the *Luftlande Sturmregiment* required reinforcements. All Student had available were several companies of *7 Flieger Division* for whom there had been no transport on 20 May. To the west of Maleme he landed a paratrooper company of *2 Fallschirmjäger Regiment* and a reinforced company of *Fallschirmflak Battalion*. Among these arrivals was Oberst Bernard Ramcke, the new commander of the *Luftlande Sturmregiment*. Ramcke was an energetic officer who quickly reorganised the remaining soldiers into a battlegroup that would bear his name.

To the east of the airfield near Platanias, Student planned to drop two more paratrooper companies from *2 Fallschirmjäger Regiment*. Using tactics strikingly similar to those employed without success on the first day, Ramcke was to organise a converging assault to clear Pirgos and Maleme, and create the safety zone required to land the mountain troops.

GENERAL DER FALLSCHIRMTRUPPE BERNARD HERMANN RAMCKE

Bernard Hermann Ramcke was born on 24 January 1889. He joined the navy as a boy and, on the outbreak of the First World War, he transferred ashore and spent the conflict on the Western Front as a marine infantryman. Ramcke ended the war as a lieutenant and a recipient of the Iron Cross, 1st and 2nd class.

After the Armistice he went to Prussia and fought with the *Freikorps* in the Baltic states. He received a commission in the *Reichswehr* and, by the outbreak of the Second World War, had attained the rank of lieutenant-colonel. Not content with being a foot soldier, he volunteered for the paratroopers and passed the course at the age of 51.

On 21 May Ramcke, now colonel, dropped into the Maleme maelstrom to assume command of the *Luftlande Strumregiment* from the wounded Meindl. The next day he handed direction of the battle to Ringel and formed his surviving paratroopers into the battlegroup that bore his name. Despite the *Luftlande Strumregiment*'s exhaustion and near annihilation, Ramcke spurred his men to action and they fought well for the rest of the campaign.

Ramcke was promoted to generalmajor on 1 August 1941 and, later that month, he received the Knight's Cross. He subsequently fought in North Africa in command of the *Ramcke Brigade* where he received the Oak Leaves to his Knight's Cross.

In 1943 Ramcke raised the *2nd Flieger Division*, leading it in Italy and Russia before his transfer to France during the Normandy campaign. On the Cotentin Peninsula he commanded the defence of Brest and denied the allies the port until forced to surrender on 19 September. Ramcke, now general der fallschirmtruppe, received the further awards of Swords and then Diamonds to his Knight's Cross. He was only the twentieth recipient of this honour.

Ramcke was captured by the Americans in Brest and spent the rest of the war as a prisoner. After Germany's surrender he was handed over to French authorities who tried and convicted him of war crimes. He received a five-year sentence. After his release Ramcke retired to Germany where he died on 4 July 1968.

Soldiers of *5 Gebirgs Division* prepare to board their transports for the flight to Crete.
National Library of New Zealand DA-01313

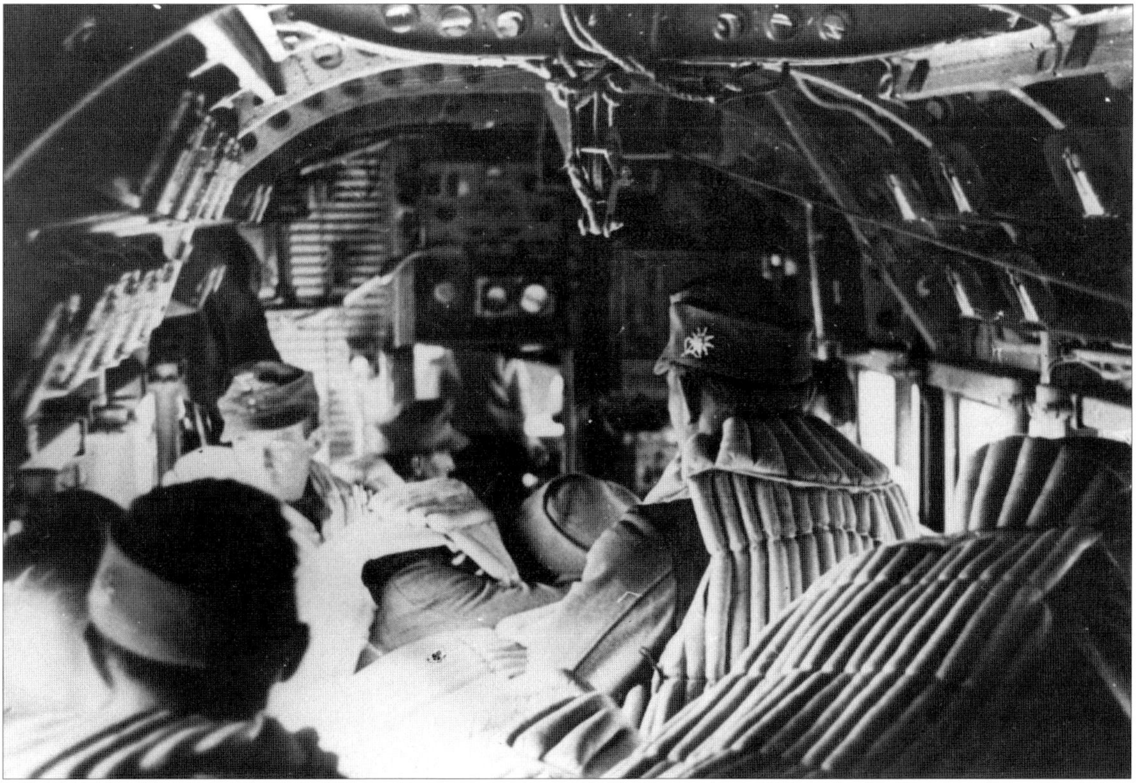

Mountain troops en route to Crete.
National Library of New Zealand DA-11979

At around 1600 hours the soldiers of B Company, 28 New Zealand (Maori) Battalion and 19 Army Troop Company were surprised by the sound of transports overhead. In a repeat performance of the previous day, the sky filled with parachutes as Student's East Group arrived. On the first day of the invasion the New Zealanders had annihilated *III Battalion, Luftlande Sturmregiment*, on this same ground. Yet again the Maori battalion made short work of the Germans who landed amongst them, while the engineers were almost as efficient. Few paratroopers had a chance to reach their weapon containers. An engineer, Captain J. Anderson, wrote, 'a Hun dropped not ten feet away. I had my pistol in my hand … I let him have it while he was still on the ground. I had hardly got over the shock when another came down almost on top of me and I plugged him too while he was untangling himself.' Those Germans who lived hid in bamboo breaks and brush until dark when they made their way westward to Pirgos.

As the Maoris and engineers greeted the new arrivals, the western arm of Student's planned assault began its task. The paratroopers pushed cautiously eastwards, occupying the villages of Maleme and Xamoudhokhori and extending their perimeter by approximately a kilometre. Then they dug in again.

At about 1700 hours Junkers 52s began to land at Maleme. These carried the promised mountain infantry reinforcements, elements of *85* and *100 Gebirgsjäger Regiments*. Also to arrive was the commander of *5 Gebirgs Division*, Generalleutnant Julius Ringel, who took command of all German forces on the island.

The New Zealanders Attempt to Reclaim the Airfield

The New Zealand Division's reserve formation was 4 New Zealand Brigade which had begun the battle as the Creforce reserve. Freyberg kept the brigade under his direct control until 1100 hours when he returned it to Puttick. In so doing, Freyberg unfortunately gave Puttick no direct instructions regarding its use, although the act in itself suggested that the Creforce commander intended something be done with the formation. However, the availability of the brigade did not spur Puttick into action. Similarly, Hargest, the commander of 5 New Zealand Brigade, allowed the day to pass without realising any sense of urgency. Even on day two of the invasion both Puttick and Hargest continued to react slowly to the German challenge. In this, Freyberg must share his subordinates' culpability because he did not take a firm hand with either. In part, the New Zealanders remained distracted by the possibility of a seaborne landing, but it is also clear that they did not realise the immediacy of the danger that the paratroopers posed.

> **Lesson 13**
>
> The function of a reserve is to allow a commander to intercede in battle at the decisive point and at the decisive moment. A reserve also provides a defender the opportunity to seize the initiative from an opponent. Husbanding a reserve in case of future need is of no benefit if to do so leads to defeat. Commanders must have the ability to recognise the decisive moment and the courage to risk victory.

As the German transports began to land at Maleme the only opposition they faced was shelling from the guns of 27 New Zealand Field Battery and 2/3 Australian Field Regiment. From a distance of about three kilometres, two Australian observers had a clear line of sight to the runway. They timed their fire carefully, striking the moment a transport appeared on the runway. Despite their worn-out weapons the gunners scored direct hits on many fully laden planes, but reinforcements poured out of the aircraft that escaped them. Whenever wrecks or burning planes blocked the runway the Germans used a captured Matilda to bulldoze it clear. A German mountain soldier left a record of the inferno that greeted his arrival at Maleme. He wrote:

> Numerous Jus [Junkers 52s] were hit, burnt fiercely and exploded, crash-landed and ran into one another. Ground crews were kept more than busy to remove the destroyed planes from the runway, and to tow them to the edge of the field. The number of wrecks increased to 30, 40, 50 … Maleme was the gate to hell through which the men of the 5 Mount. Div. had to come from the air to fight on the island, to help their paratrooper comrades.

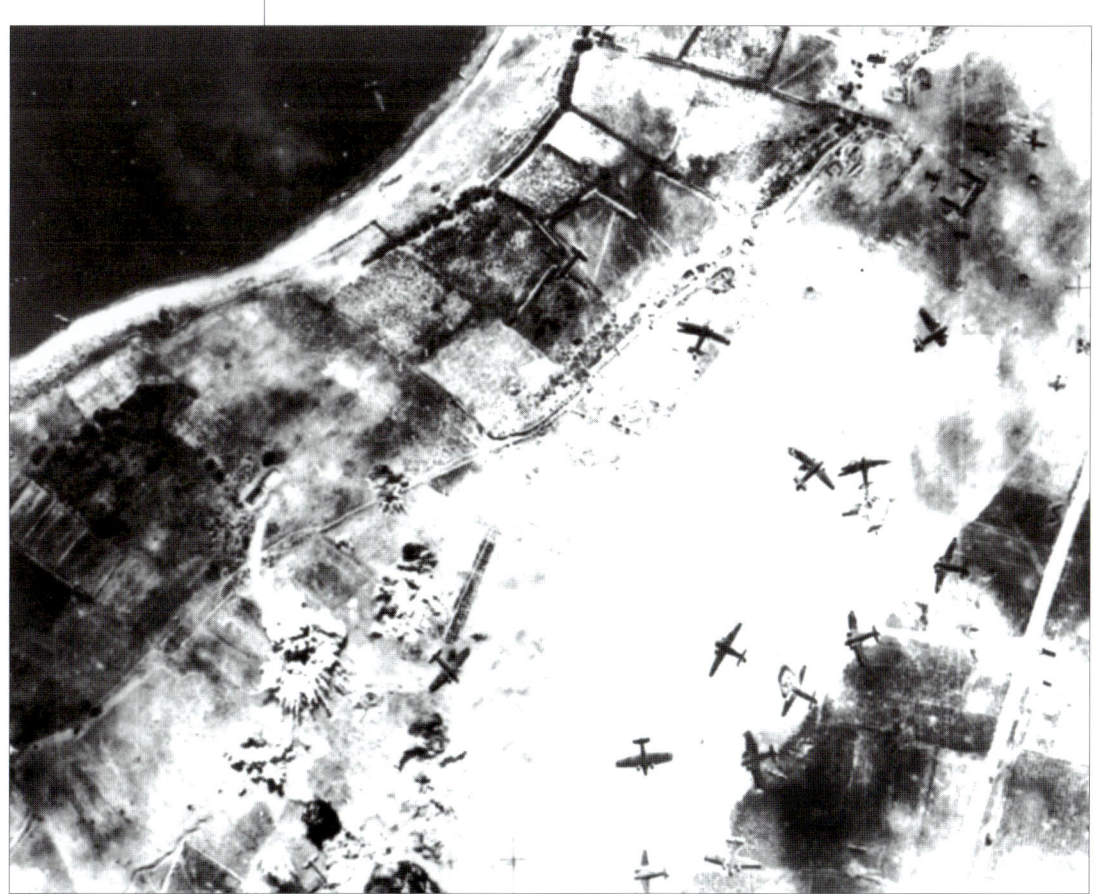

The Maleme runway under bombardment by artillery. Note the number of planes.
Imperial War Museum CM880

Wrecked Junkers 52 transports on the Maleme runway.
Australian War Memorial 069219

Student lost hundreds of men to these guns, but neither the shelling nor the growing casualty list deterred him from pushing more troops onto the island. He knew that the campaign was a critical moment and he, unlike his New Zealand opponents, did not hesitate to act.

Freyberg witnessed the stream of Junkers 52 landing at Maleme from his headquarters near Canea. 'Throughout the day,' he wrote, 'a constant stream of troop carriers continued to land, coming in and taking off again low over the sea before our eyes with a painful monotony.' It was this sight that finally spurred the New Zealand leaders to action, although it was not until late on the afternoon of 21 May that planning actually began for the airfield's retaking. Furthermore, unlike Student, no-one was willing to make a maximum effort. Instead of ruthlessly pushing the nearest units into the attack, the New Zealanders prepared a complex plan that required several preliminary steps before the operation could be launched.

The two battalions given the task of retaking the airfield were 28 New Zealand (Maori) Battalion from 5 New Zealand Brigade and 20 New Zealand Battalion from 4 New Zealand Brigade. Neither battalion was positioned near the attack's start line. Instead, the Maoris were at Platanias, about five kilometres away, and 20 New Zealand Battalion's position near Canea was even further from its line of departure. Moreover, 20 New Zealand Battalion was ordered not to move until relieved of its beach defence duty by 2/7 Australian Battalion which had to come from Georgeoupolis, a distance of twenty-five kilometres over *Luftwaffe* dominated roads. The start line itself lay behind the forward New Zealand battalions and was nearly five kilometres from the airfield. The attack was to commence at 0100 hours on 22 May.

The Australians had to run a harrowing gauntlet of prowling enemy bombers and fighters in order to relieve 20 New Zealand Battalion. By the time they arrived the planned start time had already passed. In fact, the attack did not step off until about 0330 hours, and even then both battalions had to cross a zone containing scattered parties of Germans dropped the previous day. This took time, as did negotiating a minefield laid by the New Zealand engineers. It was not until just before dawn that the two battalions passed through the forward line held by 21, 22, and 23 New Zealand Battalions and advanced on their objectives.

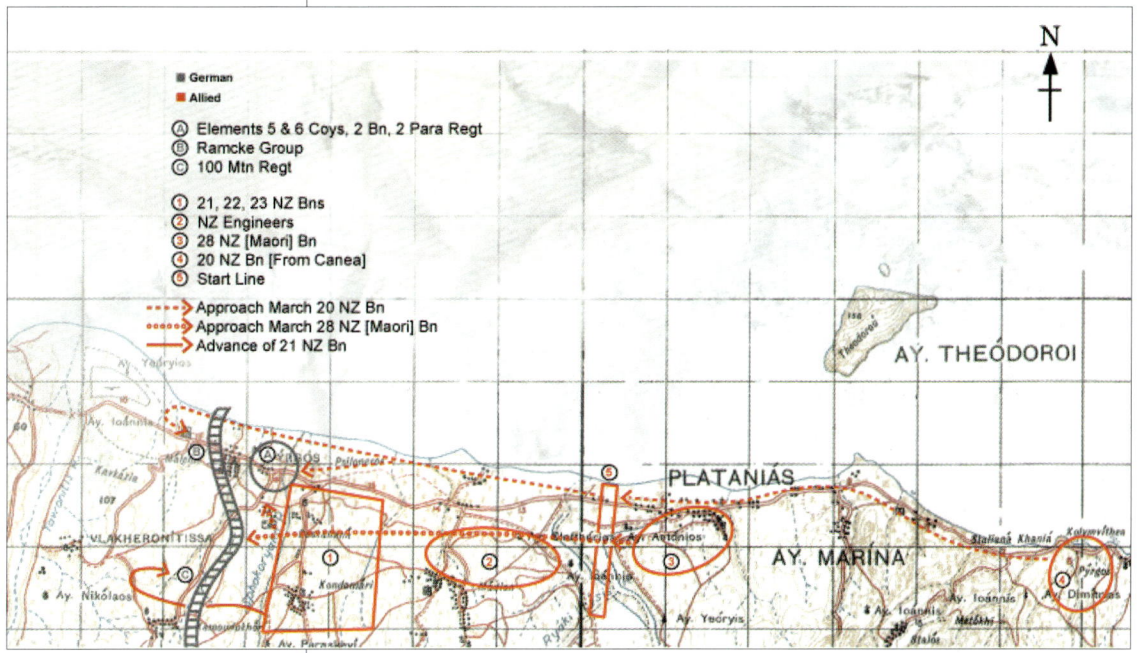

The New Zealand Counter-attack at Maleme.
Australian War Memorial Map Collection
Modified by Mark Wahlert

On the right, 20 New Zealand Battalion advanced towards the airfield, while 28 New Zealand (Maori) Battalion slanted southwards into the hills towards Point 107. The lateness of the attack surprised the Germans who initially gave way. However resistance increased the further the Kiwis pushed into the German defence. Yet, even in broad daylight, the New Zealanders continued to advance. One company of 20 New Zealand Battalion actually reached the eastern edge of the runway, although the rest of the battalion was held up at Pirgos. The Maoris made it onto the lower slopes in front of Maleme before grinding to a halt. At 0700 hours, unknown to either of the attacking battalions, Allen added his 21 New Zealand Battalion to the attack. Advancing separately on the left through Xamoudhokhori, his forward platoons had fought midway up Hill 107 before deciding to pull back.

The Maleme airfield is occupied. German troops man a 20 mm Flak 38 Anti-aircraft gun to protect the runway from British planes.
National Library of New Zealand DA-11983

The attackers had come within sight of their objectives, but did not have the mass needed to push through the enemy and retake the critical positions. The other two nearby battalions held their positions and did not help. Simply put, the New Zealanders had committed insufficient men to a critical attack, and then allowed it to start too late. Meanwhile, during the night and some distance out to sea, the New Zealanders saw the flashes of the Royal Navy's guns that spelt the destruction of the German reinforcement convoy.

If the Kiwis lost the battle for Maleme airfield on 20 May when 22 New Zealand Battalion withdrew, they lost the campaign when they did not retake the lost ground two days later. Freyberg commented on the counter-attack in his campaign report. He pointed out that the Germans suffered far more casualties than the New Zealanders, that the Kiwis had made excellent progress in their advance, and that his men had done fine work with the bayonet. He neglected to mention that the attack had failed.

THE DEFENCE OF THE GALATAS LINE

Another Go?

On 22 May Freyberg spent the whole day watching from his headquarters near Canea as German transports landed and took off from the Maleme airfield. The failure of the New Zealander counter-attack had allowed Student to push reinforcements and supplies onto the island, turning the tide of the battle against Creforce. At 1700 hours Freyberg conferred with Puttick and instructed him to try again. However, instead of organising a second counter-attack, Puttick requested permission to retreat. To do so meant to accept defeat; but rather than sacking him, Freyberg demurred. At no point did either commander consider using the largely unemployed 4 New Zealand Brigade or even 1 Welch Battalion from Creforce reserve in a second counter-attack.

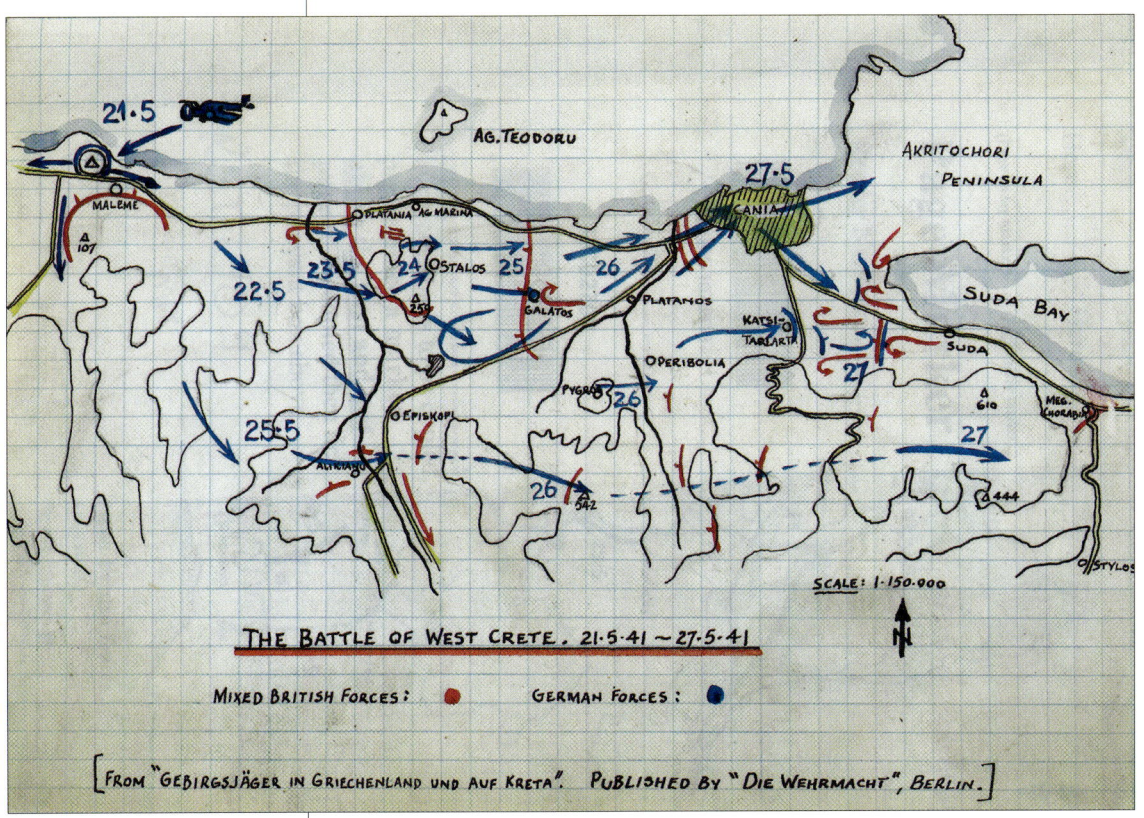

The German Advance against Canea and Suda.
Australian War Memorial RC02708

When a staff officer arrived at Headquarters 23 New Zealand Battalion to convey the news of the planned withdrawal, the battalion commander, Leckie, exclaimed, 'What! Have they tossed it in?' He had expected news of the enemy's surrender. Instead, he was told to fall back. Leckie's reaction illustrates the ease with which commanders in different locations draw different conclusions on the course of the same battle. Leckie knew that his men had dealt severely with the Germans and that they were holding their own. Puttick and Freyberg only saw the arriving transports and drew a considerably more negative conclusion. No doubt the limitations of Creforce's communication net played a significant part. As 5 New Zealand Brigade disengaged, the bone-weary paratroopers rose and cautiously followed.

During the morning of 23 May, 5 New Zealand Brigade took up its new position behind the Platanias River. Along the coast, Ramcke's group pursued until it came into contact with 28 New Zealand (Maori) Battalion near the Platanias Bridge. Ringel also sent his mountain infantry regiments on a sweep through the hills in an attempt to position themselves behind 5 New Zealand Brigade. Ringel preferred to avoid frontal assaults and, while his men faced a hard climb, he believed that sweat saved lives. It was a slower method than a direct assault, but Ringel had sufficient men to use Ramcke to hold the Kiwis at the front while manoeuvring a killing blow against their flank and rear.

Generalleutnant Julius Ringel decorates one of his mountain soldiers on Crete.
National Library of New Zealand DA-12642

> **GENERALLEUTNANT JULIUS RINGEL**
>
> Julius Ringel was born in Völkermarkt, Austria, in 1889. During the First World War he served in the Austrian army's mountain forces. Throughout the interwar period Ringel continued his career in the Austrian Army until the *Anschluss* and Austria's incorporation into Germany in 1938. By this time he had been a member of the Nazi Party for two years, having joined in 1936.
>
> During the Second World War, Ringel saw service on almost every front, leading troops in Norway, the Balkans, Italy and Russia. After serving as Chief of Staff to *3 Mountain Division* he was appointed commander of the newly formed *5 Mountain Division*. He infused the formation with his philosophy of hard work and the axiom that 'sweat saves blood'. His skill as a trainer and driver of men was clearly demonstrated by the division's performance in Crete.
>
> By 1944 Ringel was a corps commander in charge of *LXIX Corps* on the Eastern Front. In the Third Reich's dying days he commanded *Korps Ringel* against the Russians in Austria. Ringel died on 11 February 1967.

The New Zealanders were aware of the danger from the encircling German forces and Freyberg authorised a further withdrawal. The 5th New Zealand Brigade was to retreat behind 4 New Zealand Brigade on the Galatas Heights line and become the Creforce reserve. By the morning of 25 May the New Zealander position was as follows:

- 18 New Zealand Battalion – Wheat Hill to the coast facing west;
- Petrol Company and New Zealand Divisional Cavalry Squadron – Pink Hill facing south-west towards the prison;
- 19 New Zealand Battalion – ridgeline in front of Karatsos facing south;
- 19 Australian Brigade – blocking exit from Prison Valley near Perivolia facing west;
- 2 Greek Regiment – hills on south side of Prison Valley facing north; and
- 8 Greek Regiment – hills around Alikianou facing north.

As the Germans moved forward they linked up with Heidrich's cut-off paratroopers who had been fighting a separate battle against the New Zealanders on the Galatas Heights. The German dispositions were: Ramcke's group on the coast; on their right in the foothills *100 Gebirgsjäger Regiment*; and in Prison Valley *3 Fallschirmjäger Regiment*. Ringel sent *85 Gebirgsjäger Regiment* on a wide sweep through the hills south of Prison Valley to strike for Suda. The Germans spent 24 May building up their strength and preparing for the next attack. The significance of the loss of the airfield became even more painfully apparent, as Ringel also welcomed the arrival of *141 Gebirgsjäger Regiment, 95 Gebirgsartillerie Regiment*, and *95 Gebirgspionier Battalion*.

On the morning of 25 May the Germans began a softening-up barrage on the New Zealanders holding the Galatas Line. The primary targets were 18 New Zealand Battalion which barred the way to Canea along the coast, and the Petrol Company and New Zealand Divisional Cavalry Squadron which guarded the village of Galatas. To the New Zealanders it felt as if the Germans had an unlimited supply of mortar bombs. Adding to the thunder was the artillery of *95 Gebirgsartillerie Regiment* and the recoilless guns of the *Luftlande Sturmregiment*. Also joining in was the *Luftwaffe*, whose planes attacked any visible target. Against this massed firepower the defenders had only a few remaining pieces of artillery and their own mortars. Unlike the German profligacy, the New Zealanders had to watch their ammunition; the entire division had only 72 three-inch mortar bombs left.

Der abgeschossene englische Kampfwagen

A wrecked light tank from 3 Hussars.
National Library of New Zealand DA-12645

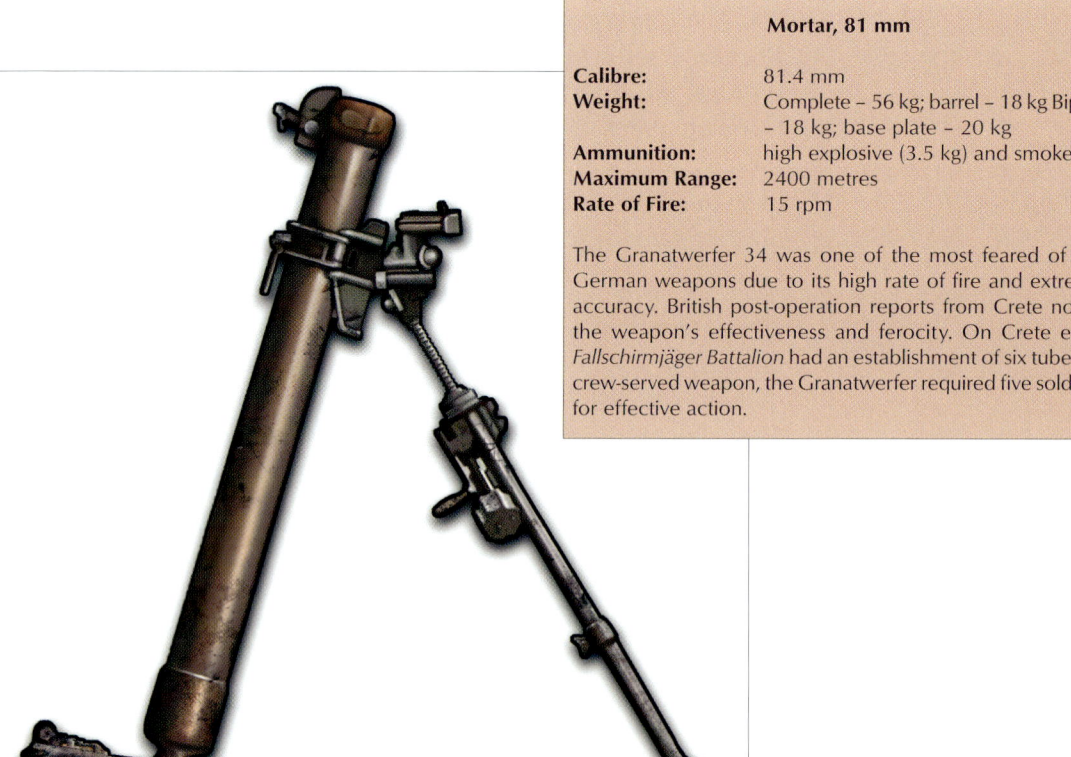

Mortar, 81 mm

Calibre:	81.4 mm
Weight:	Complete – 56 kg; barrel – 18 kg Bipod – 18 kg; base plate – 20 kg
Ammunition:	high explosive (3.5 kg) and smoke
Maximum Range:	2400 metres
Rate of Fire:	15 rpm

The Granatwerfer 34 was one of the most feared of the German weapons due to its high rate of fire and extreme accuracy. British post-operation reports from Crete noted the weapon's effectiveness and ferocity. On Crete each *Fallschirmjäger Battalion* had an establishment of six tubes. A crew-served weapon, the Granatwerfer required five soldiers for effective action.

At about 1400 hours the mortaring reached a crescendo and the German infantry advanced against 18 New Zealand Battalion's positions. The battalion's line ran for 2,700 metres, and was held thinly everywhere. The unit had only six Vickers, and two of these were without tripods. Yet the battalion fought the enemy to a standstill and the Germans retired.

The first attack was probably just a warm-up; the Germans were probing for weak points in the New Zealand line. At 1500 hours a more determined assault began. Behind a barrage of mortar bombs and artillery shells the Germans struck at D Company on 18 New Zealand Battalion's right wing near the coast. Ramcke's paratroopers worked their way up gullies and penetrated the company's perimeter. Suddenly the Germans were everywhere, and the defenders were caught in crossfire, while bombs continued to rain on their pits. Overwhelmed, the defence lost its cohesion as the Germans methodically took D Company's position apart. The enemy's superior firepower eliminated position after position. The end came swiftly and the survivors surrendered.

The Germans now shifted their focus to the opposite end of 18 New Zealand Battalion's line. A Company on Wheat Hill bore the full brunt of the enemy's renewed bombardment and assault. The New Zealanders fought valiantly and made the enemy pay for the feature, but there were simply not enough defenders to hold off two regiments of Germans who enjoyed enormous fire and aerial support. A Company gave way and broke.

With both of its flanking companies gone it was the centre's turn. The battalion disintegrated under the pressure even as bodies of men remained defiant, continuing to fire until overrun. It was a heroic defence, but it could not be maintained and the remnants of 18 New Zealand Battalion crumbled, its men heading east.

Pressure now mounted on the Petrol Company which, after six days of defiance, still stood on Pink Hill, and on the cavalrymen on their left. Enfiladed by fire from both Wheat and Cemetery Hills, with Germans infiltrating their exposed rear and mortar bombs exploding all around their pits, these resolute defenders accepted that it was time to go. They too made their way through Galatas.

Throughout the battle the sector's commanders, Inglis and Kippenberger, pushed forward their few reinforcements to shore up the line. Into the maw went service corps troops, gunners fighting as infantry, ack-ack platoons, and anyone else they could find. Also sent forward were the New Zealand Division Band and the New Zealand Division Concert Party. Neither Inglis nor Kippenberger had any formed units that could turn the tide of the enemy's advance. In reality, they were playing for time.

Grenade, No.36M

Weight:	.68 kg
Range:	25 to 35 metres thrown; up to 220 metres projected from rifle
Fuses:	4 seconds and 7 seconds
Casualty Radius:	20 metres, with a danger area of at least 100 metres

Introduced in 1917 as a rifle grenade and popularly known as the 'Mills Bomb', the 36M grenade represented the evolution of the No.5 grenade of 1915. An increase in range was obtained by attaching a base plug and gas check plate, enabling the grenade to be fired from a discharger cup fitted to the Lee Enfield rifle. Extensively used by British and Commonwealth forces throughout the Second World War, its basic design has remained unchanged to the present day.

Grenade, Steilhandgranate (StG) 39

Weight:	.61 kg
Length:	355 mm
Igniter Delay:	4-5 seconds

Grenade, Eihandgranate 39

Length:	7.6cm
Weight:	0.28kg
Fusing:	4–5 second delay

During the Second World War the German Army fielded different types of hand grenades designed for offensive and defensive roles. The Steilhandgranate, or stick grenade, was little changed from the model used in the First World War and saw service primarily as a defensive weapon. Smaller, lighter and less complex to manufacture, the Eihandgranate or 'egg' grenade was used as an offensive weapon. It was also easily modified for use in booby traps.

 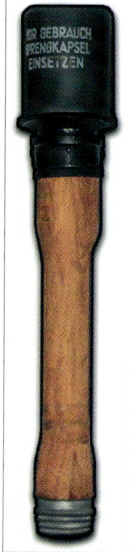

Good Work with the Bayonet

The New Zealand front line had disappeared under the weight of the German assault. As 18 New Zealand Battalion's commander, Lieutenant-Colonel J. R. Gray, rallied whatever men he could find near Karatsos, Inglis and Kippenberger desperately tried to form a new line from the village to the coast.

Kippenberger knew that the division's only hope was to stun the enemy and to seize the initiative, even if temporarily. Near Karatsos he found 23 New Zealand Battalion and ordered Major H. H. Thomason to retake Galatas. Thomason had taken command of the battalion only hours earlier from the wounded Leckie.

The Germans cautiously re-enter Galatas. Farran's tank is in the background.
National Library of New Zealand DA-12652

The attack went in just after 2000 hours. Thomason took two companies up the main road that ran from Karatsos to Galatas. Leading the way was Lieutenant Roy Farran of 3 Hussars with two light tanks. Along a secondary road the remnants of 18 New Zealand Battalion and the Petrol Company joined the assault. As the attackers advanced, other New Zealanders gripped their weapons, rose from the shelter of the olive trees and ruined buildings, and fell in. Cooks, signallers, and soldiers from other units all realised, as if by unspoken order, that every man was needed.

As the columns neared the outskirts of Galatas the men surged forward, picking up their pace, anxious to enter the village before the clatter of the enemy's machine-guns ripped through their ranks. But, surprisingly, no fire greeted them. The Germans remained unaware of their approach until the last minute when a few rifles spat and sounded the alarm. By then it was too late. With a blood-curdling battle cry the Kiwis plunged into Galatas.

As they poured into the village's narrow streets the Germans formed to meet the attack. Neither side showed quarter. Machine-guns fired at close range until silenced by grenades. Bombs were hurled through windows, followed by the bayonet as the New Zealanders cleared houses. Men fought with whatever was at hand—rifles swung like clubs and bayonets plunged into bellies. Farran was in front, spraying anything that moved with his machine-guns until his tank exploded, hit by an anti-tank shell. The New Zealanders converged on the village square by the church. Across the far side the enemy attempted to rally, covering the open ground with their weapons. After a moment's hesitation the New Zealanders charged. Lieutenant Thomas, 23 New Zealand Battalion, described the climax of the attack. He wrote:

> I decided to charge, we jostled each other for the lead, and firing from the hip we advanced across the square. … Screams and shouts showed desperate panic in front of us … By now we were stepping over groaning forms, and those which rose against us fell to our bayonets, and bayonets with their eighteen inches of steel entered throats and chests with the same horrible sound …

The Germans fired, attempting to hold their position, but the Kiwis came on. This time it was the Germans who broke, and those who could do so fled.

While the New Zealand attack on Galatas demonstrated what the Kiwi soldier was capable of when released from the deadening hand of his commanders, it did not change the outcome of the Crete Campaign. The fate of the campaign had already been decided. It was a spoiling attack, nothing more, that prevented the day's defeat from becoming a rout, and it bought time for the division to form a new line in front of Canea. Later that evening the men who had stormed Galatas received orders to fall back.

Monument in the town square of Galatas commemorating the battle for the village.
Photo courtesy of author

END GAME AT HERAKLION AND RETIMO

Stalemate at Heraklion

Despite being heavily repulsed on the first day, defeat did not weaken Bräuer's determination to secure Heraklion's airfield and port. By contrast, after enjoying great success on the first day, Chappel remained cautious and chose not to exploit his advantage over the Germans. Instead he focused on maintaining his grip on the area's prizes. The result was a stalemate at Heraklion.

Student managed to airdrop Bräuer several hundred paratrooper reinforcements over the next few days, but these made little difference. The British defences possessed tremendous natural strength. On 21 May Bräuer organised a two-pronged attack. The eastern advance probed towards the airfield but made no progress against the Black Watch on East Hill. In the west the Germans penetrated the city's walls, and some paratroopers even gained the port, but their hold was temporary. British reinforcements forced most of the Germans from the city and the Greeks hunted down and killed those who remained.

The paratroopers' strength was their aerial reach and the element of surprise in their arrival. At Heraklion neither advantage remained. In order to crack the British defences, Bräuer needed heavy infantry, tanks and artillery, not his lightly armed paratroopers supported by only a few 75mm recoilless guns. The determined Bräuer organised several more attacks, but none had any hope of success. The Germans were mired in a trap of their own making. In order to win they needed more powerful weapons, but to land these weapons they needed the port which they did not have the strength to capture. It was almost out of frustration that on 24 May the *Luftwaffe* destroyed Heraklion from the air, an act which only hardened the local people's resolve to resist.

For his part Chappel did nothing to jeopardise his hold on the port and airfield. Even after 2 Argyll and Sutherland Battalion arrived from Tymbaki he refused to use his numerical advantage to take the initiative. While he maintained his patrols, in all other respects he was content to hold the perimeter and bloody the Germans whenever attacked. On 22 May the British buried 950 Germans, a gauge of their success in denying the enemy.

The destruction of Heraklion by the *Luftwaffe*.
Australian War Memorial 128431

A line of German prisoners in Heraklion. Except for 17 officers evacuated to Egypt, all German prisoners were freed by their comrades.
Imperial War Museum E3066E

Ju 87B Stuka

Type:	dive bomber
Wingspan:	13.2 m
Length:	11 m
Engine:	Junkers Jumo 211A (883 kW)
Max Speed:	350 kph
Range:	600-800 km with bombs (depending on variant)
Armament:	one rear-facing 7.9 mm MG15, two 7.9 mm MG17 (one in each wing) and one 500 kg bomb (1000 kg bomb if rear crew left behind)

Universally known as the Stuka, the Ju 87 became synonymous with the blitzkrieg tactics employed by the Germans in the early years of the Second World War. The Stuka's role was to provide close air support to ground forces. First flown in 1935, it was accepted into service in 1937. However, by the end of 1941 the Stuka's days were numbered; it was too slow to evade fighters and one pilot described it as an 'ideal target'. While there were numerous modifications to the aircraft, the B model was the most common and was the version involved in the Crete campaign.

Ultimately, the Germans would win Heraklion—but only because of events elsewhere on the island. After dark on 28 May the Royal Navy arrived to evacuate the garrison. Throughout the night British and Australian soldiers made their way through the ruins of the city to the harbour. There they boarded destroyers which took them out to waiting cruisers.

On the passage to Egypt the *Luftwaffe* exacted a heavy toll. Repeatedly bombed, the convoy lost two destroyers and had two cruisers damaged. Over 400 soldiers died, many times the number lost in Heraklion's defence.

On 28 May the Italians joined their ally in the conquest of Crete when a force from Rhodes landed at Sitia. As he had done in the conquest of France, Mussolini had waited until the contest was decided before arriving to share in the spoils. During the ensuing occupation, Italy controlled the island's eastern provinces.

Lieutenant-Colonel Ian Ross Campbell
(photograph taken in 1945)
Australian War Memorial 120557

MAJOR-GENERAL IAN ROSS CAMPBELL

Ian Ross Campbell was born in Moss Vale, New South Wales, on 23 March 1900. He chose to pursue a military profession and, in 1922, he graduated from the Royal Military College and was commissioned a lieutenant.

Campbell spent the interwar years in various adjutant and quartermaster appointments in militia units. His breaks from the monotony of garrison life were few: a period of exchange with the Scots Fusiliers in India, and an appointment as aide-de-camp to the Governor of New South Wales. In 1935 Campbell attended Staff College at Camberley.

The outbreak of the Second World War found Campbell still a captain, which was not unusual for the army during this period. In October 1939 he was promoted to major and appointed brigade major to 16 Australian Brigade. The next year he moved to 6 Australian Division Staff before his attachment to 2/5 Australian Battalion for the attack on Bardia. He was awarded a DSO for his role in the city's capture.

In April 1941 Campbell sailed with 6 Australian Division to Greece. There he was promoted to lieutenant-colonel and given command of 2/1 Australian Battalion. It was his first command. Following the evacuation from Greece, Campbell landed on Crete where Vasey gave him responsibility for Retimo. He played a handy role in the defence of Retimo, but was captured when British resistance collapsed.

Campbell was liberated in April 1945 and promoted temporary brigadier. He commanded the Australian Imperial Forces Reception Group in Britain until his return to Australia later that year. In 1946 he was awarded a bar to his DSO for the defence of Retimo.

Campbell enjoyed a number of staff appointments including Director of Military Training. In 1949 he served in Japan and later Korea as part of the occupation force. He was appointed commandant of the Australian Staff College in 1953. This was followed in 1954 by his promotion to major-general and his appointment as commandant of the Royal Military College. He retired in 1957. Campbell died in Sydney on 31 October 1997.

Campbell Defends Retimo

By the end of the second day Campbell had the Germans pinned in two enclaves, held the enemy commander prisoner and had captured over 500 Germans. Unless the Germans received massive reinforcements, the sector would remain secure. Unlike Chappel at Heraklion, however, Campbell was not content to merely hold off the enemy. He sought to destroy them. For the rest of the campaign he sent his men against the enemy's redoubts, refusing to provide the Germans an opportunity to recover the initiative.

If Chappel can be accused of being too passive, perhaps the opposite can be said of Campbell. He was probably too aggressive and caused casualties amongst his men for no real benefit. The enemy defended formidable positions. Those in Perivolia had converted its thick-walled houses and churches into a veritable fortress, while the group in the olive oil factory near Stavromenos held an equally powerful redoubt. The Germans guarded both with a plentiful supply of mortars and automatic weapons.

St George Church near Perivolia. The Germans converted it into a fortress.
The Australians stormed it on 23 May.
Australian War Memorial 131071

An Australian aid station in the shade of a crashed German plane.
Imperial War Museum E3135E

By the end of the first day the Australian soldiers bristled with small arms. They gathered up weapons from the enemy's containers and had learned how to request a supply drop from the *Luftwaffe*. They had even captured a PaK 36 anti-tank gun that had drifted down under a cluster of parachutes. Corporal A. Hackshaw, 2/11 Australian Battalion, described the arsenal he and his mate possessed:

> We were using German arms and ammo. My mate and I have our own rifles, a German anti-tank rifle, one of our anti-tank rifles, a Luger pistol apiece and a Spandau machine-gun. When we are in fixed positions we are bristling with arms, but food supplies are another matter.

But what Campbell did not have were weapons that could fire a shell of sufficient mass to batter down the enemy's walls. Instead, his men had to rely on fire and movement tactics to cross the deadly zone in front of the German positions. In most cases the Germans broke up the Australian attacks well short of their objective. Campbell did have two Matilda tanks, but they were ineffective and constantly broke down.

Panzerkampfwagen (PzKw) Mark II tank	
Length:	4.4 m
Width:	2.2 m
Height:	2 m
Weight:	7.9 tonnes
Crew:	three (commander/gunner, loader/radio operator and driver)
Power plant:	Maybach HL57TR
Armament:	One 20 mm KwK30 L/50 gun and one 7.92 mm MG34
Max Armour:	15 mm
Speed:	40 kph (road)
Range:	200 km

The PzKw II was the main battle tank of the German Army in the opening days of the Second World War but was soon usurped in this role by the more powerful PzKw III and IV. However it remained in service as a reconnaissance vehicle. Two PzKw II from *4 Panzer Regiment* were landed on Crete on 27 May.

The Australians captured the olive oil factory, but only because the enemy abandoned it when they ran short of food and ammunition. The German defenders slipped away to the east. At Perivolia, however, the enemy repelled every Australian effort to break into the town.

Campbell received only fleeting assistance from Creforce. On 24 May a company of 1 Rangers arrived from Suda and attacked Perivolia from the west. The new arrivals made no effort to coordinate their attack with the Australians. After their bloody repulse the Rangers turned around and returned to Suda.

At about 0600 hours on 30 May the Australians heard the sound of engines approaching from the west. Half an hour later a column of German motorcycle troops supported by two Panzer II tanks came into view. The game was up.

THE RETREAT TO SFAKIA

The Death of the Welch

As the morning of 26 May dawned, the Germans began a cautious advance towards the New Zealanders' new position in front of Canea. It was not until the afternoon that an attack began to develop, and at no point was it as brutal or determined as that of the previous day. The Germans were almost certainly seeking out weak points in the defenders' new line, while also bringing forward their guns, mortars and ammunition.

The only serious threat developed in the late afternoon at the southern end of the line in the foothills near Perivolia and Mournies. Elements of *3 Fallschirmjäger Regiment* found a gap at the junction of 2/8 Australian Battalion and 2 Greek Regiment and pushed behind the Australians. The Greeks were in bad shape and would not last much longer: during the coming night the unit would dissolve. Faced with a potential crisis, 19 Australian Brigade responded by shifting its line back towards Mournies allowing the enemy to occupy Perivolia.

Meanwhile, further south, *85 Gebirgsjäger Regiment* continued its push through the hills. Ringel sent the unit on a wide sweep over the rugged terrain from Alikianou towards Stilos to cut the coast road behind the British and trap Creforce in a pocket around Canea. The *Gebirgstruppen*'s only opposition was 8 Greek Regiment. The Greeks had neither the weapons nor the skills to match the Germans in an open fight; but they knew the terrain and performed magnificently, making the enemy pay for every hill and ravine. It was solely due to their delaying tactics that Creforce escaped Ringel's trap.

Some of the hills crossed by *85 Gebrigsjäger Regiment*.
Photo courtesy of author.

During the night of 26-27 May, one of the great tragedies of the Crete Campaign unfolded—the destruction of 1 Welch Battalion. On 26 May Freyberg contacted Wavell and informed him of the need to evacuate. He knew he could not hold Canea for much longer, and with its capture he would lose his base area and reserves of supplies. Without these, Creforce would last only a matter of days. His choices were stark: evacuate or surrender.

During the night, units began the long trek towards the small fishing village of Sfakia on the south coast, the evacuation point for the troops from the Canea area. To allow Creforce's excess base area men to escape, Freyberg wanted the Germans held west of Canea for one more day. He gave the task to his 1,500-man force reserve: 1 Welch Battalion, 1 Rangers Battalion and the Northumberland Hussars.

> **Lesson 14**
>
> Economy of force demands that commanders retain only those forces which they can utilise effectively. The presence of surplus troops will, at best, serve as a drain on logistics while, at worst, these troops will impede the actions of essential units. Units for which there is no role in the battlespace must be removed to a base area or redirected to another theatre of operations.

On Weston's orders the Welch Group moved forward to replace the New Zealanders on the Canea Line. The New Zealanders were to stay until relieved by the incoming Welch. On their left the Royal Perivolians and 19 Australian Brigade would remain and extend the line into the hills. The Kiwis would form a second line further back along 42nd Street near the tip of Suda Bay.

By the time the Welch commander, Lieutenant-Colonel A. Duncan, arrived at the position he was to defend, there was no sign of the New Zealanders. They had already pulled out. Of greater concern was the fact that Duncan's men could not make contact with the British and Australians who were supposed to be on their left. Even today, it is unclear precisely what transpired during the relief. What is known is that Puttick and Weston did not coordinate their actions, probably due to the confusion of the night and the poor state of Creforce's communications. Puttick, anxious to get away, did not wait for the Welch Group to arrive and fell back early. Instead of leaving Vasey's Australians and the Royal Perivolians behind as instructed, he brought them back too. As dawn approached, Duncan realised that his left flank was exposed. It was not long before Ringel discovered this too.

Ringel believed he had been handed his chance to destroy Creforce in a pocket around Canea and the Akrotiri Peninsula. He was not yet aware that the retreat had commenced and that all he faced was a rearguard. Ringel ordered Ramcke to hold the Welch Group from the front while *100 Gebirgsjäger Regiment* moved into the gap and assaulted from the flank. He also sent *3 Fallschirmjäger* and *141 Gebirgsjäger Regiments* through the hole on a wider sweep to close the door from the enemy's rear. He instructed *85 Gebirgsjäger Regiment* to continue its push towards Stilos.

Duncan's position was hopeless. This fine battalion had impatiently waited in its position as Creforce reserve since the campaign's start for the chance to intervene at a decisive moment. Now this opportunity had simply been thrown away. Shortly after midday the action was over. Several hundred Welch, Rangers and Hussars cut their way out of the trap and rejoined the British line near Suda but most had no choice but to surrender.

The Charge at 42nd Street

After retreating from Canea, Vasey's 19 Australian Brigade joined the new line at 42nd Street, a position running from the end of Suda Bay to the hills to the south. The Australians occupied the section near the bay with Hargest's 5 New Zealand Brigade on their left.

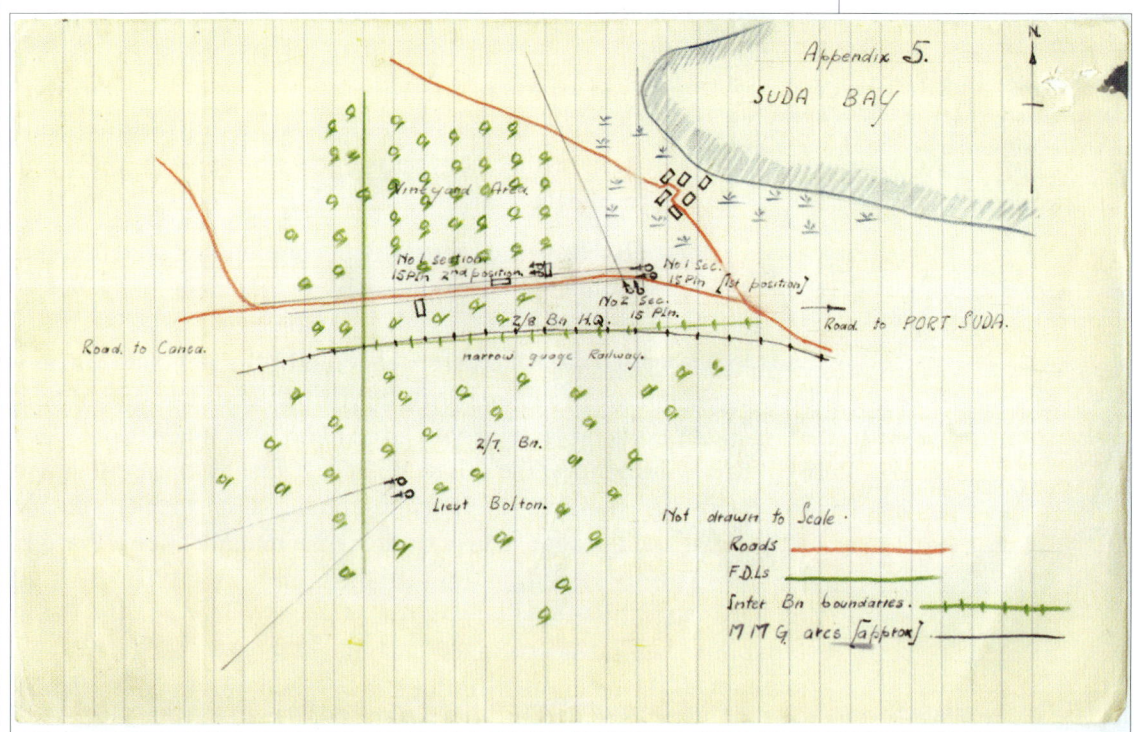

Australian Defences along 42nd Street.
2/1 Aus MG Bn War Diary, AWM52, 8/5/1, page 60

42nd Street position's name derived from the engineer company that had a camp nearby.
Australian War Memorial P0371.001

At about 1100 hours the right wing of *141 Gebirgsjäger Regiment* paraded directly in front of the Australian-New Zealand position along 42nd Street. The mountain troops were intent on cutting the coast road and reaching the bay; at that point they were unaware of the enemy's presence. Instead, they believed that the British were still around Canea and that they were slamming shut Ringel's trap.

The Australian and New Zealand battalion commanders had earlier agreed that if the enemy appeared they would attack immediately. None wanted to allow the Germans the opportunity to organise a set-piece battle in which the enemy's superior firepower would pound them to pieces. The 2/7th Australian Battalion sent a patrol out to keep the Germans under observation while its commander alerted the rest of the group of the enemy's arrival.

While the counter-attack was by no means a carefully planned operation, it was characterised by dash and determination. As its patrol opened fire, the men of 2/7 Australian Battalion charged with bayonets fixed. From their left, 28 New Zealand (Maori) Battalion and 19 New Zealand Battalion converged to join the fray. The appearance of a mob of charging Australians and New Zealanders took the *Gebirgstruppen* by surprise. Before the Germans could reorientate to face the assault, the attackers crashed into *141 Gebirgsjäger Regiment*'s flank. The German soldiers broke, unable to hold back the torrent that poured onto them. The Australians and New Zealanders pursued them for almost two kilometres before being ordered to return. Reg Saunders, of 2/1 Australian Battalion, recorded his memory of the charge. He wrote:

> We were all obsessed with this mad race to slaughter with the bayonets. … When we got there they were real men … excited like us and some of them terribly frightened. They were highly trained Germans, but they got such a shock.

The exact number of German casualties is not known, but battle reports describe the number of bodies as between 150 and 300.

No-one was under any illusion that the success at 42nd Street somehow changed the situation on Crete. Like a cornered animal, the Australians had struck at their tormentors and taught them a bloody lesson. It had been a good show, but that was all. Creforce's senior officers knew that with the loss of Canea's depots the only chance for their men to avoid spending the rest of the war languishing in a prisoner-of-war camp was to get to Sfakia and hope that the navy arrived in time.

Charge with the Bayonet – gouache on board, 2005
artist – Jeff Isaacs, OAMt

The Escape Route

Freyberg's focus was now fixed on getting as much of Creforce to Egypt as possible. It was not an easy task, neither for the soldiers who marched and fought for their survival, nor for the sailors who braved seas dominated by the *Luftwaffe*.

The march from Suda to Sfakia was 70 kilometres, much of it over a poor quality road that crossed Crete's mountainous spine. The first stage of the route followed the coast road and passed through some of the island's most fertile areas. There was a road junction at Vrises, a small town at the confluence of several rivers. The coastal road continued east towards Georgeoupolis while the other road branched off and headed south into the mountains to Sfakia. Just beyond Vrises, the road began to climb and the country became rougher, the ground less fertile, and the inhabitants poorer. Prior to his decision to evacuate, Freyberg had made no preparations to establish food or water dumps along the route. Now with the retreat underway there was no time to make these arrangements. The men carried what they could or scavenged food and water from the few villages and wells they passed. Their only respite came as they crossed the Askifou Plain, a high plateau that contained several well-watered villages surrounded by green fields.

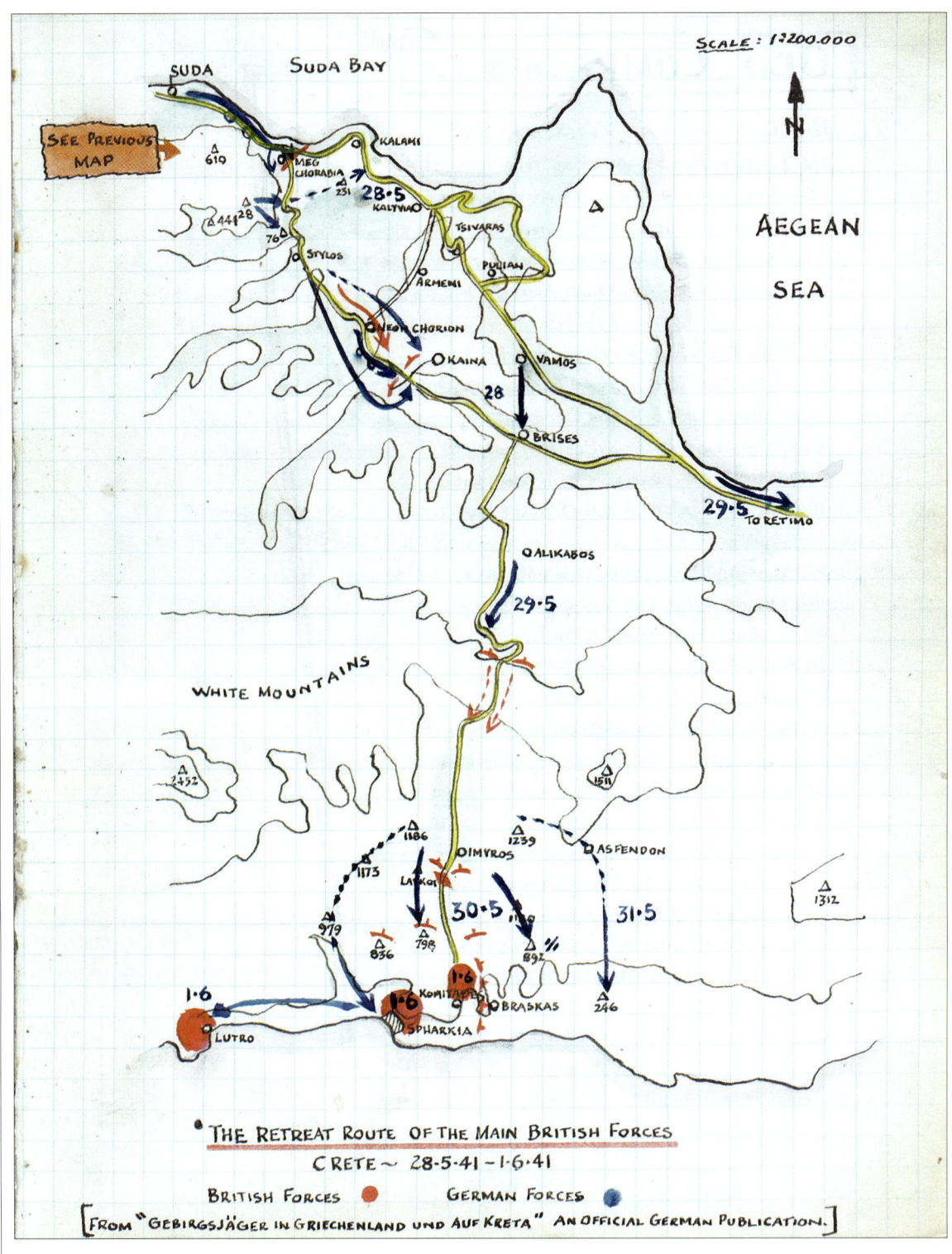

The Retreat Route to Sfakia
Australian War Memorial RC02709

A soldier fills his water bottle from a well during the retreat.
National Library of New Zealand DA-08185

The road did not actually reach Sfakia, terminating instead at the top of an escarpment about 500 metres above the parched south coast. From the escarpment's edge a rock-strewn path ran down through the Imbros Ravine to the sea. The ravine was narrow—at its narrowest point a man would be unable to stretch his arms out without touching the sides. However it provided most of Creforce with a shady refuge from the hot sun while they awaited embarkation. Freyberg made his headquarters in a cave in the ravine's lower reaches.

Creforce's cave headquarters at Sfakia. Freyberg sits in the middle.
Imperial War Museum E3023E

Freyberg chose Sfakia as the evacuation point because it was the closest port on the south coast to Canea. A south coast embarkation was essential because of the shorter sailing time between Egypt and Crete which would reduce the fleet's exposure to the *Luftwaffe*. Another reason for the selection of Sfakia was its beach. The village's harbour did not contain a pier. Instead, the local fishermen grounded their boats on a small beach measuring a mere 200 metres, around which the village's few buildings clustered. It was not a sand beach, but was covered in small stones. Most importantly, it sloped gently downwards into the sea. Over these stones the evacuation fleet's landing craft and small boats could safely pull into the shallows without risk of damage. To the south of Sfakia were the blue waters of the Mediterranean, and beyond the horizon lay Egypt and safety.

As the retreating men made their way south they noticed a dramatic reduction in attention from German planes, allowing them some respite from the torment of the continuous aerial bombardment. From the campaign's start the *Luftwaffe* had dominated the sky, making any movement in daylight hazardous. Now only a few enemy planes hindered the marching soldiers. The reason for this easing in enemy aerial harassment at the point when the columns of troops were most vulnerable was unclear at the time. Later the explanation became obvious. The *Luftwaffe* had begun to redeploy its squadrons northwards to the bases they would use for Operation *Barbarossa*, the German invasion of the Soviet Union.

The goal: Sfakia.
Australian War Memorial P04067.005

Delay and Retreat

During the night of 27-28 May the Australians and New Zealanders who had held the line at 42nd Street slipped away eastwards. Creforce's infantry: 4 and 5 New Zealand Brigades, 19 Australian Brigade and Layforce, were to serve as the rearguard. Of these, only the men of Layforce were fresh and at full strength. Layforce comprised 950 commandos who had landed at Suda on the nights of 24 and 26 May. The decision to use these men as reinforcements was a curious one. As commandos, they were more suited to raids or silent fighting with knives. They lacked the weapons required to resist the enemy's heavily armed infantry. One possible explanation for Wavell's choosing them for Crete instead of the usual infantry battalion is that, being lightly armed, they were easier to transport by destroyer, the only vessel fast enough to arrive, unload and escape Suda Bay during the night.

The rearguard's task was not to defeat the enemy but to delay them long enough for the retreating depot and support troops to reach Sfakia and for the Royal Navy to complete the evacuation. Having achieved their mission they were to escape as best they could. The morning of 28 May found the commandos, supported by some Maoris, holding a blocking position on the coast road near Kalami on Suda Bay. At Stilos were elements of several New Zealander battalions with 2/7 Australian Battalion. The 2/8th Australian Battalion was positioned in support at the village of Armenoi.

In the small hours of 28 May the German advance guard ran into the commandos near Kalami. The German party comprised the *Wittman Group*, an ad hoc force organised by Ringel from his motorised and mechanised units. It included motorcycle troops, truck-towed guns, and several newly landed tanks. The group's mission was to push eastwards on the coast road as rapidly as possible to reach their hard-pressed comrades at Retimo. The commandos would have given way sooner if not for the support provided by the Maoris. As it was, they held their line for several hours before the Germans overran part of their position. The rest of the commandos and the Maoris made their way over the hills to Armenoi.

Several hours after the enemy attacked at Kalami another threat developed around Stilos. The *85th Gebirgsjäger Regiment* finally emerged from its tortuous march through the hills only to run into the New Zealanders and Australians who defended the town. If not for the delaying tactics of 8 Greek Regiment, the Germans would have reached Stilos earlier, cut the road, and trapped Creforce against Suda Bay.

By noon the Australians and New Zealanders were falling back towards their next stop points, Neon Khorion followed by Babali Hani. At each village the defenders' plan was the same: force the enemy off the road by firing on its leading troops, make the enemy expend time by deploying for an assault, and pull back as the Germans closed in for the kill.

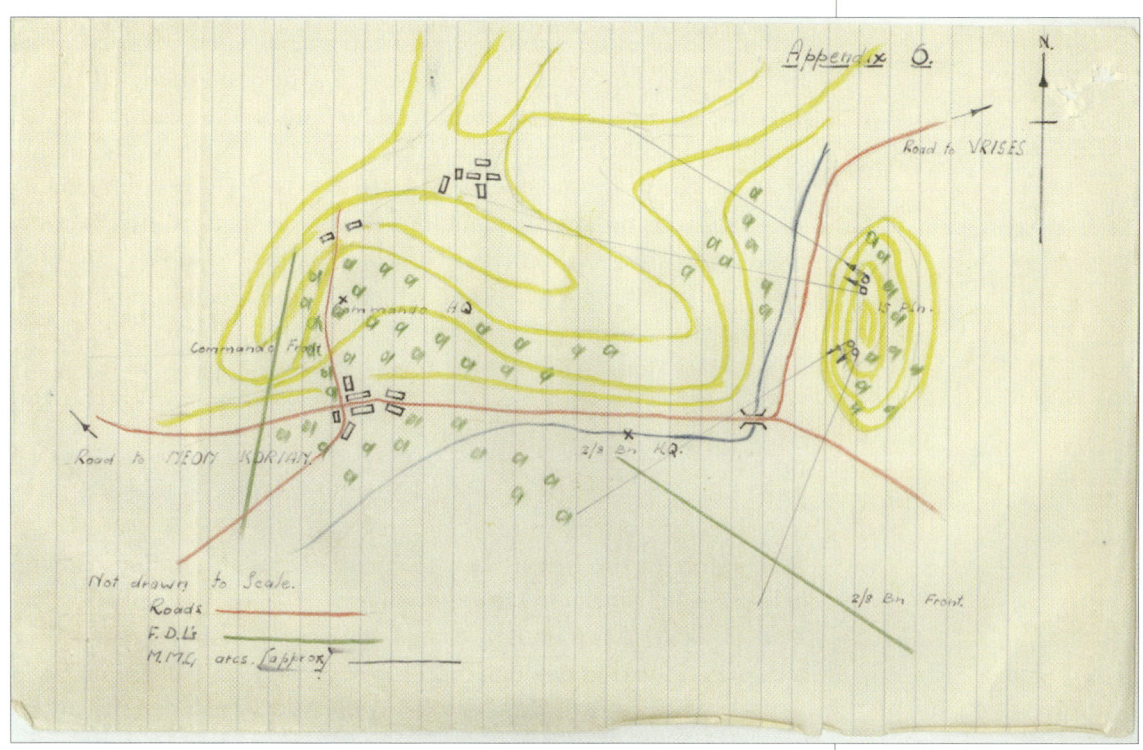

The Defence at Babali Hani
2/1 Aus MG Bn War Diary, AWM52, 8/5/1, page 61

At Vrises the rearguard took the road south. At this point the pursuing Germans split into two groups with the larger component hurrying eastwards on the coast road towards Retimo and Heraklion. Only *100 Gebirgsjäger Regiment* under Oberst Willibald Utz followed Creforce into the mountains. Ringel was obeying Student's order to make the relief of the hard-pressed *Fallschirmjäger* at Retimo and Heraklion his priority. Ringel did not know that Creforce had already abandoned the Australians at Retimo to their fate, or that the Royal Navy was about to evacuate the Heraklion garrison. He therefore kept most of *5 Gebirgs Division* on Crete's north coast heading towards the paratroopers.

There was little food and water along the road and the rearguard suffered severely from the effects of hunger and thirst. Despite this, they doggedly marched south, setting ambushes to keep the Germans at bay. One ideal ambush position lay at the great u-shaped bend near Chadiri where the road made a hairpin turn. It was a perfect spot. The long upwards approach to the hairpin forced the enemy to advance along the face of the defenders' line of fire. Once engaged, Utz responded by sending groups of *Gebirgsjäger* into the hills to work around the defenders' flanks. As the threat developed, the Australians and New Zealanders disengaged and fell back. In each case the purpose of the ambush was two-fold: to remind the enemy that Creforce remained capable of drawing blood and to buy time for the rest of the force.

View of the south coast from the escarpment above Sfakia.
Australian War Memorial 067949

Having crossed the Askifou Plain the rearguard continued to give up ground but did so more grudgingly. It was only another dozen or so kilometres to the coast. On the twisting road the defenders were able to set ambushes employing their two remaining Vickers tanks and some Bren Gun Carriers. Their machine-guns scattered the Germans and they then fell back around the next bend.

Universal carrier No. 1 (Bren gun carrier)

Weight:	4.1 tonnes
Length:	3.75 metres
Width:	1.87 metres
Height:	1.52 metres
Engine:	Ford V8 95 hp (petrol)
Speed:	65 km/hr
Crew:	three
Armament:	one .303-inch Vickers medium machine-guns and one .303-inch Bren or Lewis light machine-gun.

The Bren gun carrier was a light armoured tracked vehicle employed as a weapons carrier and light reconnaissance vehicle. The shortage of tanks on Crete often saw the carrier used as an infantry support weapon.

On 30 May the rearguard reached the final defensive positions on the ridges above Sfakia. The evacuation had already commenced. On the night of 28-29 May destroyers lifted off 800 men, mostly wounded. On the same night the Royal Navy extracted the Heraklion garrison.

The Situation at Sfakia

In the dispersal area around Sfakia, Creforce approached a state of near anarchy. Thousands of rear area soldiers milled about, discipline had collapsed, and unit structures broke down. Hargest observed that 'there were hundreds of loose members, members of non-fighting units and all sorts of people about – no formation, no order, no cohesion. It was a ghastly mess.' Each night when the ships anchored, these men became a mob, pushing towards the beach in a desperate effort to get away. The priority for Freyberg and the other senior officers lay in saving the combat troops as cadres for the rebuilding of the broken battalions, batteries and squadrons. The rear area men sensed they were to be sacrificed and were driven by a desperate need to escape. As the tension mounted, Freyberg posted a cordon of armed guards around the harbour to keep lanes open through the mob to allow the embarking combat units to reach the beach. Freyberg was now paying the price for not insisting on the evacuation of Creforce's excess depot men before the campaign began.

The beach at Sfakia.
Australian War Memorial P04067.003

New Zealand engineers awaiting evacuation at Sfakia.
National Library of New Zealand DA-10739

In its final days Creforce's fragile logistics system collapsed completely. At Sfakia there were acute shortages of food and water, and the entire force verged on starvation. While the evacuation ships brought some supplies, these were hopelessly insufficient. Efficient distribution was almost impossible as, with the exception of the combat arms, most units had ceased to exist. The men responsible for holding off the Germans suffered the most as they had to travel the greatest distance to find food and water. Creforce's communication problems blighted the force to the end. Freyberg maintained intermittent contact with Wavell on a single wireless set with a fading battery. Despite the nightly arrival of the Royal Navy, no-one in Cairo had thought to send out an extra radio or even a few batteries.

> **Lesson 15**
>
> Even in defeat, commanders and their staff have a responsibility to effectively administer the men under their command. This mandate holds true even in a doomed campaign because it is from the survivors of defeat that a new force is remade. A beaten force's ongoing support and administration is essential in order to husband the men's remaining strength and shorten the time required for them to regain their effectiveness.

What helped save much of Creforce was that Utz had no desire to pay the necessary cost in blood to storm the rearguard's positions. Now that Creforce was trapped against the sea he was content to move slowly. Instead of an assault he sent out wide flanking columns to take the defenders in the rear and to break into Sfakia.

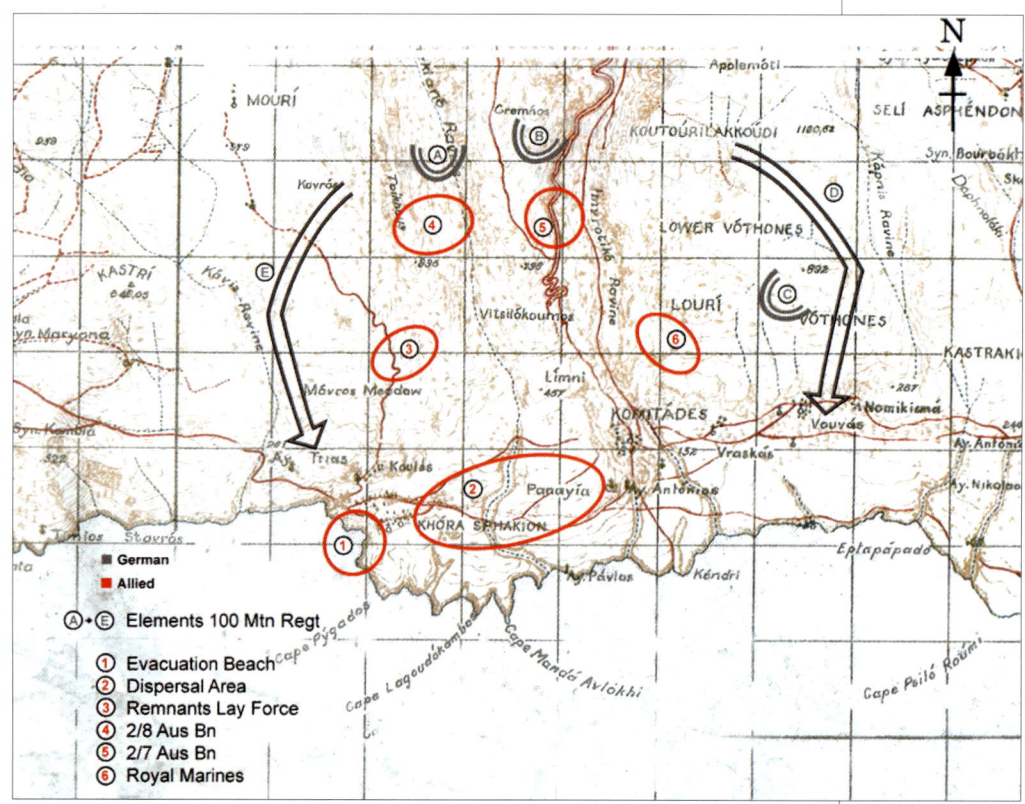

The Final Defence at Sfakia
Australian War Memorial Map Collection
Modified by Mark Wahlert

Table 2
Evacuations from Crete

- Unless otherwise noted ships are HMS.

Night Of	From	Ships Involved	Personnel Taken Off
22-23 May	Ay Roumeli	*Hero* and *Decoy*	King George of Greece and party
23-24 May	Suda Bay	*Jaguar* and *Defender*	60 wounded and non-required personnel
24-25 May	Suda Bay	*Abdiel*	50 wounded and non-required personnel
26-27 May	Suda Bay	*Hero*, *Abdiel* and HMAS *Nizam*	930 merchant seamen, RN personnel and non-required personnel
28-29 May	Heraklion	*Orion*, *Ajax*, *Dido*, *Decoy*, *Jackal*, *Imperial*, *Hotspur*, *Kimberley*, and *Hereward*	3,486 troops
28-29 May	Sfakia	HMAS *Napier*, *Kandahar*, *Kelvin* and HMAS *Nizam*	724 troops plus 20 Greek civilians
29-30 May	Sfakia	*Phoebe*, *Calcutta*, *Coventry*, *Glengyle*, *Jervis*, *Hasty*, *Janus* and HMAS *Perth*	6,029 troops
30-31 May	Sfakia	HMAS *Napier* and HMAS *Nizam*	1,510 troops
31 May – 1 June	Sfakia	*Phoebe*, *Abdiel*, *Kimberley*, *Hotspur*, *Jackal*	nearly 4,000 troops
30-31 May and 31 May - 1 June	Sfakia	Sunderland flying boat	54 VIP staff including Major-Generals Freyberg and Weston

The evacuation pressed ahead despite the Royal Navy's limited assets. Too many ships had already been sunk and many more damaged. In addition, all ships and crews had been at maximum tempo since the campaign's start. While determined to help, the Royal Navy was also cautious and its commanders would not risk any more ships than necessary.

On the night of 30-31 May Freyberg left by flying boat. Weston departed the next night. Both New Zealand Brigades were lifted off safely. The evacuation's final night was to be 31 May-1 June. The Royal Navy would not risk its ships for another night. The rearguard units pulled out one by one and made their way to the beach. Although not told that it was the last night, the rear area men knew the rearguard's movement to the harbour signalled the evacuation's end. Again they surged to the beach, fighting for a place on the ships. In the melee that resulted, the last of the infantry could not force themselves through in time. The men of 2/7 Australian Battalion stood in the water on the beach as they listened to the rattling of the anchor chains of unseen ships. The evacuation was over, although more than 5,000 soldiers remained at Sfakia. Table 2 outlines the Royal Navy's evacuation effort at Sfakia and elsewhere.

Lieutenant Keith Walker of 2/7 Australian Battalion was among those who stood at the water's edge. He later commented, 'It was terrible, left on the beach and to find out it was the last night, the navy was not coming back again – it was a terrible blow'.

Some men refused to accept their fate and escaped the Sfakia area before Utz closed the noose. These soldiers sought other means to get off the island. Some stole fishing boats and sailed to Africa. Another group repaired an abandoned British landing barge and headed south. One evening near the Preveli Monastery, HMS *Thresher* surfaced and almost eighty men swam out to the submarine. The monks had been instrumental in hiding them from the Germans and in providing them with food. The Germans rounded up many of these determined soldiers, but over 600 made their way to Egypt and rejoined their units.

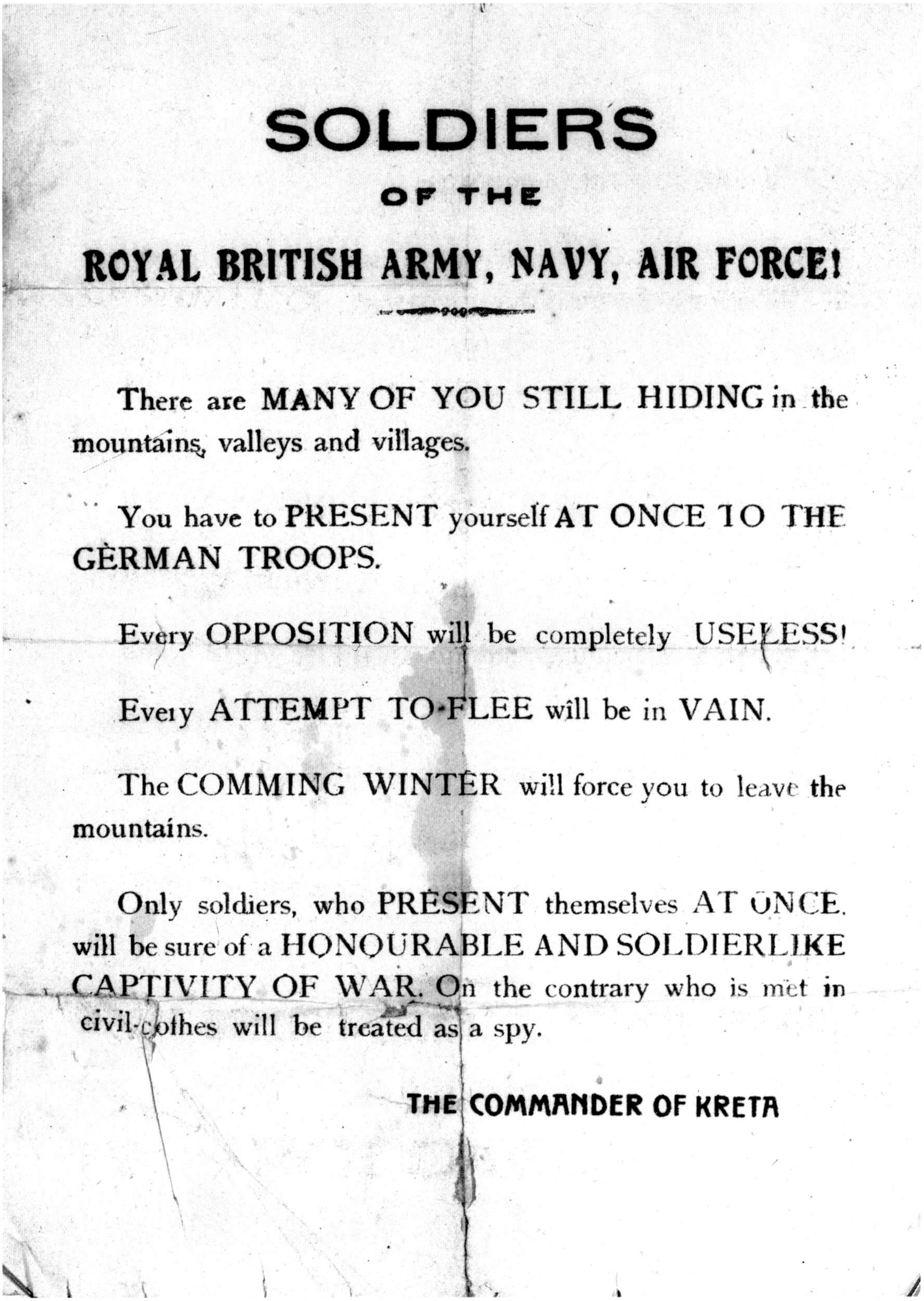

SOLDIERS
OF THE
ROYAL BRITISH ARMY, NAVY, AIR FORCE!

There are MANY OF YOU STILL HIDING in the mountains, valleys and villages.

You have to PRESENT yourself AT ONCE TO THE GERMAN TROOPS.

Every OPPOSITION will be completely USELESS!

Every ATTEMPT TO FLEE will be in VAIN.

The COMMING WINTER will force you to leave the mountains.

Only soldiers, who PRESENT themselves AT ONCE, will be sure of a HONOURABLE AND SOLDIERLIKE CAPTIVITY OF WAR. On the contrary who is met in civil cothes will be treated as a spy.

THE COMMANDER OF KRETA

German poster urging British troops to surrender.
National Library of New Zealand DA-10726

THE SEA AND AIR WAR FOR CRETE

The Naval Campaign for Crete

The Royal Navy undertook two major operations in support of British forces during the battle for Crete. These operations were:

1) the interception of the German reinforcement convoys; and
2) the evacuation of the British Army in the campaign's closing days.

Admiral Andrew B. Cunningham.
Australian War Memorial P00433.001

ADMIRAL OF THE FLEET VISCOUNT CUNNINGHAM OF HYNDHOPE
1883–1963

Admiral Andrew B. Cunningham was Commander-in-Chief of the British Mediterranean Fleet from the outbreak of the Second World War until mid-1943. Throughout his long tenure his sole objective was the maintenance of British naval supremacy in the Mediterranean. In achieving this goal he oversaw a number of the Royal Navy's wartime master-strokes, including the carrier plane attack on the Italian Fleet as it lay at anchor in Taranto Harbour (11 November 1940), and the Battle of Cape Matapan (28 March 1941). During the Greek and Crete campaigns, Cunningham repeatedly sent the fleet into harm's way, almost always in waters that were under the complete control of the *Luftwaffe*. It was his determination and willingness to take risks that led to the destruction of the two German convoys carrying reinforcements to Crete, and the rescue of the bulk of the British army from first Greece and then Crete.

Cunningham was born in Dublin on 7 January 1883. He joined the Royal Navy as a cadet at the age of fourteen, making the sea his career. During the First World War he commanded a destroyer, was awarded a DSO, and reached the rank of commander. As a result of his actions during the British intervention in the Russian Civil War he received a bar to his DSO and promotion to captain. Cunningham attained flag rank in 1932. The outbreak of the Second World War found him in the Mediterranean where he served until October 1943, apart from a brief interlude from April to October 1942 when he led the British naval mission to Washington. In October 1943 Churchill recalled him to London to become First Sea Lord, a position he held until he retired in 1946.

Cunningham was knighted in 1939. In January 1945 he was made a Knight of the Thistle, and was raised to the peerage in 1945 as Baron Cunningham of Hyndhope. He was made Viscount Cunningham the following year. Other honours accorded him included the freedom of the cities of London, Edinburgh, Manchester and Hove. Cunningham died in 1963. He was buried at sea off Portsmouth.

In addition, the British fleet also undertook several lesser tasks. These included:

- the bombardment of enemy airfields;
- the screening of the Italian Fleet, the *Supermarina*; and
- the transport of supplies or escort of supply convoys to Crete.

Since the German Navy, the *Kriegsmarine*, had no warships of any note in the Mediterranean, the story of the war at sea during the Crete campaign is largely that of the operations of the Royal Navy. Under the guidance of the Commander-in-Chief of the British Mediterranean Fleet, Admiral Andrew Cunningham, the Royal Navy performed its tasks with skill and professionalism; however in undertaking these missions it suffered heavy casualties in both ships and crews. By the campaign's end the fleet had reached the limits of its operational ability, and Cunningham withdrew it from Cretan waters in order to safeguard his ships against further loss.

The fleet's losses were indeed severe. From 20 May to 1 June Cunningham had nine ships sunk, sixteen damaged and over 2,200 sailors killed. Table 3 describes naval losses during this period. Among those damaged were three Royal Australian Navy ships, the *Perth*, *Napier* and *Nizam*.

> **Lesson 16**
>
> The measure of military power is more than the sum of manpower, platforms and weapons. Moral factors, not numbers, are pre-eminent in the waging of war. Even a military force that enjoys greater numerical strength is likely to be defeated if it lacks fighting spirit.

The Italian fleet was the wild card throughout the Crete campaign. Even after its losses in the Battle of Cape Matapan, the *Supermarina*'s warships retained considerable power which on paper was stronger than that available to the overstretched British Mediterranean Fleet. However, apart from a handful of light forces that escorted the doomed convoys to Crete, the Italian Navy spent the entire campaign in a somnolent state. Despite repeated pleas from Germany, the Italian High Command refused to allow its ships to intervene. After Matapan, dishonour was preferred to the risk of further losses. If the Italians had possessed the boldness to leave port, their simple presence at sea would have curtailed Cunningham's freedom of action. It is not too difficult to imagine that, had the *Supermarina* participated in the campaign, the entire British garrison would have ended up as prisoners of war.

Table 3
Royal Navy Losses during Crete Campaign

- Unless otherwise noted ships are HMS.
- Table does not include the loss of minor vessels.

Date	Ship	Type	Fate	Out of Action
21 May	Juno	Destroyer	Sunk	
21 May	Ajax	Light Cruiser	Damaged	minor damage
22 May	Gloucester	Light Cruiser	Sunk	
22 May	Fiji	Light Cruiser	Sunk	
22 May	Naiad	Light Cruiser	Damaged	3 weeks
22 May	Valiant	Battleship	Damaged	Not out of action
22 May	Warspite	Battleship	Damaged	7 months
22 May	Carlisle	Anti-Aircraft Cruiser	Damaged	1 month
22 May	Greyhound	Destroyer	Sunk	
22 May	Kingston	Destroyer	Damaged	1 week
23 May	Kashmir	Destroyer	Sunk	
23 May	Kelly	Destroyer	Sunk	
23 May	Ilex	Destroyer	Damaged	4 days
23 May	Havock	Destroyer	Damaged	3 weeks
26 May	Formidable	Carrier	Damaged	6 months
26 May	Nubian	Destroyer	Damaged	17 months
26 May	Glenroy	Assault Ship	Damaged	minor
27 May	Barham	Battleship	Damaged	2 months
28 May	Ajax	Light Cruiser	Damaged	3 months
29 May	Imperial	Destroyer	Sunk	
29 May	Hereward	Destroyer	Sunk	
29 May	Dido	Light Cruiser	Damaged	5 months
29 May	Orion	Light Cruiser	Damaged	8.5 months
29 May	Decoy	Destroyer	Damaged	
29 May	HMAS Nizam	Destroyer	Damaged	1 week
30 May	HMAS Perth	Light Cruiser	Damaged	4.5 months
30 May	Kelvin	Destroyer	Damaged	6.5 months
31 May	HMAS Napier	Destroyer	Damaged	1 week
31 May	Calcutta	Anti-Aircraft Cruiser	Sunk	

The Interception of the German Convoys

Student's plan involved the transport of a number of reinforcements by sea. Sea movement was essential for the transport of the invasion force's heavy equipment which included armour, artillery and transport vehicles. Such equipment could not be transported by the *Luftwaffe*'s JU-52. In addition, Student planned to send some infantry reinforcements on confiscated Greek fishing boats (caiques) as this would supplement his already overcommitted transport planes.

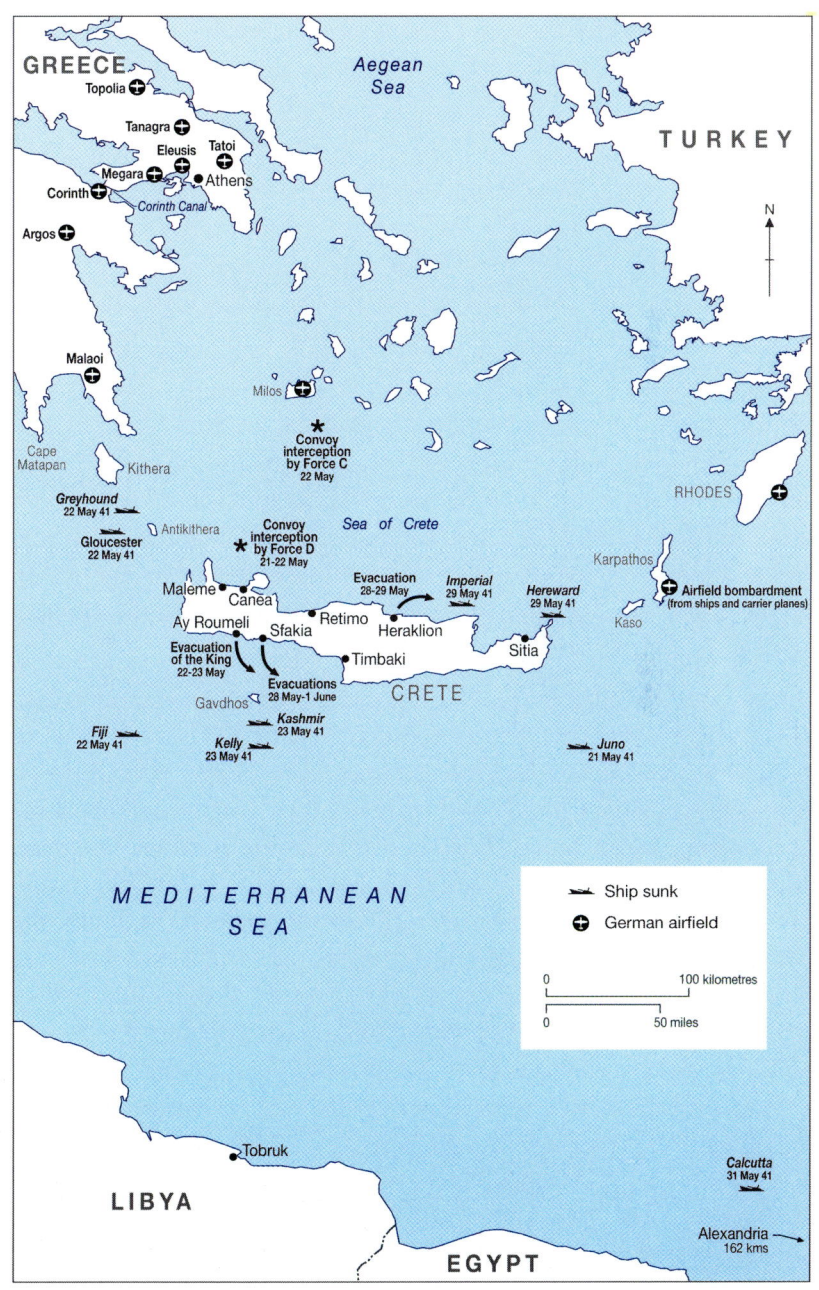

The War at Sea around Crete
Drawn by Keith Mitchell

The German naval commander for the Süd-Ost area, Admiral Karl Schüster, organised two convoys of caiques and small coastal steamers. The fishing boats were slow; even under sail their underpowered engines could barely manage four knots. The danger zone for the convoys was the 110-kilometre gap between the islands of Milos and Crete. During the daylight hours they enjoyed the protection of the *Luftwaffe*, but once the sun set the sea belonged to the Royal Navy.

Since Schüster's command had no warships he relied on his Italian ally for escorts. The *Supermarina* was willing to contribute only two small destroyers of less than 1,000 tons each, twelve motor torpedo boats, and some motor launches and minesweepers.

Alert to the convoys, Cunningham organised two task forces to patrol the waters north of Crete. On the night of 21/22 May, Force D (HMS *Dido*, *Orion*, *Ajax*, *Janus*, *Kimberley*, *Hasty* and *Hereward*), under Rear Admiral I. G. Glennie, entered the Antikithera Channel and patrolled eastward. Just before midnight, his ships' radar alerted him to the presence of the Germans. Interception took place only eighteen miles from Crete, off the coast from Canea.

The sound of heavy engines warned the Germans of the approaching ships. Shutting down the caiques' engines, the soldiers and sailors of the convoy waited in silence, hoping to avoid discovery. Then, as one of the mountain rifleman recalled, 'searchlight[s] appear[ed] like fingers of death.' Spears of light shot from Glennie's ships and locked onto the crowded caiques. As soldiers leapt into the water, salvos of fire erupted from the British ships, reducing the wooden boats to floating debris.

On the same evening, Force C entered the Aegean through Kaso Strait. Rear Admiral E. King's command consisted of HMS *Naiad*, *Carlisle*, *Calcutta*, *Kandahar*, *Kingston* and *Juno*, and HMAS *Perth*. After sweeping the Cretan coast without luck, King turned his ships northwards. Dawn found Task Force C in the northern Aegean, approaching the island of Milos. With daylight the *Luftwaffe* arrived, but King continued to press north. Then, at about 1000 hours, the British spotted a few caiques, which they dispatched. Next a destroyer reported a large party of small boats. Discovered, the German convoy scattered, making for the safety of Milos.

Greek caique loaded with German troops sinks near Crete. It is being shelled by the HMAS *Perth*.
Australian War Memorial P01345.013

A Greek caique loaded with German troops is hit by shells fired by HMAS *Perth*.
Australian War Memorial P01345.012

	Messerschmitt Bf 110
Type:	fighter/bomber
Wingspan:	16.3 m
Length:	12.3 m
Engine:	two Daimler-Benz DB 601 (809 kW each)
Max Speed:	590 kph
Range:	2410 km
Armament:	two 20 mm cannons and four 7.92 mm MG17s, all fitted in the nose of the aircraft

The *Luftwaffe*'s original concept of employment for the Bf (later Me) 110 was as a long-range Zerstörer or 'destroyer fighter'. While it enjoyed some success in the Polish and French campaigns, the aircraft performed poorly during the Battle of Britain when it was easily outmanoeuvred by the British Hurricane and Spitfire fighters. The Bf 110 was rarely used as a daylight fighter/bomber after 1940 and instead developed new roles as a night fighter and ground attack aircraft. During the Crete campaign, given the absence of effective opposition, the Bf 110 returned to its original daylight fighter/bomber role.

King faced a dilemma. He could release his ships for the chase and finish off the convoy. However, to do so would expose his ships individually to the *Luftwaffe*, which would find them easy targets. Having prevented the convoy from reaching Crete, King chose to withdraw through the Antikithera Channel, beyond which lay the Main Battle Fleet. Later Cunningham criticised King for not chasing the fleeing transports. However, King's decision was the correct one. The drowning of a few more Germans would not have materially altered the campaign, but Britain's loss of these warships would have affected not only the outcome of the struggle for Crete but the entire campaign in the eastern Mediterranean.

As the task force fled southwards, its anti-aircraft gunners put up a furious barrage as Stuka dive-bombers, Dornier bombers, and Messerschmitt 109 and Messerschmitt 110 fighters swarmed around. Miraculously, King's ships emerged from the Aegean with only the *Carlisle* and *Naiad* damaged, but once they had linked up with the Main Battle Fleet the *Luftwaffe*'s fury only increased. The British paid a heavy price for the removal of the convoys: two cruisers and a destroyer sunk, and two battleships and two cruisers damaged.

Other Missions

Of the Royal Navy's other missions the most desperate—and the most intriguing—was Cunningham's attempt to shift the campaign in Britain's favour through the projection of maritime power ashore. This called for the bombardment of enemy air bases by naval gunnery and carrier planes in order to reduce the *Luftwaffe*'s dominance of the air, thereby improving the fleet's ability to operate in daylight. The navy conducted this mission on several occasions, namely:

> **Lesson 17**
>
> It is not necessary for a commander to destroy the enemy entirely in order to meet the mission's objective. Rather, it may only be necessary to discomfort the enemy in order to remove them from the battle. To risk the destruction of your forces, after having already achieved the mission's objective, may deny a commander the necessary strength for a future operation.

- 20 May – destroyers HMS *Jervis* and *Ilex* and HMAS *Nizam* bombard the air base on Scarpanto;
- 22 May – destroyers HMS *Kelly* and *Kashmir* briefly bombard the Maleme airfield; and
- 26 May – eight aircraft from the carrier HMS *Formidable* attack the air base on Scarpanto, destroying several German and Italian planes.

The effect of these missions was negligible. In a sea space that was dominated in daylight by the enemy's planes, the British fleet was reduced to undertaking bombardment missions that were little more than raids conducted during the brief hours of darkness. Ships carrying out these missions could not remain on station sufficiently long to impede German air operations. The *Formidable* also failed to live up to its name. Its planes were obsolete, too few in number, and carried payloads too small to inflict significant damage on an airfield. At best these raids resulted in the destruction of a few enemy planes and the brief closure of a runway. None of the damage inflicted by these raids affected Germany's dominance of the air.

'N' class destroyers

Royal Australian Navy sister ships: *Napier, Nepal, Nestor, Nizam* and *Norman*

Tons:	1760
Length:	356 feet
Beam:	36 feet
Speed:	36 knots
Armament:	six 4.7-inch guns one 2-pounder forty-five depth charges ten 21-inch torpedoes
Complement:	226

HMAS *Nizam* arrives in Alexandria loaded with troops evacuated from Crete. Australian War Memorial 061018

HMAS *Perth* (1941)
Australian War Memorial P01345.001

Moreover, Cunningham paid a heavy price for these attacks. As it steamed back to Alexandria, the *Formidable's* task force was attacked by a large force of Stukas. The Germans hit the carrier twice and the destroyer HMS *Nubian* had its stern blown off. The *Formidable* was out of action for five months.

Cunningham also used his smaller ships to deliver reinforcements and supplies to Crete. These missions could not keep up with the army's demand, as the ships had only a few hours of darkness at Suda Bay to unload before racing for Kaso Strait and the relative safety of the waters south of Crete. Table 4 details the navy's supply efforts.

The Struggle in the Air

The air battle over Crete was a one-sided affair dominated by the *Luftwaffe* whose aerial strength significantly outstripped that of the Royal Air Force. Royal Air Force pilots bravely attempted to contest control of the sky, but they were too few, leading inexorably to their defeat.

The Germans allocated *VIII Flieger Corps* to the operation aimed at achieving air mastery. Its commander, General der Flieger Wolfram von Richthofen, had at his disposal about 650 aircraft, consisting of Messerschmitt 109 fighters, Messerschmitt 110 fighter bombers, Junkers 87 dive-bombers, and Junkers 88, Heinkel 111, and Dornier 17 bombers. Richthofen's mission requirements were to:

Modified Leander class cruisers

Royal Australian Navy sister ships: HMAS *Hobart*, *Perth*, and *Sydney*

Tons:	7,000
Speed:	32.5 knots
Length:	550 feet
Beam:	57 feet
Armament:	eight 6-inch guns
	eight 4-inch guns
	four 3-pounder anti-aircraft guns
	eight 21-inch torpedoes
Complement:	650

- dominate the air and sea space around Crete;
- escort the Junkers 52 transports;
- suppress British anti-aircraft fire; and
- provide the ground troops with close air support.

There were only a few British planes on Crete to oppose the enemy's air armada. The island's air defence was the responsibility of the Commander-in-Chief Royal Air Force Middle East, Air Chief Marshal Arthur M. Longmore. His was not an enviable task. His command was vast: it stretched from Crete to East Africa and from Malta to Iran. For its defence, however, he had only 650 aircraft, many of which were obsolete and of little military use. In reality, Longmore had only about 200 modern aircraft, and these he needed for the defence of Egypt and Libya.

When *VIII Flieger Corps* began its assault on 14 May, Longmore had only a handful of Hurricane and Gladiator fighters from 3, 80 and 112 Squadrons still on the island. The outcome was never in doubt. On 19 May, after losing nearly all of his planes, Longmore withdrew the surviving three aircraft to Egypt.

Table 4
British reinforcements sent to Crete

- Unless otherwise noted ships are HMS.

Date Sent	Ships	Cargo
22 May	*Glenroy, Coventry, Auckland, Flamingo*	Queen's Royal Regiment (mission aborted —returned to Alexandria)
23 May	*Jaguar, Defender*	Stores and ammunition landed at Suda
24 May	*Abdiel*	200 men of Layforce and 80 tons of stores landed at Suda
24 May	*Isis, Hero,* HMAS *Nizam*	1½ battalions of Layforce (mission aborted due to sea conditions at Sfakia)
25 May	*Glenroy, Stuart, Coventry, Jaguar*	Queen's Royal Regiment (mission aborted —returned to Alexandria)
26 May	*Calcutta, Auckland Defender,* escorting two merchant ships	Aborted due to bad weather and sea conditions.
26 May	*Abdiel, Hero,* HMAS *Nizam*	750 men of Layforce and stores landed at Suda

The Air War around Crete
Drawn by Keith Mitchell

Once battle was joined, the *Luftwaffe* subjected Creforce to intensive bombardment and strafing, and any movement in daylight quickly drew the attention of the ever-present fighters, fighter bombers and dive-bombers. The *Luftwaffe* also controlled the waters around Crete making any naval manoeuvre hazardous.

Longmore did attempt to contest German control of the sky, but his efforts were mere gestures that proved costly and futile. Bombers attacked *Luftwaffe* airbases in Greece, but with no appreciable effect on German air operations. The Royal Air Force also tried to prevent the Germans from landing reinforcements at the Maleme airfield. On 24 May, eight Wellington bombers attacked the airfield, followed the next day by a force of Hurricanes and Blenheims. These raids did cause some casualties, but were insufficient to deter the Germans from deploying *5 Gebirgs Division* to Crete.

Gloster Gladiator

Type:	fighter
Wingspan:	9.8 m
Length:	8.5 m
Engine:	one Bristol Mercury VIII AS (630 kW)
Max Speed:	414 kph @ 4500 m
Range:	700 km
Armament:	four 0.303-in (7.7 mm) Browning machine-guns

In 1937 the Gloster Gladiator was the last biplane to enter service with the Royal Air Force. By that time, however, its capabilities had already been eclipsed by the next generation of monoplane fighters, including the Spitfire and Messerschmitt. Initially sent to France, it was no match for the superior German planes. It was only in North Africa, against the Italians, that the Gladiator was able to achieve some degree of success. In the Greece and Crete campaigns it was once again completely outclassed by the German fighters.

Messerschmitt Bf 109E

Type:	fighter
Wingspan:	10 m
Length:	8.6 m
Engine:	one Daimler Benz DB 601A (1085 kW)
Max Speed:	578 kph @ 3700 m
Range:	966 km
Armament:	one 20 mm MG-FF/M nose-mounted cannon, and four 7.9 mm MG-17 machine-guns

Commonly referred to as the Me 109, the Bf 109 first flew in 1934 and saw early combat service with the German Condor Legion in the Spanish Civil War. The 109E, which was the most common model during the Crete campaign, was introduced into service with the *Luftwaffe* in 1939. The Bf 109E was superior to the British Hurricane Mark I in combat and far better than the Gloster Gladiator. Its performance equalled that of the early British Spitfires.

Throughout the battle for Crete, the soldiers of Creforce rarely saw a friendly plane—an observation often remarked upon in the campaign's documentation. Longmore was not unaware of or insensitive to the effect of the enemy's total control of the air on Creforce's operational ability. Accordingly, on 23 May, he dispatched twelve Hurricanes to Heraklion in an attempt to re-establish a presence on the island. It was another ill-considered gesture. En route the Hurricanes passed over some Royal Navy vessels that promptly shot down two and forced three more to return to Egypt. The incident was a further example of the lack of coordination between the services. Of the seven that reached Heraklion the Germans immediately destroyed one on the ground and shot down the remainder in air-to-air combat.

Destruction of the Crete Airbases

Why did the British leave the airfields intact for the enemy to capture and use? Had the British destroyed the airfields, the paratroopers, denied air-landing support, would have perished.

The explanation is two-fold. First, the airfields would have been difficult to destroy. They were simple affairs, little more than grass or packed dirt strips, from which transport planes could easily operate. Any long-term destruction would have required a major engineering program that was beyond Creforce's capabilities in the days immediately prior to the invasion. Any lesser destruction such as cratering was easily repairable with a few loads of dirt and rock.

Damage sufficient to deny the Germans use of the airfields for a period greater than the endurance limit of the *Fallschirmjäger* required extensive and considered destruction that would have had to commence much sooner, and certainly while the airfields were still being used by the British. This was not a measure that the Royal Air Force command would countenance while it still had planes capable of operations on Crete, nor did Freyberg have the right or the strength of character to undertake the necessary destruction on his own authority.

The Royal Air Force's attitude reflects a single service mentality that paid no heed to either the realities of the unfolding strategic situation, nor the nature of the threat that the ground force was about to confront. Longmore could not send aircraft to Crete in sufficient numbers within the looming campaign's time-frame in order to realistically challenge the might of *VIII Flieger Corps* because such aircraft did not exist. The Royal Air Force had preserved airfields for which it had no squadrons and, in so doing, made them available to the enemy.

German bombers attack Creforce positions.
Australian War Memorial P00090.069

Hawker Hurricane Mark I

Type: fighter
Wingspan: 12.2 m
Length: 9.6 m
Engine: one Rolls Royce Merlin engine (954 kW)
Max Speed: 510 kph @ 5400 m
Range: 966 km
Armament: eight 0.303-in (7.7 mm) Browning machine-guns (four on each wing)

When the Hawker Hurricane first appeared in 1935, it was the world's most heavily armed fighter, and Britain's first to achieve a rated speed in excess of 300 mph (483kph). Accepted into the Royal Air Force in 1937, the Hurricane played a major role in the Battle of Britain. The version employed in the Mediterranean theatres was 'tropicalised' in that it had dust filters fitted to the engine air intake and other modifications added to protect the aircraft from desert conditions.

AFTERMATH

Casualties

The Germans paid a heavy price for their victory. The German War Graves Cemetery at Maleme contains the remains of 4,465 soldiers. The Germans lost a further 2,600 wounded. Aircraft casualties were also high. The Junkers transports of *XI Fliegerkorps* suffered an approximate 50 per cent casualty rate. About 120 Ju-52s were destroyed and more than 100 damaged. In the plus column, the Germans released 14,000 Italian prisoners of war.

Although the Commonwealth forces suffered fewer fatalities, their overall casualties were much higher due to the loss of more than 12,000 men as prisoners of war. The Commonwealth War Graves Cemetery on the shores of Suda Bay contains the remains of 1,509 British, Australian, New Zealand, and other Commonwealth personnel. Table 5 details the British casualties.

Ironically, with the campaign's end, the strategic rationale for the operation passed. On 22 June 1941 Hitler sent the German Army into the Soviet Union. Henceforth, for Germany, the Eastern Front became the principal theatre and the Mediterranean declined in importance. Student's bold plan to use his paratroopers to leap across the sea and drive the British from Egypt would not come to fruition. While it was a success, the campaign, with its heavy losses, spelled the end of parachute warfare for Germany, and Hitler never again authorised a division-size parachute operation. Except for the drop on Leros in 1943, and a few commando-style missions, the *Fallschirmjäger* spent the remainder of the war fighting as line infantry.

With its loss, Crete also became a backwater for the British. The real danger to Egypt was the onslaught of the *Afrika Korps* from Libya, not a paratrooper-led invasion from the north. In addition, with the development of the long-range four-engined bomber, Crete's airfields were no longer essential as bases from which to attack the enemy's industry. Churchill, on the other hand, drew the opposite conclusion to Hitler on the effectiveness of paratrooper warfare. Consequently, the British and their future ally the United States invested heavily in a paratrooper arm.

Peace did not come to the island with the campaign's end. Instead, the British evacuation opened the resistance phase of the Cretan people's battle against the Germans. For the rest of the war partisans waged a guerrilla war against the invaders, and German soldiers ventured into the island's mountainous interior only in large numbers.

The German cemetery on Hill 107 overlooking the Maleme airfield.
Photo courtesy of author.

The Commonwealth War Graves Cemetery at Suda Bay.
Photo courtesy of author.

Table 5
British casualties on Crete

Type	KIA/DOW	Wounded	POW	Total
British Army	612	224	5,315	6,151
Royal Marines	114	30	1,035	1,179
Royal Air Force	71	9	226	306
Australian	274	507	3,102	3,883
New Zealand	671	967	2,180	3,818
Cypriots and Palestinians	9	1	396	406
TOTAL	1,751	1,738	12,254	15,743

Lessons

In the wake of Britain's ignominious end to the campaign, a number of officers presented their opinions as to what went wrong. Many of their ideas were practical, tactical-level observations which were easy to implement. These included the recommendation that all units should have small arms on their equipment establishment so that they could take responsibility for their own defence. Other recommendations concerned the importance of laying out dummy anti-aircraft positions, and the suggestion that helmets be camouflaged so as not to reflect the sun and thereby attract the attention of the *Luftwaffe*.

Yet the British lacked the honesty and introspective skills required to identify and implement more fundamental lessons. Once Inglis had recovered in Cairo, Wavell dispatched him to London to discuss the lessons of the campaign. He reported three items of note:

- the British soldier was tactically superior to the German;
- the army had fought well with the bayonet; and
- the enemy's control of the sky was the primary reason for the defeat.

Inglis's statements echoed those of Wavell. Yet these were not lessons that would produce any improvement in the army's ability to wage future battles.

Cretan partisans.
Imperial War Museum HU66036

Rifle, SMLE .303 in, No.1, Mark 3*

Calibre:	.303 inch
Operation:	manual; bolt operation; magazine fed
Magazine:	10 rounds
Weight (empty):	4.1 kg
Weight (loaded):	4.4 kg
Length:	1130 mm
Sights:	183 to 1828 metres
Effective Range:	up to 274 metres (individual fire), up to 548 metres (section fire)
Rate of Fire:	5 rpm (normal), 15 rpm (rapid)

The short magazine Lee Enfield (SMLE) No.1, Mark 3* was one of the most widely produced weapons of its day, with some 27 models manufactured. A weapon of particular significance to the Australian Army, the SMLE remained its primary infantry weapon throughout the First World War, Second World War and Korean War. Ruggedly constructed, very reliable and trusted by the troops, this rifle was accurate over extreme small arms distances and could be fitted with a scope for use as a sniper rifle. It could also be fitted with a Pattern 1907 bayonet and a grenade discharger cup for the projection of hand grenades.

The *Luftwaffe*'s domination of the air was an oft-repeated refrain both during and after the campaign. There is no doubt that airpower was a factor that Student used to his advantage. Yet the primary threat to the British hold on the island was always the enemy's ground forces rather than his planes. The lesson British ground commanders failed to learn was that, in the absence of friendly aircraft, it was their responsibility to find the means to negate the enemy's aerial prowess. For example, the defenders could have made the *Luftwaffe*'s task more difficult by maintaining close contact with the enemy, making it harder for pilots to distinguish between friend and foe. Instead, they consistently fell back, created belts of no-man's land, and established fixed lines that were easily identifiable from the air.

In the final analysis the British lost the struggle for Crete because they were unwilling to pay the price required to hold the island. During the campaign's first few days the outcome hung by a thread—particularly for the Germans in the New Zealand Division's sectors. Yet those responsible for the defence of Maleme and Prison Valley did not seize the chance to snip that thread when the opportunity presented itself. The contrast in reaction between the German and the New Zealand commanders in those first crucial days is illuminating. Student pushed transports into Maleme 'heedless of fire' and, in so doing, knowingly inflicted horrendous casualties on his men. This very act, however, made the German victory possible. Afterwards the British described Student's determination as 'criminal prodigality.'

Freyberg, by contrast, recognised the situation as 'precarious' as he watched the enemy's transports land but was unable to motivate himself or his subordinates into making the necessary maximum effort. Instead, his battalion commanders reported that nothing more could be done without 'more infantry, artillery and air support', a vain quest since, by the time these resources arrived, the chance would have passed, while Hargest, the brigade commander responsible for Maleme, in the words of one official historian, 'sat like a man bemused when the fate of the invasion … balanced on a knife edge.' Kippenberger later critiqued the performance of his fellow officers. He wrote that 'in each case they adopted a course that made victory impossible … fundamental mistakes irretrievable by the valour and devotion of those under their command.'

After the war Freyberg captured the sense of the malaise that gripped him and many of his subordinates on Crete. He wrote, 'They [the Germans] were determined to take Crete, and they were prepared to go to any length to get it.' He concluded, 'no sacrifice was too great for them to make.' What he could not admit was that he was unable to go to any length to keep it.

Rifle, Kar 98k (Kar—Karabiner—Carbine)

Calibre:	7.92 mm
Operation:	manual, bolt action
Magazine:	5 rounds
Weight (empty):	3.59 kg
Length:	1105 mm
Sights:	100 to 2000 metres
Effective Range:	up to 500 metres
Rate of Fire:	10-15 rpm

An evolution on the original Mauser Gewehr (Gew 98) which was introduced into the German armed forces in 1898, the 'k' in this model number stood for 'kurz' (short). Appearing in 1939, this was a reliable and accurate infantry weapon. The Mauser style of bolt action featured in this rifle is still in use today. The 98 k was the standard infantry rifle in use by the German forces on Crete.

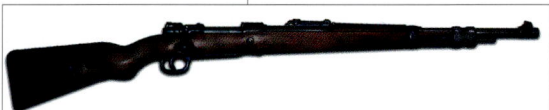

A line of British prisoners march into captivity.
National Library of New Zealand DA-12646

Further Reading

- Admiralty Historical Section, *Naval Operations in the Battle of Crete: 20 May–1 June 1941* (1960). This brief book is largely a chronological recounting of the facts associated with the Crete campaign. Its main benefit lies in its detailed appendices on technical matters, ship losses, organisation and command. However, the book's lack of historical perspective and interpretation limits its function to that of a reference source.

- Peter D. Antill, *Crete 1941: Germany's Lightning Airborne Assault* (2005). This work is listed as number 147 in Osprey Publishing's Campaign series. Well-illustrated, it provides a useful introduction to the battle.

- Anthony Beevor, *Crete: The Battle and the Resistance* (1991). A sound introduction to the Battle of Crete by a master of narrative history, Beevor's work is a balanced account which provides a useful starting point and some depth of analysis.

- Alan Clark, *The Fall of Crete* (1962). Once the best introductory work on the Crete campaign, Clark's book has now been surpassed by Beevor's volume as a quality introductory text.

- D. M. Davin, *Crete* (1953). Davin's New Zealand official history is the most comprehensive study of the Crete campaign written to date. Despite its age, it remains a basic reference work for the operation. Davin's focus is on the tactical level of war. The book's only limitation is its concentration on the New Zealand experience. A study that treats the British and Australian contingents with similar depth is yet to be written.

The Lagonikachis, one of many Cretan families who helped stranded Australian soldiers during the occupation. Australian War Memorial 131012

- Chris Ellis, *7th Flieger Division: Student's Fallschirmjäger Elite* (2002). This book is part of the Spearhead series published by Ian Allan. Its 96 pages cover the organisation, training, weaponry and operations of the *7th Flieger Division* during the Second World War. As such, it is a mini-history of German airborne forces. The book is well endowed with photographs and illustrations.

- George Forty, *Battle of Crete* (2001). Forty's work is largely a photographic account of the campaign, supported by narrative and eyewitness accounts.

- *The German Campaigns in the Balkans (Spring 1941)* (1953). This booklet forms part of a series compiled by the United States Army to examine the lessons of the Second World War from the German perspective. It relies almost totally on German sources and is a useful corrective to Anglo–American accounts. The Crete campaign receives four short chapters. Despite its brevity this is an important work.

- Michael Howard, *The Mediterranean Strategy in the Second World War* (1968). This short book is the essential starting point for a proper examination of the Mediterranean campaigns of the Second World War. Although it makes only passing reference to Crete, the book places the campaign into its broader context. It is well worth reading.

- Colonel E. G. Keogh, *Middle East 1939–43* (1959). Published by the Australian Army's Directorate of Military Training, this volume covers the war in the Mediterranean up to the capture of Tripoli, with the exception of Operation *Torch*. Despite some factual errors, it provides a reasonable account of the battle.

- Gavin Long, *Greece, Crete and Syria* (1953). Only 123 pages are devoted to the Crete campaign in this volume of the Australian official history of the Second World War. That said, Long's chapters on Crete are first rate. More maps would have been helpful, but the narrative is informative and well written.

- James Lucas, *Storming Eagles: German Airborne Forces in World War II* (1988). This is a popular history of German paratrooper forces in the Second World War. It covers initial operations in Scandinavia up to the last days of the Third Reich. There is just one chapter on Crete.

- MacDonald, *The Lost Battle: Crete 1941* (1993). Solidly written with an engaging style, this is a fine account of the battle for Crete. If Stewart's book (see below) cannot be located, then read this one.

- Jean-Yves Nass, *Fallschirmjäger in Crete* (2002). A coffee-table book on the campaign from the German perspective, this volume contains many photographs not found in English language works.

- S. O. Playfair, *The Mediterranean and the Middle East: The Germans come to the Help of their Ally: 1941* (1956). Playfair's five-volume official history of the British in the Mediterranean devotes only a single chapter to the Crete campaign. This is perhaps suggestive of a desire to forget the disaster that befell the Empire on the island, and Playfair goes to some length to justify British unpreparedness. Despite this, the chapter successfully outlines the main issues the defenders faced, and provides a reasonably balanced account at the strategic and operational levels.

- Bruce Quarrie, *German Airborne Troops 1939-45* (1983). This work is listed as number 139 in the Osprey Publishing Men-At-Arms series. It is well endowed with the photographs and art work for which this series is justly renowned. While a convenient work for accessing illustrations, its reading should be combined with a work of more substance.

- Bruce Quarrie, *German Airborne Divisions, Blitzkrieg 1940-41* (2004). This publication is listed as number 4 in the Osprey Publishing Battle Orders series. Its emphasis is on organisation and the book contains numerous orbat charts, establishment lists and wire diagrams. As is the case with all Osprey works, it is well illustrated.

- Christopher Shores and Brian Cull, *Air War for Yugoslavia, Greece and Crete, 1940-41* (1987). This book's strengths are its photographs and orders of battle. Unfortunately, the narrative is so overwhelmed by minutiae that it effectively impedes understanding. This is, however, the only readily available work dedicated to the campaign's air operations.

- Tony Simpson, *Operation Mercury: The Battle for Crete*, 1941 (1981). This book had the potential to be an important contribution to Crete campaign literature, but is ruined by the author's agenda. A New Zealander, Simpson set out to show that the New Zealand defeat was the result of a Churchillian conspiracy to force the Germans to attack the Balkans.

- I. McD. G. Stewart, *The Struggle for Crete: A Story of Lost Opportunity, 20 May–1 June 1941* (1966). This is the outstanding book on the Crete campaign. Readers should start with Beevor's book and then move on to the deeper analysis and coverage provided by Stewart. A veteran of 1 Welch Battalion on Crete, Stewart does not allow his status as an eye witness to overwhelm his work. The result is a well-balanced, engaging book that is critical and fair.

- David A. Thomas, *Crete 1941, The Battle at Sea* (1972). While written entirely from published sources, Thomas's book does a decent job of capturing the flavour of the naval war around Crete, although the first half of the book actually concerns the preceding Greek campaign.

British-German Officer Rank Equivalents

German Rank	British Rank
Generalfeldmarschall	Field Marshal
Generaloberst	General
General der . . . (insert name of arm, for example General der Flieger)	Lieutenant-General
Generalleutnant	Major-General
Generalmajor	Brigadier
Oberst	Colonel
Oberstleutnant	Lieutenant-Colonel
Major	Major
Hauptmann	Captain
Oberleutnant	Lieutenant
Leutnant	Second Lieutenant

Bibliography

Unpublished Sources

Australian War Memorial

    AWM52 – 2 AIF Unit War Diaries
    AWM54 – Written Records, 1939-45 War
    AWM67 – Official History, 1939-45 Records of Gavin Long
    Map Collection
    Film Collection
    Photographic Collection
    Bunning Papers, PR03192
    Campbell Papers, PR82/186
    Eager Papers, PR84/106
    Hackshaw Papers, 3DRL6398
    History of 2/3 Field Regiment, MSS1222
    Nagle Papers, PR89/148
    Smith Papers, PR91/085
    Traub Collection, PR90/186
    Walker Collection, PR00178
    Wilson Papers, PR01343/3

Imperial War Museum

    Photographic Collection

National Library of New Zealand

    Photographic Collection

Published Sources

Anon, *The First at War*, 1987.
Anon, *White over Green*, Angus and Robertson.
Admiralty, *Naval Operations in the Battle of Crete* (Historical Section).
Antill, Peter D., *Crete 1941: Germany's Lightning Airborne Assault*, Osprey Publishing, 2005.
Beevor, Anthony, *Crete: The Battle and the Resistance*, Penguin, 1992.
Bolger, W. P., and J. G. Littlewood, *The Fiery Phoenix: The Story of the 2/7nd Australian Infantry Battalion, 1939-1946*, 2/7 Battalion Association.
Chamberlain, P., and H. Doyle, *Encyclopedia of German Tanks of World War Two*, Cassell, 1999.
Clark, Alan, *The Fall of Crete*, Anthony Blond, 1962.
Clarke, Michael, *My War 1939-1945*, Michael Clarke Press, 1990.
Cody, J. F., *New Zealand Engineers, Middle East*, Department of Internal Affairs: War History Branch, 1961.
Darman, P. (ed.), *Small Arms of the World*, Grange Books, 2004.
Davin, D. M., *Crete*, Department of Internal Affairs: War History Branch, 1953.
Dawson, W. D., *18 Battalion and Armoured Regiment*, Department of Internal Affairs: War History Branch, 1961.
Dear, I. C. B. (ed.), *The Oxford Companion to the Second World War*, Oxford University Press, 1995.
Edwards, Roger, *German Airborne Troops, 1936-45*, Macdonald and Jane's, 1974.
Ellis, Chris, *7th Flieger Division: Student's Fallschirmjäger Elite*, Ian Allan, 2002.

The victors examine the ruins of Canea.
Imperial War Museum HU66983

Ethell, J. L., *Eagles over North Africa and the Mediterranean, 1940-44*, Greenhill Books, 1997.
Farran, Roy, *Winged Dagger: Adventures on Special Service*, Arms and Armour Press, 1986.
Forty, George, *Battle of Crete*, Ian Allan, 2001.
Harper, Glyn, *Kippenberger: An Inspired New Zealand Commander*, Harper Collins, 1997.
Henderson, Jim, *22 Battalion*, Department of Internal Affairs: War History Branch, 1958.
Hocking, Philip, *The Long Carry: A History of the 2/1st Australian Machine Gun Battalion, 1939-46*, 2/1 Machine Gun Battalion Association, 1997.
Hogg, I. V., *The Encyclopedia of Infantry Weapons of World War II*, Regent Books, 1984.
——, *Allied Armour of World War Two*, Crowood Press, 2000.
Horner, David, in John Ritchie and Diane Langmore (eds.), *Australian Dictionary of Biography*, vol. XVI, Australian National University, pp. 440-42.
Howard, Michael, *The Mediterranean Strategy in the Second World War*, Greenhill Books, 1993.
Jackson, R., *Air Aces of World War II*, Airlife Publishers, 2003.
Kidson, A. L., *Petrol Company*, Department of Internal Affairs: War History Branch, 1961.
Kippenberger, Howard, *Infantry Brigadier*, Oxford University Press, 1949.
Latimer, J., *Operation Compass, 1940*, Osprey Publishing, 2000.
Long, Gavin, *Greece, Crete and Syria*, Australian War Memorial, 1953.
Loughnan, R. J. M., *Divisional Cavalry*, Department of Internal Affairs: War History Branch, 1963.
MacDonald, Callum, *The Lost Battle: Crete 1941*, Macmillan, 1993.
McGibbon, Ian (ed.), *The Oxford Companion to New Zealand Military History*, Oxford University Press, 2000.
Murray, Williamson and Allan R. Millett, *A War to be Won: Fighting the Second World War*, Belknap Press, 2000.
Nasse, Jean-Yves, *Fallschirmjäger in Crete*, Histoire & Collections, 2002.
Nowarra, H. J., *The Flying Pencil: Dornier DO 17 & 215*, Schiffer Military Aviation Series, 1990.
——, *Junkers Ju 52*, Schiffer Military Aviation Series, 1993.
Parrish, Thomas, *The Simon and Schuster Encyclopedia of World War II*, Simon & Schuster, 1978.
Quarrie, Bruce, *German Airborne Troops, 1939-45*, Osprey Publishing, 2003.
——, *German Airborne Divisions: Blitzkrieg 1940-41*, Osprey Publishing, 2004.
Regnat, K., *Heinkel HE 111*, Midland Publishing, 2004.
Roskill, S. W., *The War at Sea, 1939-1945, vol.1, The Defensive*, HMSO, 1954.
Ross, Angus, *23 Battalion*, Department of Internal Affairs: War History Branch, 1959.
Sarson, P. and T. Hadler, *German Light Panzers 1932-42*, Osprey Publishing, 1998.
Scutts, J., *Bf109 Aces of North Africa and the Mediterranean*, Osprey Publishing, 2003.
Simpson, Michael (ed.), *The Cunningham Papers*, Navy Records Society, 1999.
Stewart, I. McD. G., *The Struggle for Crete: A Story of Lost Opportunity*, Oxford University Press, 1991.
Thomas, David A., *Crete 1941: The Battle at Sea*, Andre Deutsch, 1972.
Trevor-Roper, H. R. (ed.), *Blitzkrieg to Defeat: Hitler's War Directives 1939-1945*, Holt, Rinehart and Winston, 1971.
Weal, J., *Junkers JU87: Stukageschwader of North Africa and the Mediterranean*, Osprey Publishing, 1998.
——, *Messerschmitt Bf110 Zerstorer*, Osprey Publishing, 1999.
Weeks, John, *Airborne Equipment: A History of its Development*, David & Charles, 1976.

Websites

Admiral of the Fleet Viscount Cunningham of Hyndhope, at www.royal-navy.mod.uk/static/pages/3522.html

Aircraft at www.battleofbritain.net/

Andrew Cunningham, Royal Naval Museum Information Sheet No. 3, at www.royalnavalmuseum.org/info_sheets_andrew cunningham.html

Bf109 aircraft at www.bf109.com/frameset.html

Digger History at www.diggerhistory.info/

JU52 Factory at www.ju52-3m.ch/about

JU52 Museum at www.ig-ju52.de/ju52engl.htm

Luftwaffe Resource Group at www.warbirdsresource group.org

Major-General Ian Ross Campbell at www.awm.gov.au/units/people_2038.asp

New South Wales Lancers Memorial Museum Association at www.lancers.org

New Zealand Biographies at www.dnzb.govt.nz

RAF Museum at www.rafmuseum.org.uk/

Index

A

aircraft
    Dornier Do 17 41
    Gloster Gladiator 158
    Hawker Hurricane 159
    Heinkel 111 83
    Junkers 52 26, 27, 41, 110, 160
    Junkers 87B (Stuka) 123
    Messerschmitt Bf 109E 158
    Messerschmitt Bf 110 153
Akrotiri Peninsula 64-65
Alikianou 59, 63, 69, 72
Allen, J. M. 38, 104
Altman, Gustav 64
Anderson, J. 108
Andrew, Leslie W. 33, 36-38, 47-51, 104-105
Armenoi 138
Askifou Plain 141
Australian Army
    I Corps HQ 22
    I Corps Signals 22
    2/1 Battalion 22, 87, 89-90, 91, 99-101
    2/1 Field Ambulance 22, 56
    2/1 Field Company 22
    2/1 Machine Gun Battalion 22, 87-90, 91, 94, 130, 138
    2/1 Ordnance Store Company 22, 87, 91
    2/2 Battalion 15, 22
    2/2 Field Ambulance 22, 56
    2/2 Field Park Company 22
    2/2 Field Regiment 22, 55
    2/2 Ordnance Store Company 22
    2/3 Battalion 15, 22
    2/3 Field Company 87
    2/3 Field Regiment 21, 22, 55, 86, 87-88, 90, 91, 99, 109
    2/4 Battalion 22, 74, 77, 82-83
    2/5 Battalion 22
    2/6 Battalion 22
    2/7 Battalion 22, 87, 88, 110, 132, 139, 144
    2/7 Field Ambulance 22, 56, 87, 91
    2/7 Light Anti-Aircraft Battery 22, 32, 35, 55, 75
    2/8 Battalion 22, 72, 86-88, 90, 127, 139
    2/8 Field Company 22, 87-88, 91
    2/11 Battalion 22, 87, 90, 98, 126
    5 General Hospital 22
    6 Division 5, 18, 22
    6 Division Australian Army Service Corps 22
    6 Division Field Cash Office 22
    6 Division HQ 22
    6 Division Intelligence Section 22
    6 Division Postal Unit 22
    6 Division Reception Camp 22
    6 Division Signals 22
    7 Division Provost Company 22
    9 Division 9
    16 Brigade Composite Battalion 15, 55
    16 Brigade HQ 22
    17 Brigade Composite Battalion 22, 55
    17 Brigade HQ 22
    19 Brigade 19, 25, 86, 89-90, 115, 128-130, 137
    19 Brigade HQ 22, 87, 88
    40 Light Aid Detachment 22
    80 Light Aid Detachment 22
    AIF Postal Unit 22
    Australian Army Service Corps 55
    Australian Signals Detail 87, 88
    Australian Stevedores 55
    Base Area Unit Finance Section 22
    Ordnance Proving Section 22
    RAASC 85, 91
    Signals Construction Section 87, 88
    Staging Camp 22

B

Babali Hani 138
Balkan campaign, German 5
Beamish, G. R. 24, 53
Blamey, Thomas 24
Bräuer, Bruno 76, 79, 85, 121
Braun, Franz 43
British Army;
    chain of command on Crete 24
    failure to improve Crete's defensive capability 13-15
    1 Field Bakery 56
    1 Light Troop, 57, 61, 69
    1 Petrol Depot 56
    1 Rangers (9 Battalion KRRC) 54, 55, 127, 129-130
    1 Welch Battalion 54-55, 61, 66, 73, 113, 129-130
    2 Argyll and Sutherland Battalion 74-75, 121
    2 Black Watch 75, 76, 121
    2 Leicesters 75, 76, 84
    2 Yorks and Lancs 75, 76, 84
    3 Hussars 57, 74-75, 103, 116, 119
    4 Field Ambulance 56
    5 Independent Brigade Workshop 56
    7 General Hospital 57, 67
    7 Medium Regiment 74-75, 76
    7 Royal Tank Regiment 21, 31, 32, 34, 74, 75, 87, 91
    11 Search Light Regiment 55
    14 Brigade 17, 73-74, 75
    14 Brigade Signal Section 75
    15 Coast Regiment 55, 75
    26 Field Bakery 56
    42 Field Company 55, 75

48 Field Hygiene Section 56
52 Light Anti-aircraft Regiment 55
52 Light Anti-aircraft Workshop 56
101 Petrol Company 56
106 Battery RHA 54, 87, 88
129 Light Anti-aircraft Battery 55
151 Heavy Anti-aircraft Battery 55
156 Light Anti-Aircraft Battery 32, 35, 55, 75
168 Field Ambulance 56
189 Field Ambulance 56, 75
231 Motor Transport Company 56
234 Heavy Anti-aircraft Battery 55, 66
234 Medium Battery 75
304 Search Light Battery 55
606 Palestine Pioneer Company 56
1003 Docks Op Company 55
1004 Cypriot Pioneer Company 56
1005 Cypriot Pioneer Company 56
1007 Cypriot Pioneer Company 56
1008 Cypriot Pioneer Company 56
1017 Dock Op Company 75
1038 Arab Stevedore Company 75
Base Pay and Field Cash Office 56
Commander Royal Engineers 75
Crete Composite Company 55
Creforce HQ 53
Creforce HQ Signals 53
Layforce 137-138, 156
Northumberland Hussars 54-55, 65, 129-130
Royal Army Service Corps 56, 75
Royal Engineers Stores Depot 55
Royal Perivolians 55, 61, 129
Suda Bay Detachment 56
Suda Sector Signals 55
Queen's Royal Regiment 156
Burckhardt 79, 83

C

Campbell, Ian 19, 89, 93, 95, 98-99, 100-101, 124, 127
Campbell, T. C. 45
Canea sector 28, 39, 52, 57-58, 67, 73, 120, 127
casualties
    Commonwealth 160, 162
    German 160
Cemetery Hill 58, 60, 69-70
chain of command
    British 24
    German 23
Chappel, B. H. 14, 74-76, 121, 124
Churchill, Winston S. 7, 9, 162
Clark, Michael 86
Creforce 22, 26
    Appointment of Freyberg 17-18
    headquarters organisation 53
    inadequate communication system 19-20, 27, 103, 114, 142
    lack of equipment 20-22, 27, 95
    lack of staff officers 17-18, 52

Crete
    geography 13, 28
    strategic interests for Germany 11
Cunningham, Andrew 24, 147-148, 151, 153, 155

D

Davin, D. M. 66
Dittmer, G. 38
Duncan A. 129-130

E

East Hill 77, 121
Enigma 25
evacuation 143
    from Heraklion 123, 141
    from Sfakia 134, 140-144

F

Fallschirmjäger (see German Army)
Farran, Roy 119-120
Force C 151-153
Force D 151
Forrester, Michael 72
42nd Street 129-132
Freyberg, B. C. 14, 18, 24, 27, 51, 52-54, 58, 74, 96, 108, 110, 112-113, 115, 129, 133, 135-136, 140, 142, 144, 160, 164
    challenges 17-18
    comments on lack of equipment 20
    concerns over a sea-borne assault 25-26
    defence plan 28
    relationship with Inglis 102

G

Galatas, battle of 118-120
Galatas Heights 70-72, 102, 115, 117-118, 120
Galloway, A. 14
Gambier-Parry, M. D. 14
Genz, Alfred 66
Georgeoupolis 86, 88-89
Gericke, Walther 39, 105
German Army
    I Battalion, 1 Fallschirmjäger, Regiment 79, 85
    I Battalion, 2 Fallschirmjäger, Regiment 68, 71, 95
    I Battalion, 3 Fallschirmjäger, Regiment 63, 67-69, 71-72
    II Battalion, 1 Fallschirmjäger Regiment 79
    II Battalion, 2 Fallschirmjäger Regiment 79, 84
    II Battalion, 3 Fallschirmjäger Regiment 63, 68, 72
    III Battalion, 1 Fallschirmjäger Regiment 79, 84
    III Battalion, 2 Fallschirmjäger Regiment 95, 98
    III Battalion, 3 Fallschirmjäger Regiment 63, 67, 72
    I Battalion, Luftlande Sturmregiment 39, 40, 43, 62-64
    II Battalion, Luftlande Sturmregiment 39, 44, 45, 46
    III Battalion, Luftlande Sturmregiment 39, 41-42
    IV Battalion, Luftlande Sturmregiment 39, 44, 45
    3 Fallschirmjäger Regiment 62-63, 67, 115, 127, 129
    5 Gebirgs Division 23, 46, 105, 107-108, 139

7 Flieger Division 23, 39, 62, 106
85 Gebirgsjäger Regiment 108, 115, 128-129, 138
95 Gebirgspionier Battalion 46,115
95 Gebirgsartillerie Regiment 115
100 Gebirgsjäger Regiment 108, 115, 129, 139
141 Gebirgsjäger Regiment 115, 129, 132
Afrika Korps 9, 162
Fallschirmflak Battalion 62-63, 79
Fallschirmmaschinengewehr Battalion 62-63, 95
Fallschirmpionier Battalion 62-63, 69, 72
Luftlande Sturmregiment 38-39, 41, 105-106, 115
Wittman Group 139
German plans (see 'plans')
Glennie, I. G. 151
Gray, J. R. 118
Greek Army 5, 9
    1 Greek Regiment 31-32, 46-47
    2 Greek Regiment 55, 61, 69, 115, 127
    3 Greek Regiment 75, 76
    4 Greek Regiment 87, 90, 91
    5 Greek Regiment 87, 90, 91
    6 Greek Regiment 57-58, 61, 69, 71
    7 Greek Regiment 75, 76
    8 Greek Regiment 57, 61, 69, 72, 115, 128, 138
    Cretan Infantry Division 13
    Cretan Police Academy Force 87, 90, 91
    Greek Garrison Battalion 75, 76
Greek campaign 9, 15, 47, 90

H

Hackshaw, A. 126
Hargest, James 31, 34, 48, 51, 100, 104-105, 108, 140, 164
    placement of forces at Maleme 32-38
Heidrich, Richard 63, 70
Heraklion 28-29, 73-74, 76-77, 80, 140
    battle for 82-85, 121-123
    British organisation 75
    German plans 76, 79-80
Heydte, von der 72
Hill 107 33, 36, 39, 40, 43, 45, 47, 104-105, 161
Hill A 93, 95, 99-101
Hill B 93, 98
Hitler, Adolf 6, 9, 11, 160

I

Inglis, Lindsay Merritt 58, 102, 117-118, 163
intelligence
    British 25-26
    German 26
Italy
    in Crete 123
    in Greece 8-9
    in North Africa 8

J

Johnson, S. H. 48
Jones, Frederick 102

K

Kalami 139
Kastelli 46-47
King, E. 151, 153
Kippenberger, Howard K. 57-61, 69, 102-103, 117-118, 164
Koch, Walter 39, 43
Kriegsmarine 148
Kroh, Hans 95

L

Leckie. D. F. 38, 48, 51, 104, 114, 118
lessons
    administration in defeat 142
    advantage of single commander 26
    best use of time 14
    campaign aftermath 162-164
    communications 20
    defending bridges 37
    discomfort the enemy 153
    flexibility in procedures 97
    individual unit defence 41, 66
    irregular units 46
    logistics 81
    moral factors 148
    reserves 34, 109
    responsiveness of units to the local commander 36
    selection of positions 70
    surplus troops 129
logistics 26-28, 81
Lohr, Alexander 23
Longmore, Arthur 24, 157-158, 160
Luftwaffe (for paratrooper units see German Army) 26-27, 40, 158
    VIII Fliegerkorps 23, 79-80, 156-158
    XI Fliegerkorps 11, 23, 79-80, 160
    Luftflotte 4 11, 23

M

Maleme
    Battle of 40-51, 104-106, 108-112
    German plans 38-40, 105-106
    organisation of defence 31-38
    significance to campaign 164
McDonagh, W. G. 71
Mediterranean
    strategic interests for Britain 7
    strategic interests for Germany 6, 8
Meindl, Eugen 38-40, 45, 46, 105
Morse, R. A. 24, 54
Müerbe, Peter 46
Mussolini Benito 8, 123

N

Nagle, William 97
Nazi Party 6
Neon Khorion 138
Neuhof 68

New Zealand Army
- 2 General Hospital 56
- 4 Brigade 57-58, 61, 102-103, 108, 110, 113, 115, 137
- 4 Field Hygiene Section 57
- 5 Brigade 31, 32, 36, 38, 56, 108, 110, 114-115, 130, 137
- 5 Field Ambulance 57
- 5 Field Park Company 55
- 5 Field Regiment 57
- 6 Brigade 18, 58
- 6 Field Ambulance 57
- 7 Field Company 32
- 10 Brigade 20, 57, 58, 59, 61, 69
- 18 Battalion 57, 67, 115, 117, 119
- 19 Army Troop Company 32, 108
- 19 Battalion 57, 60-61, 67, 103, 115, 132
- 20 Battalion 57, 110-112
- 21 Battalion 31-32, 38, 41, 45, 51, 104, 111-112
- 22 Battalion 31-34, 36-38, 41-45, 47-51, 104
- 23 Battalion 31, 38, 41, 48, 50-51, 104, 118, 120
- 27 Field Battery 109
- 27 Machine Gun Battalion 31-32, 57
- 28 (Maori) Battalion 31-32, 38, 48, 50, 108, 110-111, 132, 137-138
- New Zealand Army Service Corps 57
- New Zealand Composite Battalion 57-58, 60, 67-69, 89
- New Zealand Dental Corps 57
- New Zealand Division 5, 17-18, 108
- New Zealand Division Band 117
- New Zealand Division Cavalry Squadron 57, 61, 69, 115
- New Zealand Division Commander Royal Engineers 56
- New Zealand Division Concert Party 57, 117
- New Zealand Division Field Punishment Centre 31
- New Zealand Division HQ 56
- New Zealand Division Postal Unit 57
- New Zealand Division Provost Company 57
- New Zealand Division Signals 56
- New Zealand Division Supply Column 55, 61
- New Zealand Stevedores 55
- Petrol Company 68, 71, 115, 117, 119

O

oil 6-7
Operations
- *Barbarossa* 136
- *Compass* 8
- *Crusader* 34
- *Marita* 9
- *Merkur* 12, 25

order of battle, Australian 22

P

parachute warfare 11-12, 25, 160, 162
paratroopers (see German Army)
partisans 162-163

Perivolia 72, 95, 98, 124, 125, 127
Pink Hill 68, 71-72, 117
plans
- campaign 28-30
- centre sector 62-63
- Heraklion 76, 79-80
- Maleme sector 38-40, 105-106
- Retimo 95, 97

Plessen, Wulf von 40-41
Prison Valley 86, 89, 102-103, 115, 164
- defensive positions 58-61

Puttick, Edward 17, 57, 58, 61, 63-64, 100-103, 108, 113, 129

R

Ramcke, Bernard Hermann 106, 114
Retimo 28-29, 89-101, 140
- battle at 97-101, 124-127
- defences 93, 95
- organisation of British forces 86-87, 88-90

Richthofen, Wolfram von 23, 156
Ringel, J. 108, 114, 128-129, 138-139
Rommel, Erwin 9
Royal Air Force 9, 156-160,
- 3 Squadron 157
- 30 Squadron 32
- 33 Squadron 32
- 80 Squadron 157
- 112 Squadron 75, 157
- 220 AMES 75
- 252 AMES 32

Royal Australian Navy
- HMAS *Napier* 143, 149
- HMAS *Nizam* 143, 148-149, 154, 156
- HMAS *Perth* 143, 148-149, 151-152, 155

Royal Marines
- A Heavy Anti-aircraft Battery 55
- C Heavy Anti-aircraft Battery 55, 75
- S Search Light Battery 55
- X Troop, Coastal Defence Battery 87, 88
- Z Troop, Coastal Defence Battery 32
- 2 Heavy Anti-aircraft Regiment HQ 55
- 2 Heavy Anti-aircraft Workshop 56
- 23 Light Anti-aircraft Battery 17, 55, 57, 73
- Mobile Naval Base Defence Organisation (MNBDO) 17, 35, 55
- MNDBO Maintenance and Labour Units 56
- MNDBO Signals Company 55

Royal Navy 147-148, 153-155;
- 1 Tented Hospital Royal Navy 56
- 805 Squadron FAA 32
- *Abdiel* 143, 156
- *Ajax* 18, 143, 149, 151
- *Auckland* 156
- *Barham* 149
- *Calcutta* 143, 149, 151, 156
- *Carlisle* 149, 151, 153
- *Coventry* 143, 156
- *Decoy* 143, 149

Defender 143, 156
Dido 143, 149, 151
Fiji 149
Flamingo 156
Formidable 149, 154-155
Glengyle 143
Glenroy 149, 156
Gloucester 149
Greyhound 149
Hasty 143, 151
Havock 149
Hereward 143, 149, 151
Hero 143, 156
Hotspur 143
Ilex 149
Imperial 143, 149
Isis 156
Jackal 143
Jaguar 143, 156
Janus 143, 151
Jervis 143, 154
Juno 149, 151
Kandahar 143, 151
Kashmir 149, 154
Kelly 149, 154
Kelvin 143, 149
Kimberley 143, 151
Kingston 149, 151
Naiad 149, 151, 153
Nubian 149, 155
Orion 143, 149, 151
Phoebe 143
Stuart 156
Thresher 144
Valiant 149
Warspite 149
Russell, J. T. 69

S

Saunders, Reg 132
Scheïber, Otto 39
Schuster, Karl 23, 151
Sfakia 129, 132-137, 140-144
Stentzler, Edgar 39, 45, 105
Stewart, I. McD. G. 15
Stilos 138, 139
Student, Kurt 11-12, 23, 110, 164
    invasion plan 29-31
    plan for the Centre Group 62-63
    plan for Maleme sector 38-40, 105-106
    plan for Retimo sector 95, 97
    plan for sea transport 150
Sturm, Alfred 95, 98
Suda sector 27-29, 72-73, 88, 115, 161
    British organisation in the 52-56
    defences 54
Suez Canal 7
Supermarina 148, 151
Süssmann, Wilhelm 62-63, 79

T

Tavronitis River 32-33, 37-38, 43
Thomas, Lieutenant 120
Thomason, H. H. 118
Tidbury, O. H. 14

U

Ultra 9, 25, 40
Utz, Willibald 139, 142-143

V

Vasey, George 19, 24, 86-88, 90, 130

W

Walker, Keith 144
Walther, Major 85
Wavell, Archibald 17-19, 21, 24, 163
weapons
    Bofors Mark 1 40mm anti-aircraft gun 35, 54, 74, 81
    Boys Mark 1 anti-tank rifle 95
    Bren Mark 1 light machine-gun 42
    coastal defence gun 4-inch 35
    equipment air drop container 42
    Flak 38 anti-aircraft gun, 20mm 81, 112
    grenades 39, 118
    heavy anti-aircraft gun 3-inch 35, 74, 82
    heavy anti-aircraft gun 3.7-inch 65
    Kar 98k rifle 164
    Leichte Geschutz 40 75mm recoilless gun 45, 115, 122
    Lewis Mark 1 .303 light machine-gun 69
    Matilda Mark II infantry tank 21, 31, 34, 48, 126
    MG34 machine-gun 100
    mortar, 3-inch 76; 81mm 116
    MP40 sub-machine gun 66
    Panzerabwehrkanone (Pak) 36 37mm anti-tank gun 85, 126
    Panzerkampfwagen (PzKw) Mark II tank 127
    Short Magazine Lee Enfield Mark 3* .303 rifle 163
    Thomson M1928A1 sub-machine gun 83
    Universal carrier No. 1 (Bren gun carrier) 140
    Vickers Mark 1 machine-gun 99
    Vickers Mark VI tank 103, 116
Weston, Eric C. 14, 17, 52, 54-55, 61, 129, 144
Wheat Hill 117
Wiedemann 95, 98
Wittman Group 138

X

Xamoudhokhori 111

Y

Yugoslavia 9

Made in United States
North Haven, CT
15 May 2025

68921024R00052